A Belizean Rain Forest

The Community Baboon Sanctuary

* A BELIZEAN RAIN FOREST *
the

Community Baboon Sanctuary

by

Robert H. Horwich
and
Jonathan Lyon

Orang-utan Press

Gays Mills, WI

Published by:

Orang-utan Press
Community Conservation Consultants
RD 1, Box 96
Gays Mills, WI 54631   USA

Published   August, 1990
Second edition.   September, 1993.

Library of Congress Catalog Card No. 90-91973
ISBN   0-9637982-0-0

Cover :   Poster by Caroline Beckett

Printed in the United States
Hynek Printing
Richland Center, Wisconsin 53581

CONTENTS

Preface

The Community Baboon Sanctuary is an experiment in grassroots conservation which is succeeding due to the enthusiastic cooperation of the rural people of Belize. It depends on their continued support and the sharing of their privately owned lands with the wildlife of Belize. The sanctuary has evolved a great deal and is still changing as we see what works and what doesn't. This book about the sanctuary, too, has changed radically and grown, from an 8 page symbolic representation of the sanctuary, through 60 and 100 page guidebook editions to this second edition of a general text on many facets of the Belizean rain forest including much of the background material from the sanctuary museum which opened in April, 1989. It has become a textbook of the northern forests of Belize with examples which introduce the complexities of the tropical rain forest. The material is organized in an attempt to combine general knowledge of rain forests with specific information about Belize, using the Community Baboon Sanctuary as an example which we have been researching.

- September, 1993

Dr. Robert H. Horwich
RD 1, Box 96
Gays Mills, Wisconsin
54631 U.S.A.

Jonathan Lyon
Program in Ecology
Penn State University
University Park, PA 16802

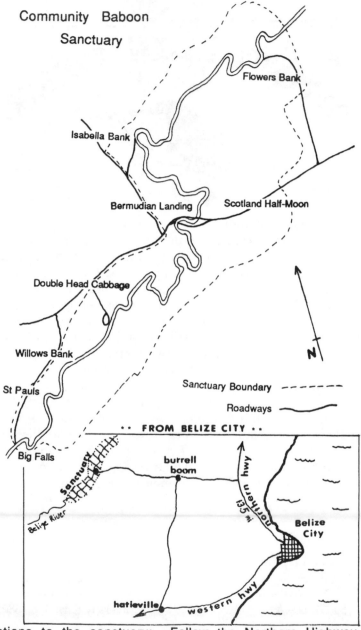

Community Baboon Sanctuary

Flowers Bank

Isabella Bank

Bermudian Landing

Scotland Half-Moon

Double Head Cabbage

Willows Bank

St Pauls

Sanctuary Boundary — — — —
Roadways ——————

Big Falls

·· FROM BELIZE CITY ··

sanctuary

burrell boom

Belize River

northern hwy

13.5 mi

Belize City

hatieville

western hwy

Directions to the sanctuary: Follow the Northern Highway from Belize City for 13.5 miles then bear left on the road to Burrell Boom. Pass through Burrell Boom and follow road for about 7 miles to Bermudian Landing Village.

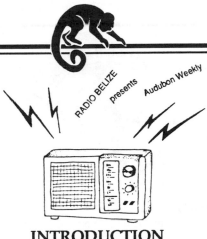

INTRODUCTION

Audubon Weekly - April 8, 1985.

"On February 23 of this year, the village members of Bermudian Landing, at their village meeting, endorsed a program proposed by Dr. Robert Horwich to form a Community Baboon Sanctuary. Earlier last year, the Village Council and 16 landowners, on whose land baboons live, had pledged their support in the planning of the sanctuary.

By giving their approval, the village members of Bermudian Landing are pioneering a new concept in environmental conservation in Belize. This grassroots conservation approach is one direction that conservation must take because the preservation of nature cannot be done without the support of local people and landowners. At Bermudian Landing and surrounding areas, the villagers have agreed to participate in a plan to voluntarily use their land to promote a better environment both for themselves and the baboons. They are developing a sanctuary, not in the legal or traditional sense but in a completely voluntary community way. These landowners are generously giving of what they own-- their land, which is the source of their livelihood, for the sake of the environment and to preserve the natural heritage of Belize.

Thus, the villagers of Bermudian Landing have taken an important step and the project has the potential to serve as a prototype for other areas in Belize and for other communities in the world. "

Audubon Weekly - April, 1987. The Community Baboon Sanctuary: An Experiment in Grassroots Conservation.

"The rural citizens of Belize are now conducting a small but significant experiment in wildlife conservation in the Bermudian Landing area along the Belize River. The area is not a sanctuary in the traditional or legal sense but one which is based on and depends on the rural people and their community government. Here, private landowners, many of them subsistence farmers, have voluntarily pledged to use their lands in accordance with a management plan which will benefit the black howler monkey and other wildlife, as well as the river and its forests. In turn, the program will benefit landowners by reducing erosion, conserving the water table, and allowing more rapid replacement of the forest and its nutrients following slash-and-burn agriculture.

This community sanctuary is the first of its kind in the world, providing unlimited possibilities for similar community-based sanctuaries in Belize and other countries. Its establishment has already begun to influence conservationists throughout the world in such varied countries as Sierra Leone in Africa, Venezuela in South America, and Australia."

" More than a dream come true, much more than a place to save a few monkeys... This community project has ricocheted all around the world, as a model that doesn't preach distance between man and conservation but sees conservation of the environment and wildlife for what it is, the conservation of mankind itself . "

Hon. Dean Lindo,
Minister of Agriculture, 1989

DEVELOPMENT OF THE SANCTUARY

𝒟espite the decreasing numbers of the black howler monkey throughout its range, the area around Bermudian Landing has for many years been known as a place where one can see howler monkeys in Belize. The film, *"Amate - The Fig Tree"*, filmed by Richard Foster, a resident of Belize, shows footage of a troop of howlers in the large fig tree overlooking the ferry crossing. It was this film that led Dr. Robert Horwich to begin field studies of the howlers in the area in 1981.

Since there was some confusion about whether or not the black howler was a different species from the closely related golden mantled howler, Dr. Horwich, with Ed Johnson, carried out a survey of the range of the black howler monkey. They found that in contrast to the golden mantled howler, the black howler was found only in low altitude areas under 1,000 ft (300 m) above sea level, and primarily in the riverine forests. They also noted that its range was rapidly shrinking into small island populations, especially in Mexico.

Geographic Distribution of the Black Howler Monkey
in Central America

3

Thus, noting the successful populations of howlers in the Bermudian Landing area and the positive feeling that the villagers had toward the monkeys which they call "baboons", Horwich and Johnson in 1984, approached the villagers and Village Council to ask for support to investigate the possibility of a community-based sanctuary in the area. They received signatures of all 7 council members and 16 landowners on a petition requesting that they study the potential for a baboon sanctuary. With this community support, World Wildlife Fund-U.S. consented to finance the work, and the Government of Belize approved the project.

WWF

On February 23, 1985 at a village meeting with the area representative, Mr. Samuel Rhaburn present, Dr. Horwich presented the findings of his investigations and explained the community sanctuary concept to the villagers and landowners. He then asked for and received enthusiastic support and permission to declare the area the "Community Baboon Sanctuary". Following the granting of permission, the villagers constructed a tourist shelter out of native materials with volunteer labor, and a sign denoting the sanctuary was erected. At that time, 3 square miles (8 sq km) along the Belize River were mapped by plant ecologist, Jon Lyon, as to vegetation types and property boundaries. Eleven original villagers signed a voluntary pledge to maintain their land according to a suggested management plan for the baboons and other wildlife. The landowners then received maps of their land and a copy of the management plan, as well as a certificate of participation.

4

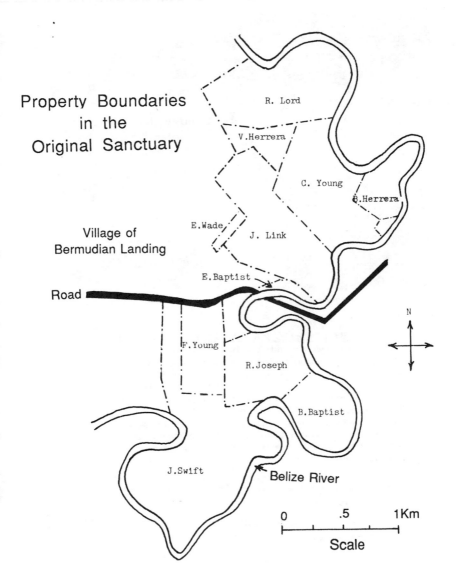

Property Boundaries
in the
Original Sanctuary

R. Lord

V.Herrera

C. Young

Herrera

Village of
Bermudian Landing

E.Wade

J. Link

E.Baptist

Road

N

F.Young

R.Joseph

B.Baptist

J.Swift

Belize River

0   .5   1Km

Scale

I, ___BENJAMIN BAPTIST___, a landowner in
the Bermudian Landing vicinity, voluntarily pledge to
accept the following management plan regarding my land and
my farming practices, to enhance the environment of the
baboon on my land.   I understand that this pledge is
not legally binding but I will nevertheless attempt to live up
to its stipulations.   If I cannot do so, I will inform
the Village Council of Bermudian Landing or any biologist
working on the community baboon sanctuary, to attempt to
make my farming practices work in harmony with the needs of
the baboon and other wildlife.

1) Leave strip of bush along river to the south and east
   of the peninsula

2) allow trees along property-force line to grow
   creating an aerial corridor

3) Leave food trees for baboons when clearing land

B C. Baptist
landowner

10th April, 1985
date

C. Young (BLVC)
Village Council rep.

WITNESS: Fallet Young

6

In 1986, with additional funds from World Wildlife Fund-U.S. and under the auspices of the Belize Audubon Society, Jon Lyon took aerial photographs and mapped an additional 15 sq miles (24 sq km) of private lands on both sides of the Belize River from Big Falls to Flowers Bank.

Over 100 landowners have now pledged to use their lands to benefit the black howler monkey (known locally as the baboon). We have also obtained formal support from 7 other villages along the river, including Big Falls, St. Pauls Bank, Willows Bank, Double Head Cabbage, Isabella Bank, Scotland Half-Moon, and Flowers Bank. The sanctuary is continually growing as additional landowners sign pledges. We hope to connect the community sanctuary lands with an established National Park to the north, the Crooked Tree Wildlife Sanctuary, and a prospective sanctuary to the east at Mussel Creek, which both support healthy howler populations.

The sanctuary, located along a 20 mi (33 km) stretch of the Belize River, was initially estimated to contain a healthy population of about 800 monkeys. Since the sanctuary was created there has been an increase in the howler population level of 20-30% .

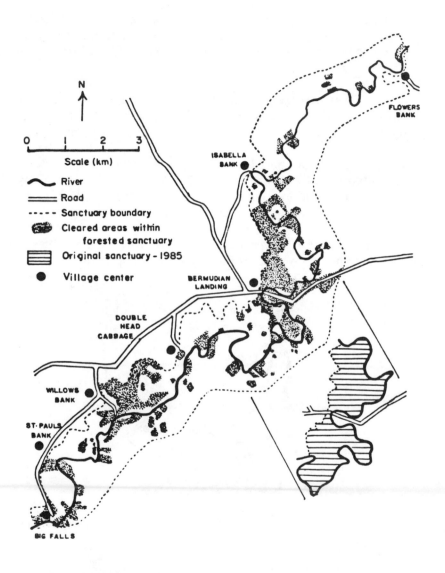

N

0 1 2 3
Scale (km)

~~ River
═══ Road
---- Sanctuary boundary
🌫 Cleared areas within
    forested sanctuary
▤ Original sanctuary - 1985
● Village center

FLOWERS BANK
ISABELLA BANK
BERMUDIAN LANDING
DOUBLE HEAD CABBAGE
WILLOWS BANK
ST·PAULS BANK
BIG FALLS

COMMUNITY BABOON SANCTUARY
1987

Estimates by the Sanctuary Manager are that approximately 90% of the landowners are abiding by their pledges. In the coming years, we will continue to accurately evaluate landowner participation using aerial photographs.

The sanctuary education program has included developing a marked trail system for tourists, a lecture program for both rural and city schools, and the publication of educational materials. Research is being carried out on the howler monkeys, the river turtle, local bird species, and the riverine forest system.

The natural history museum building was constructed in 1987 by villagers under the supervision of Mr. Camille Young. It houses a number of small exhibits about the area's natural resources and their conservation. Exhibits include aspects of howler monkey ecology, zoology, botany, forest ecology, local history, archeology, and Creole culture. Area residents have been welcoming tourists to share the beauty and wildlife of the area. Through the sanctuary, villagers have started a small "bed and breakfast" tourism which both generates income for the community and provides travellers with a glimpse of rural Belizean life.

In 1987, the operations of the sanctuary were formalized by hiring Mr. Fallet Young as the first Sanctuary Manager. His main duties include working with local landowners, tourists, students, and researchers to maintain the goals of the sanctuary. The Sanctuary Manager is supervised by and under direction of the Belize Audubon Society. His duties are guided by an Operations Manual.

COMMUNITY BABOON SANCTUARY
MEMBERS

The following list gives the names of those landowners currently participating in the sanctuary effort. Through their sustainable land use practices and voluntary cooperation, these landowners are helping to ensure the future of the black howler monkey and its habitat in Belize. We apologize for any omissions of landowners who have recently joined.

1. Edward McFadzean
2. Wallace Revers
3. Herman Williams
4. Matthew Thompson
5. Martin Rogers
6. Manny McFadzean
7. Lloyd Stephenson
8. Basil Thompson
9. Eustace Pakeman
10. Joe Rocca Family
11. Oswald McFadzean
12. Reuben Belisle
13. Albert McFadzean
14. George Stephenson
15. Leopold Pook
16. John McFadzean
17. George Flowers
18. Emmanuel McFadzean
19. Randolph Young
20. Peter Harris
21. Maud Armstrong
22. Charles Wingo
23. Roy Talbert
24. Casmore Martinez
25. Lloyd Martinez
26. Edwin Pitts
27. John Humes
28. Fallet Young
29. John Swift
30. Bert Young
31. Lloyd Flowers
32. Cardinal Nicholas
33. Charles Stump
34. Benjamin Baptist Jr.
35. Roy Joseph
36. Francis Baizar
37. Paul Joseph
38. Sydney Russell
39. Benjamin Baptist
40. Roy Young
41. Elston Wade
42. John Perez
43. Edna Baptist
44. Clifton Young
45. Bernard Herrera
46. Raymond Lord
47. Vicente Herrera
48. Edward Herrera
49. Thomas Myvett
50. Thomas Flores
51. Joseph Arana
52. Solar Taniko
53. Orlando Dawson
54. Gilbert Flowers

55. Camille Young
56. Selvin Jeffers
57. Marsella Cassasola
58. Orlando Salas
59. Joe Lanza
60. Horace Hulse
61. Allan Herrera
62. Walter Banner
63. Dudley Hendy
64. Henry Dawson
65. Rueben Rhaburn
66. Calbert Inks

67. Hughson Baptist
68. Cecil Flowers
69. Lincoln Flowers
70. Robert Mitchell
71. Emilio Lanza
72. Dan Lanza
73. Eduardo Eck
74. Melford Hendy
75. Edwin Hendy
76. William Hyde
77. Harry Sutherland

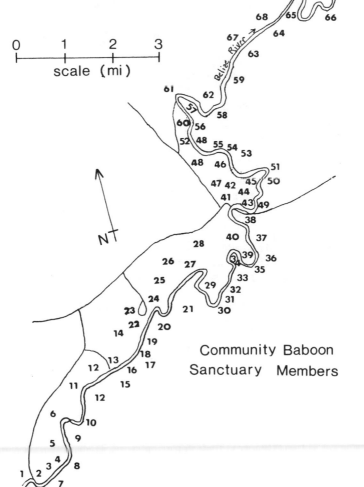

Community Baboon
Sanctuary Members

COMMUNITY
BABOON
SANCTUARY

Belize

In recognition and appreciation,
this certifies that

by voluntarily pledging the use of private land
for the conservation of
the black howler monkey, *Alouatta pigra*,
is an active participant in
the Community Baboon Sanctuary

Date

President - Belize Audubon Society   President - World Wildlife Fund

Chairman - Village Council of

THE COMMUNITY BABOON SANCTUARY:
A Model for the Conservation of Private Lands

𝒯he Community Baboon Sanctuary began as an experiment in grassroots conservation to ensure the conservation of wildlife on traditionally "unprotectable" lands: privately owned lands. The sanctuary's survival depends on the cooperation of rural landowners and subsistence farmers to live up to their responsibility as land stewards. Landowners have been presented with a map of their lands and an accompanying management plan. They have also each signed a voluntary pledge to abide by the plan. The community sanctuary shifts the center of conservation to include rural people as custodians of their own land.

The Sanctuary's 4 Goals:
Conservation, Education, Research, and Tourism

Conservation

One of the most densely populated black howler regions is located on the private lands of subsistence farmers along the Belize River in Belize. The traditional approaches to conservation, mainly land purchasing and human exclusion, were not valid options in this context. Instead, we started from the premise that only a limited amount of tropical forest can be maintained in its pristine state. This leaves the majority of tropical forest lands in private hands and often outside the realm of sound management. Introducing management practices on those private lands under cyclic slash-and-burn cultivation could help ensure a better environment for the howler monkeys and other wildlife.

The main emphasis of the sanctuary is its conservation program. The most important function of the Sanctuary Manager is to work one on one with landowners . Each year the Manager checks on the landowners' agricultural practices to make sure they are maintaining their practices in accordance with the management plans they pledged to uphold. Discussions occur yearly during the dry season prior to cutting and burning of clearings known locally as "milpas" or "plantations".

Secondarily, the Sanctuary Manager has started the mapping of additional lands to expand the sanctuary to include

Sanctuary Manager Fallet Young and Jon Lyon work with landowners to draw up manangement plans

all riverine and cohune palm forests providing good habitat for the howlers. Besides being asked to leave riverbanks uncut, landowners are asked to leave strips of forest on property boundaries, to leave aerial pathways for howlers across large cleared areas, and to leave specific howler food trees when clearing land. The Manager is also working with local farming cooperatives to integrate wildlife conservation into their future farming plans.

In this manner, the sanctuary acts as a catalyst for the development of new conservation ideas and projects which spring up in Belize from the grassroots level. In addition, the voluntary nature of the sanctuary both respects the capacity of rural farmers to follow wise management practices and fosters an environment for individual acts of wildlife conservation. In this vein, individuals have started creative new projects including tree cuttings or "living fenceposts" being planted to create "baboon bridges" across roads and clearings.

Howler Crossing Bridge Constructed With Living Fence Posts

Howler censusing of the original 3 sq mile (8 sq km) sanctuary is continued yearly to feed back information on the status of the population within the sanctuary. Approximately 25-30 troops are involved in the census. The population has increased approximately 20% from 1985 to 1988. It has increased from an estimated 840 monkeys to over 1,000 howlers within an 18 sq mile (47 sq km) area of forest along the Belize River.

A second endangered species, the Central American river turtle (*Dermatemys mawei*), called "hickatee" locally, has also been targeted for research. The turtle research is especially important due to the probability of its disappearance from the area from overhunting if present trends continue. Study of the turtle's seasonal reproduction and its local exploitation will help sanctuary staff to make management suggestions to local and federal government bodies for the hickatee's protection and sustained use.

One long-term goal of the sanctuary is ultimately to reintroduce both plant and animal species which have disappeared from the area. Mahogany and other hardwoods which were very important economically to Belize in the past have virtually disappeared from the area. We have built a small greenhouse and hope eventually to encourage replanting of mahogany, cedar, and other hardwood species for long-term economic gains. The greenhouse will also be used for production of other local trees for replanting riverbanks and other erosion prone areas as well as for the growing of fruit trees.

We would additionally like to reintroduce some game birds back to the area. This will entail agreement on the part of landowners and a general concensus of area residents not to hunt the introduced species with the potential for managed hunting in the distant future. Potentially reintroduced species include the ocellated turkey, an endemic and protected bird in Belize. Two other birds, the crested quan, and the great curassow are game species which have been hunted to extinction within the area. Plans are also being made to reintroduce black howlers into other secure areas in Belize from which they have disappeared.

Female Curassow

Education

The education program centers around this guidebook, a museum, and an interpretive forest trail system. The museum, Belize's first, opened in April, 1989. By locating the museum within the sanctuary, we shifted the center of conservation by having a conservation oriented museum located rurally where the future protectors of the forests live and work. The museum is composed of a series of laminated poster exhibits integrated with biological specimens and materials from the area (many of which were donated by local residents). The majority of the subject matter focuses on natural history materials with some local cultural, archeological, and historical materials. The natural history exhibits are strongly conservation oriented and they specifically deal with local animals and plants.

Museum Opening April, 1989

Dr. Robert Horwich addresses audience. Seated from left to right: Fallet Young (Sanctuary Manager), Hon. Dean Lindo (Minister of Agriculture), Mrs. Lindo

The museum grounds have been planted as a young arboretum with forest seedlings as well as herbs for display. A small greenhouse is being used to start seedlings for reforestation projects. These projects complement a 3 mile (4.8 km) trail system which is marked with tree names and numbers corresponding to sign texts in this book. The trail is interpreted by sanctuary staff to tourists and students of all ages. The field experience is often complemented by prior classroom lectures.

View of Museum Interior

Research

Research at the sanctuary has concentrated on the ecology of the howler, including studies on infant development, home range, feeding, and seasonal ecology. A population of 50 howlers have been individually marked to study social behavior and population changes. Complementary studies of the riverine forests and on farming practices help both in howler management and in aiding farmers develop sustainable management plans for their farms. Additional research projects include studies on river turtle biology, the impact of the sanctuary policies on the area, pesticide use in the sanctuary, and studies of Creole culture.

Tourism and Local Economics

A key objective of the sanctuary is to integrate human interests with the conservation of forests and wildlife. One potential economic benefit expressed by villagers was an interest in inviting tourists to the area. This has been explored slowly but the numbers of tourists (both Belizean and foreign) has steadily and rapidly increased. With the recent building of a bridge across the Belize River, the ferry became a part of Belizean history, and easier access to the area resulted in a growing tourism industry. Villagers initially built a tourist shelter for overnight visitors but they are now being accomodated in villagers' houses in a "bed and breakfast" style of tourism. At present there has been a small but significant economic benefit for local families from tourism. Low-interest loans have also been made to villagers for tourist cabin construction to increase the economic benefits to villagers.

Sanctuary Staff Reuben Rhaburn and Fallet Young Lecture
Tourists on an Interpretive Trail

FUTURE OF COMMUNITY SANCTUARIES

The idea of forming community based sanctuaries based on voluntary management programs for privately owned lands has wide ramifications throughout the world and in other disciplines such as in archeology. We have been exploring the potential for similar sanctuaries in other countries and the Community Baboon Sanctuary is beginning to become a model for other sanctuaries around the world.

Creating A Community Sanctuary

Seven steps were followed in creating the sanctuary and are guiding the formation of other community based sanctuaries:

1. Identify the Site for Conservation - The area along the Belize River historically had a healthy population of howlers which was contiguous with other howler habitats. The howlers were considered harmless to crops and people by local Creole villagers who liked having them in the area.

2. Contact Local People - We asked locals if they were interested in a sanctuary and had them sign a petition of support.

3. Formalize Plan - We brought the idea before a Village Council meeting and with the local support got approval of the appropriate Government Minister.

4. Develop Site - We mapped the area as to vegetation and property boundaries, often including local landowners in the mapping. Then we censused the howlers, developed a management plan, an education program, and began developing tourism at the villagers' request. Each landowner was asked to sign a voluntary pledge to abide by the plan. No direct benefits were promised but all sanctuary participants received T-shirts and copies of their land maps and management plans. We also arranged free dinner lectures/get-togethers for landowners.

5. Publicize Sanctuary - This was done through radio, TV, and newspaper and magazine articles.

6. Expand the Sanctuary - All participating landowners signed a land management plan. We expanded from the original 12 landowners and one village to over 100 landowners and 8 villages; from 3 square miles to 18 square miles. Each landowner was given a certificate of participation in a public ceremony.

7. Formalize the Structure - We hired a Manager, created an Operations Manual, and a long-term Master Plan.

Community Eagle Sanctuary

A second community sanctuary has been initiated to protect the wintering roosting areas of the American bald eagle (*Haliaeetus leucocephalus*) on the lower Wisconsin River near Sauk City, Wisconsin in the United States. Presently over 60 landowners have signed a petition requesting a local conservation group to coordinate management plans, similar to those for the black howler, for the bald eagle. Using the technique established in Belize and working with the Ferry Bluff Eagle Council, we have mapped areas and created land management plans for farmers and landowners in the area. The "Sauk-Prairie Community Eagle Sanctuary" a second community sanctuary was officially formed in January, 1990.

Basic goals of the eagle management project include: protecting seven specific winter roosts which shelter eagles from severe winter weather; increasing and coordinating feeding of carrion from roadkills, fish killed by dams, and piglets which have died on local farms; and developing nesting sites in the area to entice breeding pairs to the area. Additional requests may be made to specific farmers to include a wider variety of conservation techniques, including forming forest corridors and protecting wetlands, prairies, and specific areas of ecological significance.

Specific research and public education goals have been developed. A bald eagle day was run with the Wisconsin

Department of Natural Resources in January, 1989 and 1990 for public education. Roost counts will be made to monitor the winter eagle population each year and additional behavioral studies and feeding studies are planned.

American Bald Eagle   (*Haliaeetus leucocephalus*)

A Sanctuary For Sea Turtles

In 1989 Greg Smith, an American living on northern Ambergris Cay, in Belize heard about the Community Baboon Sanctuary and decided that it might be an alternative way to protect some nesting areas for sea turtles. Although the land was costly and mainly owned by foreigners, Greg was able to convince them that their shoreline had an important natural resource in the three species of sea turtle (green, loggerhead and hawksbill) which come in during the summer months to lay eggs on the beach.

Working with the Fisheries Department and the private landowners, he has mapped the frequency of turtle nesting along a 6 mile (10 km) stretch of beach and has developed a management plan which all landowners are being asked to follow. The requests being made are to restrict construction to 60 ft (19 m) from high tide as turtle nesting areas, restrict domestic animals from disturbing nests, restrict lighting during nesting season, and to prohibit anyone, including workmen from poaching sea turtle eggs.

This program also includes Belizean teachers and student volunteers who live on Greg's land for 1-2 weeks and patrol the beaches to safeguard the newly laid eggs from poaching. This volunteer program has successfully reduced the nest poaching from 38% to only 1% of the eggs and has allowed Belizeans to play a large role in protecting their own natural resources.

Green Sea Turtle (*Chelonia mydas*)

THE BABOON OR BLACK HOWLER MONKEY
(*Alouatta pigra*)

Howler Range

The black howler monkey known as "baboon" in Creole or "saraguate" in Spanish is one of the largest monkeys found in the Americas. It lives only in Belize, southern Mexico, and in parts of Guatemala and in many areas of its range it is very rare and is in danger of disappearing altogether. Belize is very fortunate to still have a healthy population of these fascinating primates.

Belize has two monkey species: the black howler monkey (*Alouatta pigra*) or baboon and the spider monkey

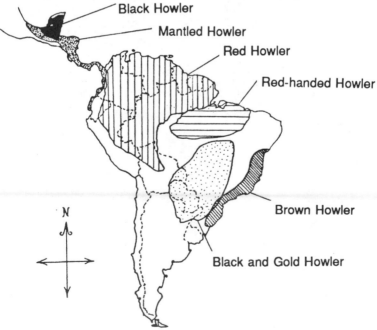

Geographic Range in Central and South America of the
6 Howler Monkey Species

(*Ateles geoffroyi*) called monkey in Creole. The baboon, weighing 15 to 20 lbs (6-7 kg), is larger and heavier than its small, slender relative. With the exception of the young infants which are brown, the baboon is entirely black in color.

There are only six species of howler monkeys in the world all of which live throughout Central and South America. The map on the previous page shows the range of each species. There is a small chance that a second howler species, the golden mantled howler (*Alouatta palliata*), is found along the Sarstoon River on the southern border of Belize. Small populations of mantled howlers have been confirmed in

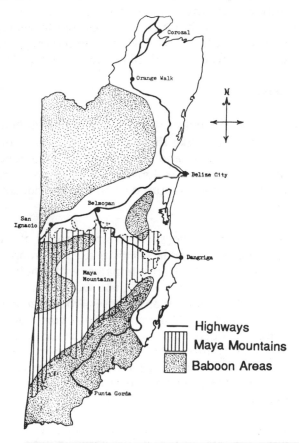

Geographic Range in Belize of the Black Howler Monkey

the Rio Dulce area in Guatemala south of the Sarstoon. The golden mantled howler is so closely related that for many years it was thought to be one and the same species as the black howler monkey. It is so named because of a light golden brown stripe on its sides.

Since the baboon prefers to live in low lying tropical rain forests under 1,000 ft (300 m) above sea level, Belize provides a good habitat for the monkeys. They are most common in the riverine forests, especially on the Belize River and its major branches. They can also be found in the foothills of the Maya Mountains. The Community Baboon Sanctuary in the Bermudian Landing area supports a relatively high density of howlers which are easily accessible to visitors and researchers who visit the area. The map on the previous page indicates the range where the black howler occurs in Belize.

Social Behaviors

Like other monkeys, the baboon displays behaviors and habits very much like those of people. They use their hands to feed, they nurse and tend their babies, defend their property, and use facial expressions similar to humans. Some of these behaviors have been captured on film in the documentary film *"Amate -the Fig Tree "*.

Black howler monkeys live in small troops of mostly 4 to 8 members with no troops larger than 10. The troop usually consists of an adult male and females with their young. Occasionally, more than one adult male will live in a troop or a male will live alone without any troop. Troop size may vary from a pair to as many as 10 members. The entire troop feeds, sleeps, and travels together. On occasion, a troop will split up to feed, then later, re-form into the original troop. The troop unit is relatively stable from year to year. Mostly young males and rarely females are believed to migrate between troops before settling down.

Each troop has its own property or territory in which it lives. Although some howler species are not strictly territorial, no troops of any species tolerate other groups in

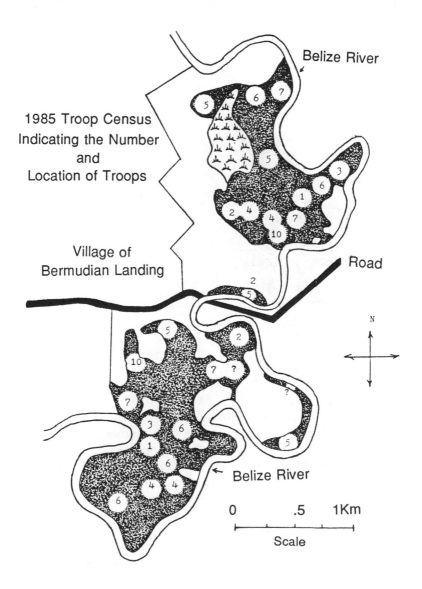

Belize River

1985 Troop Census
Indicating the Number
and
Location of Troops

Village of
Bermudian Landing

Road

N

Belize River

0   .5   1Km

Scale

their immediate areas. The territory size depends on the troop size and availability of food within the area. Territories range from 3-25 acres (1-10 ha). An average territory in the sanctuary is about 12-15 acres (5-6 ha).

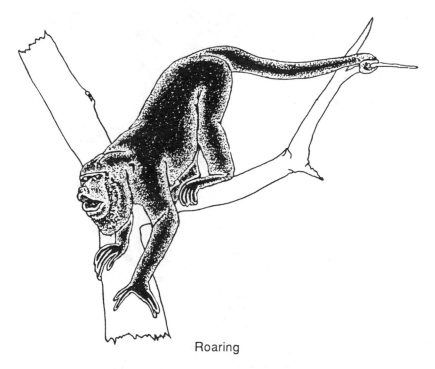

Roaring

Maintaining the howler troop is often a balance of friendly and aggressive behaviors both within and between troops. Baboons defend their territory from intruding troops by using their remarkable voices to let other troops know their location. The howling is so strong and loud that it has been compared to that of a jaguar. Howler monkeys have evolved an elaborate set of throat structures for magnifying the sounds they produce. Their roars can be heard as far as a mile away. These throat structures are most well developed in males who do most of the roaring although females join the choruses with higher pitched calls. In order to produce such sounds, howlers narrow their throat region around their relaxed vocal chords. This increases the pressure of the expulsed air and extends the chambers in the hyoid   cartilage which funnels the sounds into the large, hollow hyoid bone. The hyoid bone acts as a resonating chamber, much as a guitar body amplifies the sounds of its strings.

Throat Structures Used in Roaring

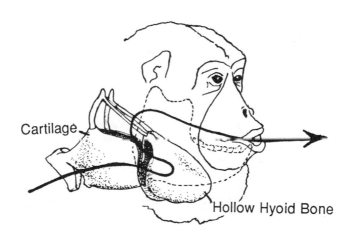

Cartilage

Hollow Hyoid Bone

Howlers often begin or end their day by roaring. It seems that this helps the troops to space themselves so they will not meet and fight. Although troop living areas may overlap, specific territories do seem to be accepted by adjacent troops who roar and display ritual threats across boundary lines. When troops do meet, the intruding troop is chased back to their own territory and both troops roar or "bawl" from their respective territories. They may also use ritualized aggressive displays and lunges toward each other while roaring at the adjacent troop.

In Belize there are local sayings as to why howlers roar; two of the more common sayings predict that roaring occurs before it rains and when other animals are feeding. From our studies, we have found that the sound of rain, car motors, and other loud repetitive sounds will cause the baboons to roar.

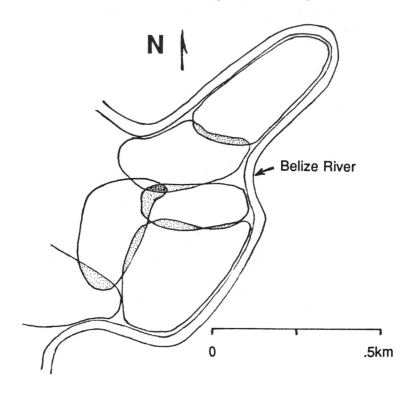

Howler Territories Showing Small Overlap Areas

N

Belize River

0   .5km

Roaring most commonly occurs in early morning and late afternoon but baboons are frequently heard at all hours of the night. Roaring is subdued during the midday. During the rainy season when days are often overcast, morning and afternoon peaks may not be as pronounced and calling is more common during the midday.

Another aggressive behavior which appears to act as a warning is performed by adult males who raise their body hair to give them a larger, more formidable appearance. They raise and hunch their shoulders and lean quickly forward, grasping a tree branch. They may also rub their chest and throat area along a tree branch, often while hanging below the branch. A gland in the throat region leaves a scent when the male rubs and thus males can convey an angry message both visually and by smell.

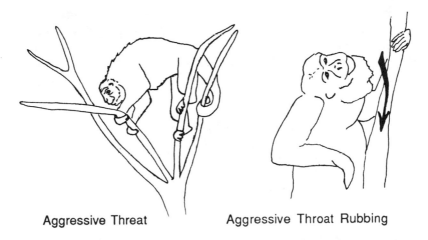

Aggressive Threat   Aggressive Throat Rubbing

Within the troop, certain friendly behaviors help maintain the group peacefully. Grooming a partner, which is a common behavior in many monkeys, is seen only rarely in howlers. Grooming is usually done in a relaxed situation between two animals who know each other well, often a male and female. In similar relaxed situations males and females have been seen to hold hands.

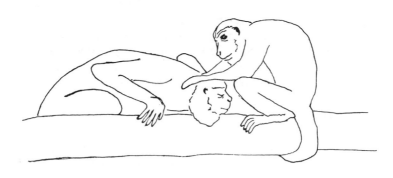

Grooming

Play is common between young in a troop but even adults will chase and wrestle with each other, sometimes displaying an open mouth with teeth and giving low-pitched play grunts. Young subadult males seem to try and elicit play from the dominant male. Perhaps this elicitation prolongs their stay in the troop since many black howler troops have only one adult male and it is thought that the old male harasses his matured sons so they move out of the troop.

Howlers also exhibit a behavior of catching urine in their hands, feet or tail. They may be preparing to scent mark a trail on branches high in the canopy. The urine smell, which would be deposited from their body to the branches, would tell lagging troop members to where their troop had moved.

Apart from direct mating or copulating, one other sexual behavior has been commonly seen in mating pairs of howler monkeys. When facing each other, they make prolonged eye contact. One or both of the pair may lick the tongue out at the partner. This seems to indicate an attraction for the partner and has been seen given by a captive howler to a preferred zookeeper.

Like other monkeys, howlers raise their young much like humans do. They nurse them a great deal when they are newborn. Usually only a single infant is born after a six month pregnancy and it is brown in color, eventually changing to the longer black hair after three months. The young clings to its mother's belly at first, nursing from her breasts which are located under each arm. Other females are attracted to the infant, perhaps due to its different coloration, and they may try to touch it or even pull it onto them.

When the infant is older and rides on its mother's back, other females will often rest near the mother to encourage the infant to crawl onto them. Eventually the infant will move readily over other troop members and may even be carried by adult males for short periods. The females reach adulthood and are capable of having young between 4-5 years of age and the males mature at 6-8 years of age. Although howlers do not thrive well in captivity, if they do survive, they may live as long as 20 years.

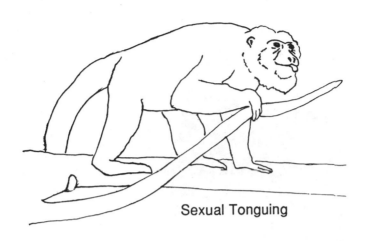

Sexual Tonguing

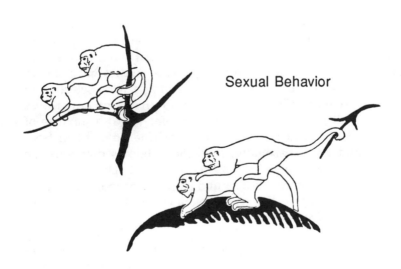

Sexual Behavior

Infant Sharing

Feeding Behavior

Howlers are vegetarians. They will eat flowers and flower buds, but tender leaves and fruits are the largest and most important part of their diet. They eat more leaves than any other monkey in the Americas. Our studies have shown that the baboon balances its diet by eating a wide selection of foods every day. While they can and do survive on only leaves if that is all that is available, they prefer to eat a mixture of flowers, fruits, and leaves within the same day. Most trees flower and fruit seasonally; thus the baboon's diet must be flexible to adjust to these seasonal changes. During the dry season when most trees flower and fruit, the baboon has a more diverse diet than in the wet season when they eat a higher percentage of leaves.

Many plants produce toxins or poisons in their leaves to prevent or deter animals like the howler from eating them. Eating too much of these toxins could harm or make the monkey sick thus its diet must avoid or minimize exposure to the dangerous toxins. Mature leaves most often have the highest

Feeding on Cecropia
Leaves

concentration of toxins while fruits, flowers, and new leaves have much less. For many trees such as dogwood, gumbo limbo, and hogplum, only the fruit, flower and/or the new leaf will be eaten. The mature leaves of some trees such as the fig, and prickly yellow will be eaten but usually only the tip which has the least toxin will be bitten off and eaten. These choicer foods are generally more nutritious for the howlers as well. Fruits are high in sugars and the new leaves have a higher amount of protein and less of the indigestible cellulose.

Since they are large bodied monkeys who often feed at the slender tips of branches, howlers depend on their prehensile tails as an extra hand to prevent them from falling as they jump from branch to branch. Apart from being very prehensile, the last part of their tails have a long pad with dermatoglyphs or "fingerprints".

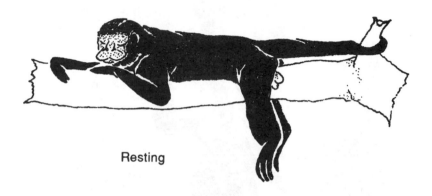

Resting

Baboons are fairly inactive monkeys, resting sometimes as much as 70% of the day in addition to sleeping at night. They generally do not move much during the day, often travelling only about 200-1,200 ft (65-400 m) per day. They have a main rest period at midday. Following this rest period, they will again feed and move. Before settling down for the night, they commonly roar to telegraph their position.

To observe the baboons first hand in their natural environment is a pleasure many Belizeans share, living close to the riversides where the baboons reside. But this is not the case everywhere and will not be the case in Belize if care is not taken. The baboon's natural enemies are the large cats and the harpy eagle and in the 1950's sylvatic yellow fever greatly reduced the howler population numbers. The main danger to the howler, however, is forest destruction. Throughout the baboon's range, much of the forest is being cut without regard to the baboons and they are disappearing very fast. We have little or no control over natural predators but there is something we can do in regard to protecting the howlers forest habitat.

As in the Community Baboon Sanctuary, landowners can help the baboons thrive and maintain healthy population levels in Belize, without adversely affecting their farms. Landowners can leave trees such as figs, trumpet, hogplum, ramon, sapodilla, bucut, bri bri, and roseapple, that are special food trees for the monkeys and also leave strips of forest between fields and along rivers and other waterways.

A. pigra seems to prefer low elevation habitat and high mountainous areas may have aided its separation from *A. palliata* . *A. pigra* also is in high abundance in riverine areas partially due to high number of figs. *Ficus* spp. are an important food source and may affect population and troop size. The figs can attain large size and produce great food quantities. In addition, since they are asynchronous and howlers can eat the mature leaves, they can be extremely important to a troop supplying a steady supply of nutritious food. One troop in the sanctuary has been noted to stay for weeks at a time in a single *Ficus glabrata* tree depending heavily on it for food.

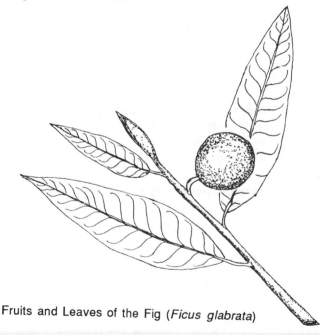

Fruits and Leaves of the Fig (*Ficus glabrata*)

CONSERVATION OF HOWLER MONKEYS

*B*ecause rain forests are disappearing at such a rapid rate, and because howler monkeys depend on the rain forest for their existence, all howler species are vulnerable to extinction. However, generally howlers are more adaptable than other Neotropical monkeys. Although their large size, diurnal lifestyle, and their inability to live in open country work against howlers, their broad opportunistic diet and small home ranges aid in their survival.

Howlers occupy a wide range of habitats and adapt to a wide range of ecological conditions. The six howler species are similar in their habitat requirements. They are adaptable to changes in forest due to slash-and-burn agriculture and may even benefit from low rates of such farming. They can use some secondary growth areas and they may effect faster recolonization of trees by dispersing seeds in their fecal droppings.

Agricultural Threat

There are 3 main threats to the survival of howlers and other forest dwellers: habitat disturbance due to agriculture, logging, and hunting. The main problem is habitat disturbance which is occurring at an increasingly rapid rate due to increases in human population. Most disturbance is due to direct forest destruction which is occurring at the rate of 124,000 sq miles (200,000 sq km) annually. Roughly half of this destruction is from small-scale, shifting slash-and-burn agriculture done by subsistence farmers. It is the dominant form of land use and thus the most important factor in the conversion of tropical forests. Shifting agriculture, however, has allowed howlers to survive better than many other new world primates due to their adaptability to change and their generalist, opportunistic vegetarian diets. The Community Baboon Sanctuary is a direct example of how farmers are trying to balance land use and conservation for the howlers.

Logging Threat

Commercial exploitation of tropical forests for lumber is a serious problem for most primates but how logging is carried out can make a great difference. Although logging initially causes mortality, primate populations can recover rapidly if the forest is left to regenerate. Large clearcutting of areas for eventual use in agriculture or for monoculture forestry is the most devastating practice and few animals can survive it. Even under selective logging, designed to remove only a few of the most valuable timber trees, there is a high loss of other trees due to operational damage. The survival of primates in logged forests is influenced by both their ability to tolerate initial logging and their ability to adjust to different environmental conditions of the regenerating forest.

Logging initially causes major changes as monkeys attempt to avoid human activity. It causes a high level of infant mortality as well as adult injury due to tree felling and disorientation. However, in the long run, monkey populations can return to normal levels. But not all primates or other forest dwellers are as flexible to changing conditions and specialist feeders are particularly vulnerable to logging.

Since only 3.6% of the worlds broadleaved tropical forest are legally protected from exploitation, the conservation of tropical areas is dependent on sustainable use of unprotected forest lands. Light to moderate disturbance (about 25% destruction) generally have only minor effects on the forest. However, heavy disturbance (about 50% destruction) seriously disrupts forest and soil dynamics including promoting higher tree fall rates in severely logged plots due to wind and increased erosion.

The secondary effects of logging cause the greatest problems. Logging roads open up areas for hunters and slash-and-burn farmers. This colonization eventually causes the local extinction of most wildlife in the area. Thus, restriction of secondary agriculture or hunting in areas of regenerating forest can play an important role in primate/wildlife conservation. The requirements of timber exploitation and wildlife conservation are not always mutually exclusive.

Hunting Pressure

Predation by humans is clearly one of the most important factors affecting monkey densities in many countries of Central and South America, particularly along major rivers. Together with fish, monkeys form the principal source of protein for many forest dwelling peoples. The most common game monkeys are howlers. Their large size, loud vocalizations, sedentary habits, and comparatively slow movements place them among the most vulnerable and easily hunted game animals. In addition, larger species such as howlers are less able to respond reproductively to compensate for their losses due to their late maturity and low reproductive rates. They are also shot for sport and captured for the pet trade. Mothers are killed in order to capture the infant, an act both cruel and senseless for the baby howlers are not likely to survive without their mothers. A large percentage of the infants die during the capture or shortly thereafter while acclimating to captivity. Large numbers of howlers also die in transport before they arrive at their final destination.

Vulnerability to Extinction

Very small geographic ranges predispose populations to extinction. In this respect, the black howler, *Alouatta pigra*, is probably the least secure of howlers being confined only to parts of Belize, Guatemala, and Mexico. It is listed as threatened by the U.S. Department of Interior and indeterminate by IUCN. Its range is rapidly shrinking into isolated island populations. There are still a number of healthy populations, especially in Belize, which seem to be increasing in numbers in some areas. However, there are no totally protected regions for large populations of the species.

However, howlers are able to live in small home ranges and have been found thriving around villages where they are not hunted. One small troop of three in the Community Baboon Sanctuary has moved into a small residual broken ridge forest along a small creek bed where howlers had not occurred for at least 35 years. They have been living in a 2-3 acre (0.8-1.2 ha) area for almost a year.

Both the golden mantled howler, *Alouatta palliata*, and the brown howler, *Alouatta fusca*, also have relatively small geographical ranges. The mantled howler is listed as endangered by the U.S. Department of Interior and on appendix 1 of CITES listing. However, mantled howlers have a very long, thin range and thus occur in a great number of countries. They are protected in a number of parks in Costa Rica and appear to be doing well there. In Mexico and Guatemala there are isolated populations which are in danger.

Brown howlers, *Alouatta fusca*, are endemic to the dwindling coastal forests of southeastern Brazil. The remaining populations are found in small pockets threatened by new roads and rapid encroachment. In the southern subspecies, males are rufus colored and females are brown.

Little is known about the red-handed howler (*Alouatta belzebul*). One subspecies is considered endangered but more will be under threat with the construction of the Transamazonia and Bele-Brazilia highways.

The black and gold howler (*Alouatta caraya*) is fairly wide ranging and adapts well to the proximity of humans if not hunted, and can adapt to deforestation. The red howler (*Alouatta seniculus*) has the largest range of all species even occurring in Trinidad. They are perhaps the most adaptable howler occurring frequently in secondary forests. They can also travel far distances on the ground across llanos (grassy plains).

Conservation Solutions

The association of howlers with humans has not always been detrimental. Two major food sources for the howlers in the Yucatan, the ramon or bread fruit (*Brosimum alicastrum*) and zapote or chicle (*Manilkara zapota*) have been of considerable economic importance to human inhabitants of the area and continue to be so today. Ramon was a useful tree for the Mayan culture and has been frequently left uncut and perhaps encouraged to grow by them. Ramon trees are still commonly found around ruin sites such as at Lamanai. Zapote, also exploited for its chicle gum, may have benefitted the monkeys and occurs in close proximity to humans.

Cohune palms in Belize, although a poor howler food source due to their hard seed hulls and inedible fronds, are nonetheless important for forest regeneration. They are historically left in pastures for a number of reasons. The abundance of cohunes has been affected by the Mayans who traditionally left them uncut because of their usefulness. Cohunes produce thatch, palm oil, and edible palm hearts among other items. Perhaps partially due to these Mayan cultivation habits the cohune palm is very common, forming large forests in which it is a dominant species. It is now left by Creole ranchers in pastures both because of its usefulness and the fact that it is difficult to fell. Strangler fig seeds dropped by vertebrates often fall into frond scale openings where they take root and if allowed, envelop the palm.

Because howlers are adaptable to small areas and can utilize all ages of forests, reintroduction becomes a distinct possibility once an area has been made safe for them from hunting and major forest cutting. A serendipitous translocation of howlers occurred near Sandhill in Belize. An informant noted that two captured juveniles escaped into an unpopulated area which is not favorable howler habitat. However, they have survived for two years and the informant noted that they are now breeding.

Management Suggestions

1. Leave or encourage fig trees or other trees on which howlers eat both the fruits and mature leaves. Food trees also include sapodilla, bay cedar, bri-bri, bucut, copna, ramon, gumbolimbo, hogplum, madre cacao, and mampola.

2. Encourage any size forest strips along river banks, in run-off gulleys, swamps, between yearly farm plots, between property boundaries and/or along fence rows.

3. Fence rows can be developed using a variety of "living fence posts" which can benefit howlers and other wildlife.

4. Encourage corridors to connect existing or potential forest strips to encourage gene flow. Investigate larger corridors to connect major reserve or forest areas.

5. Encourage proper agricultural cycling by leaving land fallow long enough for the soil and forest cover to regenerate (generally 15-30 years).

6. Encourage smaller agriculture plots or attempt to maintain forest strips across any larger cut areas. This will allow monkeys aerial pathways to travel across and maintain a seed bank for future forest recolonization.

7. Establish large national game reserves for howlers and other wildlife.

8. When forestry is an inevitable development, follow size-limit restrictions and encourage the establishment of restrictions on consequent development from new built roads. Also encourage the replanting of valuable timbers.

9. Do not hunt howlers or take them as pets. They need a specialized diet and often die in captivity. The Government of Belize, through the Wildlife Protection Act, prohibits the killing and/or capturing of this animal.

HISTORY OF THE AREA

from information provided by Leo H. Bradley

*T*he area west of Burrell Boom, including the Bermudian Landing area was first settled by the Mayans who looked to Altun Ha as their center. Evidence of the early Mayan occupation is seen in small mounds dotted throughout the sanctuary and in the area around Rancho Dolores where many of the people have Mayan surnames. With the arrival of the Europeans around 1650, began a growing logwood and timber trade. Logwood is a small dye-producing tree which grows in dense thickets along waterways such as the Belize River. This trade quickly spread along inland creeks and lagoons where small bands of European buccaneers established encampments to base their logging operations to pull out the timber along the riversides and farther inland. Later, when the logging trade shifted to mahogany, larger more permanent camps, generally composed of a few Europeans and their slaves were established.

Out of these encampments came the present day town names such as "bank", "landing", "walk", "boom", and "pen". These town names came from the loggers and usually reflected a settlement progression. When the loggers first landed to log an area, it was termed a "landing" or "bank" such as Bermudian Landing which was earlier called Butchers Landing. In areas where they spread a boom (a long iron chain) across the river to trap logs floating down river, the towns were known as "booms" such as St. James Boom or Burrell Boom. The original chain or boom may still exist at Burrell Boom. Most of the logs were

floated out in the 18th and 19th centuries to Burrell Boom until roadways were constructed for oxen and wagons and later for motor vehicles to pull out commercial timbers such as mahogany which was often called red gold in those days.

As the areas became more settled, for example when settlers or landowners planted crops (plantations) at an embankment, the areas would then be called a "walk". Thus the village of Flowers Bank was earlier called Flowers Walk and Orange Walk has a similar name. If an area specialized in keeping cattle, it might be called a "pen" such as Maypen, a town downriver from Bermudian Landing, is named. Other areas got their names from the people who settled there. In the Burrell Boom area there were a number of Scotsmen in the communities and there are still a number of fair skinned people in the area of Burrell Boom and Crooked Tree. The village of Scotland Half-Moon across the river from Bermudian Landing also displays the Scottish influence. Some town names were named after specific men, such as pirates. Admiral Ben Bow's name adorns Ben Bow Creek.

The area west of Belize City had a history of cattle rearing. When herdsmen brought their cattle from the pine ridge areas to Belize City, they had to cross the Belize River at Haulover Creek which is so named because the cattle were roped by their horns and hauled across the river at that spot. Later a ferry was constructed there and it remained as the mode of crossing until 1935 when the first bridge was built. The first region where most of the cattle were raised was near the present airport and was called Tillets Pond. Eventually cattle ranching spread west to Burrell Boom, Bermudian Landing, and surrounding areas. As this movement proceeded, Bermudian Landing became a center for the butchering of cattle and became

known as Butchers Landing because ranchers would bring their cattle to the area from surrounding lands. However, it was also an encampment for logging so that it took on the title of landing. As the loggers purchased land and began cattle farms it became established as Butchers Landing.

The origin of the name Bermudian Landing is attributed to a buccaneer band of Bermudians who fled upriver after being raided by other pirates back in the 1600's. The village rested on the first high bank where they could camp away from the flood waters. Because it was a logging encampment, it took on the title of landing. The original name reasserted itself possibly during the late 18th century when large tracts of land were given out and timber cutters leased large areas. One of the landowners was from Bermuda or was of mixed descent, being half Bermudian and he became a land leaser during the 19th century. Another story which may have equal validity, maintains that Bermudian Landing got its name from the Bermuda grass which was grown for the cattle. Whichever explanation is correct, there was nonetheless a settler in the area who was at least half Bermudian. As the river became increasingly settled with towns and encampments, the river took on a major transportation function in the 1800's. Since there were no real roads across land, the river played its part in history as the main travel route west, just as the ocean continued to be the method of travel along the coast.

Pitpans and Cayo Boats

Besides the many small, hand-carved dories, the first boats used on the rivers for moving people and goods were called pitpans. These hand-carved boats reached to 40 ft (12.5 m) long and 5 ft (1.5 m) across and were mostly flat-bottomed. Both the bow and stern of the boat were squared and several oarsmen paddled the boat. Pitpans were used extensively from the 1600's up until the early 1900's. A pitpan trip from Belize City to San Ignacio took anywhere from 8 to 21 days, travelling both day and night. Because the Belize River has strong currents along some stretches, the pitpans would be emptied of persons and cargoes and pulled by rope or hand over the rapids. One such area was Big Falls located within the Community Baboon Sanctuary. Other rapids had names such as Baboon Eddy, Monkey Run, 4 Pounds of Pork, and Triantilobo.

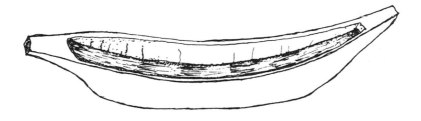

Pitpan

In the early 1900's the pitpan gave way to the mechanical age as engine driven boats began to run on the Belize River. These boats ran from Belize City to San Ignacio and became known as the "Cayo Boats". The first Cayo Boat to travel up the Belize was the *Clarence Mengel* in 1905. The earliest boats burned kerosene and then gasoline and the later boats burned diesel fuel. Cayo Boats were flat-bottomed and could travel in as little as 2-3 ft (0.6-1 m) of water. The boat's propeller was protected by being located in a large oval groove in the stern. The boats ranged from 43-52 ft (13-16 m) long and from 7-10 ft (2-3 m) wide. The deck of the boat was covered only with a small canvas awning. Officially the boats were known as "River Tunnel Boats". A typical Cayo Boat could carry between 7 and 10 tons of cargo and make the round trip from Belize City to San Ignacio in 6 to 12 days. Travel was faster in the rainy season due to the higher water level in the river and as many as 5 trips per month were made. Cayo Boats made stops at Bermudian Landing, Double Head Cabbage, Willows Bank, Cockloft, St Paul's Bank, and Big Falls all located within the present day sanctuary.

Typical Cayo Boat

A typical Cayo Boat crew consisted of a captain engineer, purser, oiler, and 3 to 4 sailors. Each Cayo Boat was also equiped with a winch to pull the boat forward against strong currents or rapids. Passengers had to sit, eat and sleep on the deck for the trip's duration. As many as 15 Cayo Boats might have been on the Belize River at any one time. Many boats tugged pitpans behind them to carry goods such as chicle, bananas, lumber, food, mail and even livestock. The Cayo Boats ran until the mid 1940's when the Western Highway connecting Belize City to San Ignacio was completed.

BELIZEAN TREES AND HISTORY

*B*elizean forests support over 700 tree species including a large variety of economically and historically important trees. Economically valuable trees have played a vital role in the history of the country. Indeed, the history and the very existence of Belize as a colony is inseparable from the logging industry. Among the most important historical tree crops are logwood, mahogany, and chicle.

Logwood - *Born To Dye*

The early history of Belize [British Honduras] is largely based on the exploitation of the logwood tree (*Haematoxylon campechianum*). As early as the mid 1500's, the Spanish were cutting logwood off the Atlantic coasts of Guatemala, Honduras, and Mexico and shipping it to European ports. Logwood grows in abundance in low forests, swamps, and wet thickets on the eastern half of the northern plain of Belize. The species ranges from the Yucatan Peninsula south into the Bay of Honduras. The logwood tree is usually small, 25 ft (8 m) high or less, with a crooked, deeply fluted trunk and often grows in dense thickets.

The heartwood of the logwood tree contains a valuable dye which was much in demand in the European woolen industry. The dye was also used in the manufacturing of inks. The dye, known as *haematoxylon*, was extracted by mashing the logwood into small bits and boiling them in water. The extracted logwood dye was used as a basic fixing dye and depending on the additives used, dyes ranging from yellow to black could be obtained. The southern Yucatan contained virtually the sole source of the valuable wood.

British buccaneers using the mouth of the Belize River (also called the the Old River) as a base, were probably the first foreign settlers in Belize in the late 1630's. These buccaneers raided Spanish ships carrying logwood cargoes and brought them to England where they were paid as much as £500 per ton. Even before buccaneering was outlawed in 1670, many buccaneers were cutting logwood themselves along the Belize and Sibun Rivers and in Campeche in Mexico.

Logwood cutting continued as small groups of slaves were brought in to do the cutting from 1670 on. Logwood cutting required only small groups of slaves and former buccaneers. Because logwood sinks in water, rafts were made (commonly out of cabbage palms) to float the logwood down the rivers to be loaded on ships. The logwood was usually cut into three foot (1 m) lengths and loaded onto the rafts. Because logwood grows in dense thickets, initially the loggers had large reserves of logwood to harvest along the riversides but by the early 1700's, many of the inland logwood regions were overharvested. Today along the rivers and lagoons in northern Belize, large stands of logwood can still be found. Logwood groves still exist on the shores of the lagoons in the Crooked Tree Wildlife Sanctuary and logwood can be seen near the old ferry crossing in the Community Baboon Sanctuary.

The logwood industry was booming in Belize up until the 1770's when logwood prices bottomed out as alternative dyes were developed and mahogany replaced logwood as the major forestry crop. Despite the logwood crash, logwood was being exported from Belize in small quantities up into the 1930's. Today there seems to be a slight resurgent interest in logwood as the modern world is again interested in natural dyes.

Mahogany - " Sub Umbra Floreo "

The coat of arms of Belize has the motto: "*Sub Umbra Floreo*"; under the tree we flourish. The tree is mahogany. During the logwood boom, mahogany was largely overlooked as a marketable timber and was cut and used mostly for ship repair. From the mid-1500's, mahogany was being cleared along the lower Belize River. Mahogany was a logical choice for repair work because the wood was strong yet easy to work and found in abundance along the rivers. But by the mid 1700's,

as the logwood industry was in decline, mahogany became the timber of choice as the beauty, durability, and workability of the wood was discovered by European manufacturers.

Even as early as 1670, Scottish loggers with slave crews were penetrating beyond the riverbanks deeper into Belize in search of mahogany. Many of the areas they logged were on lands claimed by the Spaniards. This territorial dispute over mahogany rights led to a 200 year struggle for control of the territory. It wasn't until 1783 and 1786 under Article 6 of the Treaty of Versailles, that concessions were formally given to the British by the Spanish for logging, and even at that time, concessions were exclusively for logwood.

Mahogany cutting was more complex than logwood cutting mainly because mahogany trees grow scattered about in mixed forests, sometimes there being only one tree in two acres or more of forest. This meant that harvesting the timber required dragging the logs to the nearest river so they could be floated downstream to be shipped to Europe or America.

Before any logging operations were started, a buccaneer and mahogany "hunters" would paddle their canoes up river to set up camp at a promising site. The first rivers travelled up were the Belize, New, and Hondo. The party would set up a temporary camp called a "bank". During the voyage they would keep track of the high water mark, especially over rapids or rocks where the logs would have to be floated past. From the bank camp, hunters would go into the bush looking for mahogany. Each tree would be marked and a series of right angle trails would be cleared connecting all the trees. After the hunt was complete, a semi-permanent cutters camp would be built.

The next step involved preparing areas to accomodate the oxen used in pulling out logs from the bush to the river's edge. Areas had to be cleared to grow fodder. After the camp was established the operator of the camp would then return back to the coast to recruit labor for the cutting. Slaves were usually indentured for six months of the year to work in the logging camps. Mahogany crews ranged in size from 10 to 50 men and typically included a foreman, crew captain, two cattle drivers, 30 laborers (mostly axeman), 80 working steers or oxen, and four log sleds. The successful harvesting of mahogany was, and still is for the most part, linked to the weather and the timing of the rainy and dry seasons. Cutting began in December just before the dry season began. From 1670 on, logging camps sprang up along the Belize River as far west as the Cayo District.

Because mature mahogany trees often have large buttresses, the tree cutters, known as fellers, would have to build scaffolding up to 15 ft (5 m) up the trunk. This scaffolding was called a "barbeque". The trees were felled with axes and cross-cut saws. After felling, the trees would be cut into 20 ft (6 m) lengths and dragged out by four, eight or more yoke of oxen depending on the size of the log. Because such an operation was costly, a five mile (8 km) haul by an ox drawn sled was generally the operations limit. As many logs as possible would be cut during the dry season at any number of established banks. The area where the logs were hauled was called a landing. Logs would not be floated downstream until sufficient rains arrived in June or later. When the rivers rose high enough, the logs would be floated down river to an area where a large chain or barrier was erected in the river called a "boom". Here

Barbeque Scaffolding

the logs would be picked out of the river and transported onto land vehicles or directly onto ships. Some of the logs would be roughly squared by hand before loading onto the ships. Due to the colonial, export-orientated nature of the logging trade, the first sawmill in Belize was not established until 1933, in Belize City. In a similiar bent, systematic forestry under the auspices of a Forestry Department did not begin in Belize until 1922.

Mahogany was primarily used in Europe and America for furniture building and wood working. The market fluctuated a great deal and estimates of production are very sketchy. However, mahogany exports were the mainstay of the economy of British Honduras from the late 1770's to the

1950's. In the 1840's there was a boom as the expanding European railway industry used the wood for building elegant railway carriages. Another resurgence in the trade occured early in this century as trade to the U.S. increased. Today much of the mahogany in the country has been removed and little systematic effort has been made to replant seedlings after logging operations.

GALLON JUG

One of the last huge stands of natural mahogany forest in Belize was at the frontier with Guatemala west of Hill Bank Lagoon in northwestern Belize. In the late 1920's and early 1930's this area was exploited when a light railway was developed heading west from Hill Bank Lagoon. Eventually the railroad reached a logging camp called Gallon Jug. The mahogany was carried by rail to Hill Bank and then rolled into the lagoon where the logs were connected in rafts of 400 to 500 logs and then floated by lagoon, river, and estuary to the sawmill on Haulover Creek in Belize City, some 180 miles (290 km) away! The Gallon Jug logging boom employed many people from the seven villages comprising the Sanctuary. Gallon Jug was abandoned in 1965 and all the equipment was moved to Hill Bank where many rusty remnants still remain.

MAHOGANY CONSERVATION AND REFORESTATION

One reason mahogany stocks are depleted in Belize today, has been the lack of consistent replanting of the tree after harvest. Although some reforestation efforts have been made in the past in areas like the Silk Grass Reserve and at Hill Bank, much more reseeding and replanting is needed to ensure future supplies of the timber. In other attempts to preserve timber stocks, size limits have been set for mahogany and other valuable hardwoods. The minmum cutting limit for mahogany is 24 in dbh (63 cm in diameter at breast height). Size limits are needed to prevent overharvesting and to ensure that at least some trees capable of reproducing will be left as seed sources to reseed the cutover forests.

Another noteworthy conservation effort links past and present techniques. The ancient Mayans frequently planted belts of mahogany trees on their raised terraces to shade some of their plantings. This practice may account for the high density of mahogany in some regions. Nevertheless, in the 1950's a group of Kekchi Maya tried to revise this type of old Mayan replanting strategy. Under the new system, the Kekchi plant mahogany seeds with corn in their recently cleared milpas. They tend to both their crops and the mahogany seedlings. After three years the milpa is abandoned, but after this period there has been sufficient time for the mahogany seedlings to take hold. In 50 years or so there will be large harvestable mahogany on the site again. Repeated plantings in this manner, year after year, could provide a sustainable crop of mahogany as well as a wide variety of food stuffs.

Chicle

The preparation and use of chicle dates back to the ancient Maya. Chicle is formed from the coagulated milky latex of the sapodilla tree (*Manilkara zapota*), a native tree of the mixed hardwood forests of Belize, the Peten in Guatemala, and the southern Yucatan. While chicle gum (and the fruits of the sapodilla tree) were used for centuries, it was not until the early 20th century that the commercial chicle industry was born. Chicle became an important export as a gum base for the commercial chewing gum industry in England and America. The chicle industry in Belize reached prominence in the 1920's and chicle continued to be exported through the 1960's. The sapodilla tree has also been introduced to several other regions of the world including Venezuela, the Caribbean islands, India, Burma, Indonesia, Sri Lanka, and the Phillipines.

The chicle industry in Belize was centered in the northern and western regions of the nation. The sapodilla is a large tree with thick fissured bark and is common on limestone soils in well developed forests. The trees were harvested by chicle tappers called "chicleros". Chicleros generally travelled in parties of four or five persons (but sometimes in much larger groups). The equipment used to harvest the latex included razor sharp machetes, canvas collecting bags lined with rubber obtained from the local rubber tree (*Castilla elastica*), rope, climbing spikes, and iron pots to boil the latex. Chicleros lived in the forest often for months at a time eating rationed supplies supplemented with game meat hunted around camp sites.

Trees are tapped during the rainy season from July to February when the latex is most abundant. Only trees greater than 30 years old are generally tapped. Tapping the sapodilla tree involves making a series of oblique cuts or V-shaped slashes from near the base of the tree up to around 30 ft (9 m) with a machete. The machete cuts are carefully made to

Chiclero Climbing to Make
Zig-Zag Cut On Chicle Tree

pierce only the outer bark and not the cambium layer. This zig-zag pattern of cuts is made so the milky latex will slowly drip down the trunk into a rubber lined bag attached to the base of the tree. Because the latex coagulates quickly on exposure to wind or sun, tapping is generally done early in the morning while the air is humid and still. The latex usually runs for only four to six hours after cutting. A chiclero could tap anywhere from 6 to 15 trees in one morning. A single tree might yield 4-5 lbs (2 kg) of latex.

The latex is then collected from each tree and placed in an iron pot to be boiled. Thirty gallons (110 liters) or more of chicle are usually boiled at one time. The latex is boiled until it has a water content of about 33% and then is poured into wooden molds called blocks or bricks. The blocks are lined

Collecting Chicle

with rubber, canvas or palm leaves and soaped to prevent the chicle from sticking. Blocks are then dried for 2- 3 days. Each dried block weighs around 25 lbs (11 kg) and is packed into "bales" of about 4 blocks each and loaded onto mules. A chiclero's entire collection of blocks is called a "cache". The mules then carry the bales to the nearest river to be transported by boat to the city for export. In a season, a chiclero on average could set one ton (910 kg) of chicle and tap some 200-300 trees.

After a sapodilla tree is tapped, it is retappable only after 6-8 years or after 3 years on an area of tree trunk left previously uncut. A tree can be harvested (tapped) up to three times, although the yield drops with each successive tapping. If you look in the forests of Belize today, nearly every large sapodilla tree has the scars of the chiclero's cuts. The chicle industry in Belize peaked in the late 1920's and early 1930's when around 12 million lbs (5.5 million kg) per year were produced and was valued at some 70 million U.S. dollars. After that time, the industry faced a steady decline as the supply of virgin sapodilla trees became exhausted and chicle from other sources filled the market.

BELIZEAN FORESTS

*I*n Belize there are nearly 4,000 species of flowering plants including over 700 tree species and 250 different orchids. Belize also supports a wide range of forest types and associations. The location and extent of a given forest type (or plant species) depends on several factors including the type and quality of soil, seasonal rainfall amounts, climate patterns, and the topography of a given region. For example, the limestone soils in Orange Walk that receive about 60 inches (150 cm) of rain per year, support very different forests than the hilly sandstone-shale soils in the Toledo District which receive about 160 inches (400 cm) of rain per year.

Another factor affecting forest structure and cover in Belize is human activity. Due to both the extensive logging in the country for the past 300 years, and agricultural activity, many of the forests in Belize have been modified and no longer resemble the undisturbed, mature forests of previous eras. Many forests in the nation are "secondary forests", meaning they have been disturbed in the recent past, are not fully developed, and contain many species that only grow in disturbed areas. Mature undisturbed forests, often called "climax forests", are less common in Belize and are generally found in remote regions.

To say that Belize is covered with tropical rain forest is misleading. The general term "tropical rain forest" refers to a wide variety of different forest types ranging from wet cloud forests to dry subtropical-like forests. While Belize is in the tropical realm and much of the nation remains under a mixed hardwood forest cover, many forests in the nation are not lush, well-developed, high canopy rain forest. For example, in the northern and coastal parts of the nation there are many dry, broken canopy forests, mainly pine or pine-oak forests and savanna. These low forests occur on sandy soils, have a broken canopy, contain relatively few species, and often are dominated by only a handful of tree species. Other forests occurring along lagoons and swamps are also often scrubby, broken forests little resembling well developed rain forest. Many high altitude forests in the Maya Mountains also support low, scrubby forests.

In addition to the dry, scrubby character of some Belizean forests, many forest trees in Belize are deciduous (shed their leaves) during the dry season giving the forests a semi-deciduous and subtropical flavor. Nonetheless, in some regions of Belize, such as in the western Orange Walk and Cayo Districts and in the Toledo District, well-developed, species-rich "rain forests" do occur.

Northern Belizean Forests

As was mentioned earlier, the climate, soils and topography of a region dictate what type of forests can grow. Northern Belize is a relatively flat plain underlain by limestone. Soils range from coastal muds to sand to clay to fertile-limestone soils. There are many forest types in northern Belize which grow on these soils and not all have been well studied or documented. Many forest types also grade together and it's difficult to determine when one forest type ends and the next begins. A few key forest types, however, are relatively common and provide a broad classification scheme for all forest types.

It should be noted that in Belize, different forest types are commonly referred to as different "ridges". The word ridge refers only to forest type and not topography. For example, the most commonly used ridge terms are "Pine Ridge" (refers to Pine or Pine-Oak forest), "Broken Ridge" (mixed-hardwood, broken canopy forest), "High Ridge" (well developed, high canopy forest), and "Cohune Ridge" (cohune palm forest). The following is a brief description of some of the more distinctive forest types found in northern Belize and/or within the vicinity of the Community Baboon Sanctuary. It is by no means a complete list of the many forest associations found in the region.

Coastal - Mangrove Forests

Mangroves are defined as any group of woody plants growing on subtidal or intertidal soils; they do not have to include species of mangrove trees, although most do. Mangrove forests occur mostly along the mainland and island coasts and in tidal lagoons and coastal swamps. Most of Belize's coastal fringe is or was at one time occupied by mangroves. The mangroves are important habitat for many fishes, crabs, birds and other sea life. They are also an important breeding ground for many species. The main tree species found in the mangroves are red mangrove (*Rhizophora mangle*), buttonwood (*Conocarpus erecta*), white mangrove (*Laguncularia racemosa*), and black mangrove (*Avicennia germinans*). Other coastal plant species include the sea grape (*Coccoloba uvifera*), swamp caway (*Pterocarpus officinalis*), provision tree (*Pachira aquatica*), coconut (*Cocos nucifera*), and marsh fern (*Acrostichum aureum*). This latter group of species often forms a tidal levee forest which is found behind the mangroves on slightly higher and less salty ground.

Pine Forest - Pine Ridge

"Pine Ridge" refers to the pine-oak-palmetto forest and savanna in Belize. Pine ridge forests occur on sandy soils along the coastal plain and in dry, sandy areas on the northern plains. Two narrow north-south bands of pine ridge occur inland on the northern plain. The first is about 11 miles (18 km) wide and located from 5 to 25 miles (8 to 40 km) from the coast and the other is much narrower and is 25 to 40 miles (40 to 56 km) inland. Pine ridge plants must be well adapted to the dry, acidic, nutrient-poor conditions found on the sandy soils, especially in the dry season. The dominant species is the honduran or caribbean pine (*Pinus caribaea*). Another pine species (*Pinus oocarpa*) occurs in Belize but at much higher elevations than   *P. caribaea*   and is centered mostly in the Mountain Pine Ridge and ranges west into Guatemala.

Pine ridge forests contain several characteristic species but do not have the diversity of tree species found in other forest types.   The common pine ridge tree species associated with the caribbbean pine are the calabash (*Cresentia cujete*), oaks (*Quercus* spp.), yaha (*Curatella americana*), craboo (*Byrconima craccifolia*), and the palmetto palm (*Acoelorraphe wrightii*).   In some areas there may be as many as 3,400 palmetto stems per acre (0.4 ha). However, the forest canopy in the Pine ridge is rarely closed and often forms a savanna/grassland. The ground cover in pine ridge areas consists of grasses, many sedges, and numerous species of wildflower.

Pine ridge areas not part of protected Forest Reserves are often deliberately burned during dry periods. The areas are burned in an attempt to improve grazing for cattle and sometimes to attract deer for hunting. The ashes from the fires act as fertilizer for the young grasses and forbs which resprout after the fire. These pine ridge fires, however, often kill many younger shrubs and trees including pines, and the density of many trees depends on the frequency and severity of fire. Many mature pine trees are protected from the flames and heat by their thick, corky bark.

Because the pine (*Pinus caribaea*) in Belize is a timber of economic value, the Forestry Department protects pine forests from uncontrolled burning in both the Mountain Pine Ridge and the southern coastal plain. While the adult pine is fairly fire resistant, young pines are susceptible to burning. Controlled burning after pines reach a certain size, however, can actually be beneficial to the trees because the fire kills or damages competitors. It should also be noted that the minimum cutting limit for pine is 13.5 in (34 cm) in diameter at breast height.

Swamp Forest - Bajo

Northern Belize has many inland, freshwater lagoons and waterways with swamp forests on their perimeters. In these areas and in other low-lying wet areas, you also often find herbaceous marshes (called "ponds") with swamp forests surrounding them. These swamp forests have wet soils througout the year although they may dry out somewhat during the dry season. The swamp forests often have a low canopy rarely over 40 ft (12.5 m) with few emergent trees. Some of the more common species are the pokenoboy (*Bactris major*), give-and-take (*Chrysophila argentea*), and cabbage palms (*Euterpe macrospadix*), as well as wild grape (*Coccoloba belizensis*), copna (*Erythrina* spp.), provision tree (*Pachira aquatica*) and bamboo. Swamp forests are often dense and form inpenetrable thickets, especially where spiny bamboo is found.

Another type of swamp forest is the logwood thicket. The logwood tree (*Haematoxylon campechianum*) is found in low, wet areas, especially along inland lagoons, in the northern plains of Belize. It often forms dense monotypic stands.

Broken Canopy Broadleaved Forest - Broken Ridge

Broken mixed broadleaf forest is an intermediate stature forest occuring between sandy pine ridge soils and more fertile alluvial clays or rich limestone soils. Mixed broadleaf forest associations are also found on well-drained limestone hillsides and in the low-lying, wetter regions of the pine ridge. These hardwood islands in the pine ridge are called "cayes" and resemble the hardwood islands found in the Florida Everglades. The extent of the mixed broadleaf forest is highly variable ranging from a few hundred feet in some areas to many miles in others. Broken ridge forests also vary in species composition. The canopy is frequently broken and many species found in the broken ridge are light-demanding species capable of rapid growth. The mixed forest is more species rich than the pine ridge but not as diverse or well structured as the mature cohune forests and closed canopy, mixed hardwood forest.

Tree species typically found in mixed broadleaf forest include yemeri (*Vochysia hondurensis*), trumpet (*Cecropia peltata* and *C. obtusifolia*), negrito (*Simarouba glauca*), white maya (*Miconia argentea*), wild cotton (*Cochlospermum vitifolium*), cowfoot (*Piper auritum*), nargusta (*Terminalia amazonia*), polewood (*Xylopia frutescens*), and bay cedar (*Guazuma ulmifolia*). Within the Community Baboon Sanctuary, the mixed broadleaf forest is best represented on the west bank of the Belize River between the river and the pine ridge. Other examples can be found on the Western Highway moving towards Belmopan. The highway cuts through pine, broken, and cohune ridge forests before it reaches the rich riverine forests along the Belize River and Roaring Creek.

Cohune Palm Forest - Cohune Ridge

The cohune palm (*Orbigyna cohune*) occurs throughout Belize from near sea level to 2,000 ft (650 m) and is one of the most abundant and distinctive trees in the nation. The cohune is prominent in many plant communities but is often the dominant species forming a plant association known as cohune forest or cohune ridge. Reports of over 120 cohune trees per acre (0.4 ha) have been recorded and cohunes commonly form dense monotypic stands. Cohune forest is most common on fertile organic soils which are moderately well drained but still moist. Cohune forests are found throughout all Districts in Belize.

Cohune forest shares many attributes with the broadleaved hardwood forest (high bush). The main differences are in the relative proportion of species and in the nutrient dynamics in the soils under the forest. Cohunes provide both shade year round which inhibits shade-intolerant species from becoming established, and a deep mulch of frond litter which provides a constant nutrient source. The forest floor is often cluttered with fallen cohune fronds and nuts in a mature cohune forest. The towering cohune fronds, some reaching up to 35 ft (12 m) long, also give the understory a cathedral like quality.

Despite the abundance of cohunes in the cohune forest, other tree species are common and attain canopy height including hog plum (*Spondias mombin*), tubroos (*Enterolobium cyclocarpum*), quamwood (*Schizolobium parahybum*), bucut (*Cassia grandis*), dogwood (*Lonchocarpus guatemalensis*), mampola (*Luehea seemanii*), and gumbolimbo (*Bursera simaruba*). Because of the fertile soils beneath cohune forests, many Belizean farmers use the cohune's presence as an indicator of rich, arable land for agriculture. Cohunes are also left in plantations or milpas because of the difficulty in felling them with machetes or axes; the persistent leaf sheaths and the base of the trunk are very hard. Cohunes are also commonly left in pastures as a source of year round shade for cattle further contributing to their abundance in certain regions.

Broadleaved Hardwood Forest - High Ridge

Closed canopy broadleaved forests cover large areas in northern and western Belize as well as in the Peten region of Guatemala and the southern part of the Yucatan in Mexico. These forests have been described as semi-deciduous rain forest, deciduous seasonal forest, or broadleaf forests rich in lime-loving species. Under the broad classification of broadleaved hardwood forest, many different forest associations can be found. Cohune forests are often interspersed with or are contiguous to the hardwood forests. Two major associations common within the northern Belizean hardwood forests are riverine forests and upland limestone forests.

Riverine or riparian forests are found on alluvial clay soils associated with inland rivers and waterways. These riverine gallery forests cut through regions of pine ridge, broken ridge, cohune forest, and other broadleaved forest associations. Riparian forest compositon overlaps with other forest types and is distinguished by the relative abundance of certain species and the seasonal dynamics of flooding. Species along waterways must be adapted to seasonal patterns of flooding and drying out. Common riverine species include the bri bri (*Inga edulis*), bullet tree (*Bucida buceras*), wild grape (*Coccoloba belizensis*), swamp dogwood (*Lonchcarpus hondurensis*), provision tree (*Pachira aquatica*), Cabbage palm (*Euterpe macrospadix*), and many fig species (*Ficus* spp.).

The banks of rivers are often a dense tangle of bamboo, vines, lianas, shrubs, and trees. This luxuriant growth is due to the high levels of sunlight along open waterways. One of the most common species along waterways is spiny bamboo (*Guadua spinosa*), a grass which grows quickly and in dense tangles which are virtually inpenetrable unless one yields a machete.

Proximity of the Belize River throughout the Community Baboon Sanctuary, makes riverine forest the predominate forest community found in the sanctuary. Because of the fertile soils beneath this forest type, riverine forest areas are also one of the most disturbed forest communities in Belize. Clearings for milpas and pastures often run to the rivers edge increasing erosion, damaging soils, slowing forest regeneration, and destroying valuable wildlife habitat. Understanding the value and importance of riverine forests is a crucial step in improving both agricultural methods and environmental quality in Belize.

The other common hardwood forest type in Northern Belize is the broadleaved limestone forest. These forests occur both north and west of the Belize River on moderately drained soils rich in limestone. These forests are very diverse with no one species attaining dominance. Characteristic species of this forest are mahogany (*Swietenia macrophylla*), cedar (*Cedrela mexicana*), ramon (*Brosimum alicastrum*), santa maria (*Calophyllum brasiliense*), sapodilla (*Manilkara zapota*), cherry (*Pseudolmedia spuria*), allspice (*Pimenta dioica*), chicle (*Manilkara chicle*), silly young (*Pouteria izabalensis*), cojotone (*Stemmadenia donnell-smithii*), and figs (*Ficus* spp.). Limestone forests do not occur in the Community Baboon Sanctuary but are common west of the sanctuary in Rancho Dolores and north past Lemonal. The lands purchased as part of the Rio Bravo Reserve in northeast Belize also support high ridge forests.

FOREST TYPES WITHIN THE SANCTUARY

*L*ike most of Belize, the forests of the Community Baboon Sanctuary have been periodically logged for some 300 years. Most of the area is thus a patchwork of secondary forests of varying ages from 10-75 years old, interspersed with cleared areas and secondary growth. Within these varied successional stages of forest, there are five distinct forest communities: pine-oak forest, mixed broadleaved forest, cohune palm forest, riverine forest, and bajo forest. There are also herbaceous plant communities within the sanctuary including wetland marshes, grasslands, and aquatic vegetation.

The sanctuary is located in the climatic region of north central Belize classified as lowland, semi-deciduous rain forest. The region gets around 60-70 in (150-175 cm) of rain per year with a pronounced dry season from February through May. The Belize River winds through the heart of the sanctuary and is a key ecological component of the area. Locally, forest is commonly called "bush" and is used with modifiers such as high, medium, or low.

The pine ridge forests are found on the sandy, drier soils in a north south band in the western portion of the sanctuary. Pine ridge soils are somewhat acidic, have a low fertility and are well drained. The sandy soils are commonly 18-20 in (45- 55 cm) deep. These soils support a pine-oak-palmetto palm forest and/or savanna with a herbaceous ground cover. The main shrub and tree species found in the pine ridge are the caribbean pine (*Pinus caribaea*), pimenta palm (*Paurotis wrightii*), wild cotton (*Cochlospermum vitifolium*) , white maya (*Miconia argentea*), craboo (*Byrsonima crassifolia*), yaha (*Curatella americana*), calabash (*Cresentia cujete*), oak (*Quercus* spp.) and wild coco plum (*Chrysobalanus icaco*). The ground cover includes many grasses including *Ischaemum latifolium, Andropogon leucostachys, Paspalum serpentinum, Panicum parvifolium, Mesosetoum filifolium,* and *Leptocorphium lanatum* and sedges of the genera *Rhyncospora,*

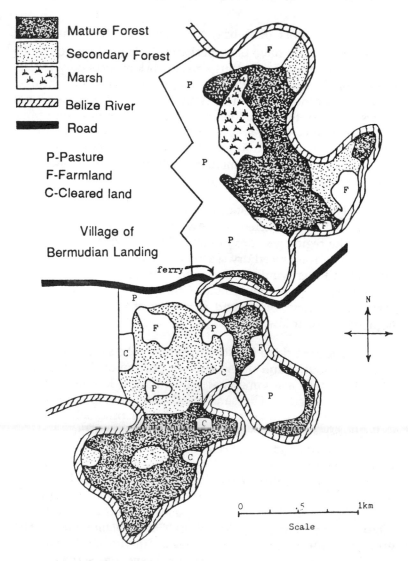

Legend

- Mature Forest
- Secondary Forest
- Marsh
- Belize River
- Road

P-Pasture
F-Farmland
C-Cleared land

Village of
Bermudian Landing

ferry

N

Scale
0   .5   1km

Vegetation Map of the Original Sanctuary

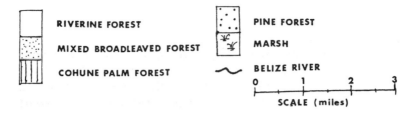

RIVERINE FOREST   PINE FOREST

MIXED BROADLEAVED FOREST   MARSH

COHUNE PALM FOREST   BELIZE RIVER

0   1   2   3

SCALE (miles)

VEGETATION MAP OF CBS

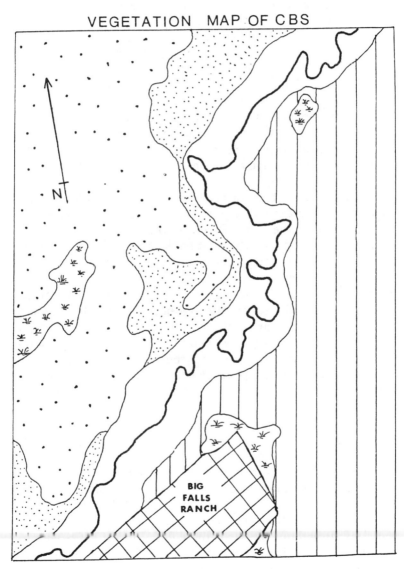

N

BIG
FALLS
RANCH

Eleocharis, and *Cyperus.*

Most of the village centers are located on the pine ridge because there is better drainage, there are fewer insects and there is often a steady breeze. Within the sanctuary, all village centers are located in the pine ridge except Flowers Bank and Scotland Half-Moon. Much of the quality pine in the sanctuary has been recently logged off mostly due to the presence of a sawmill in Isabella Bank. Pine trees have also been cut down near dwellings because it is widely believed that they attract lightning. Pine trees are also cut for their resin-laden wood which burns when green and produces a thick smoke used to repel insects. Oaks are the primary source of firewood for most villages and hence large oaks are also rare. A large number of cashew (*Anacardium occidentale*), mango (*Mangifera indica*), and coconut palm (*Cocos nucifera*) trees have also been planted on the pine ridge near homes and village centers.

The mixed broadleaved forest is a transition forest situated between the sandy pine ridge soils and the fertile clay soils found along the Belize River. In the sanctuary, the mixed forest is most evident on the west bank of the river between the north south running pine ridge and the riverine forest. Often, the mixed forest canopy is broken and does not reach a great height. Locally, the forest is called broken ridge. Much of the broken ridge in the sanctuary has been cleared for pasture because the moderate-fertility, moderately-drained soils support pasture grasses. Patches of mixed forest still stand however, especially surrounding the low-lying areas in the pine ridge and running parallel in a band west of the Belize River.

Cohune forest, characterized by the cohune palm (*Orbigyna cohune*), is found on the more fertile, clay soils where a moderate amount of water is available throughout the year. Cohune forest is located primarily in the eastern portion of the sanctuary and runs all the way to Mussel Creek. Along the rivers, however, where flooding is frequent during the rainy season and where abundant quantities of water are available throughout the year, the cohune forest gives way to riverine forest. Although the cohune and riverine forests share many of the same species, certain species are much more common or occur only in the riverine forest because these species are better adapted to the seasonal flooding and drying out cycles

Cohune Palm

which exist along the river. Proximity of the Belize River throughout the sanctuary makes riverine forest the predominate forest community found in the sanctuary.

The riverine forest is found in a band of variable width running along both sides of the Belize River and contains some 60-70 tree and shrub species and hundreds of other lianas, vines, epiphytes, and herbs. Of the numerous tree species found in the riverine forest, certain species are much more common. These common species include the bucut (*Cassia grandis*), tubroos (*Enterolobium cyclocarpum*), mampola (*Luehua seemanii*), bay cedar (*Guazuma ulmifolia*), bri bri (*Inga edulis*), hogplum (*Spondias mombin*), figs (*Ficus* spp.), cotton tree (*Ceiba pentandra*), dogwoods (*Lonchocarpus* spp.), bullet tree (*Bucida buceras*), wild grape (*Coccoloba belizensis*), cohune palm, and gumbolimbo (*Bursera simaruba*). These trees reach a moderate height when mature. The pronounced dry season coupled with the effects of seasonal flooding prevent the forest trees along the rivers from attaining the height they might achieve in other areas of Belize or Central America. The pronounced dry season also causes the soil to dry out and many trees such as the hogplum, bucut, tubroos, gumbolimbo, and mampola drop their leaves during the dry season in response, in part, to the lack of available moisture. This leaf dropping gives the forest a semi-deciduous character.

The riverine and other forest communities which remain today in the sanctuary, have been greatly modified by two major activities: commercial logging and agriculture. Logging activity has removed, and continues to remove, many of the valuable timber species from the forest. The most commonly exploited trees have been logwood, mahogany, cedar, santa maria, nargusta, and pine. Consequently, many of the logged tree species are only rarely found in the forests today in spite of their past abundance. The traditional milpa system of agriculture has also changed the forest. The clearing and burning of patches of forest for the growing of crops and raising of livestock combined with the effects of logging have left varying portions of the forest today in different stages of growth and at different ages. All the forests found in the sanctuary can be considered secondary forests because of their extensive modification. If left undisturbed, however, the forest will regenerate itself. The different patterns and phases of forest regeneration are part of the natural cycle of succession which is discussed in another section.

FOREST PHENOLOGY

*T*he seasonal rhythms of biological activity are important in all plant communities but are especially important in tropical forests. Seasonality in the leaf formation, leaf shedding, flowering, and fruiting of tropical trees (and other plants) plays a crucial role in the functioning of the entire forest community including both plants and animals. The study of seasonal biological activity is called "phenology". The phenology of tropical forests is closely linked with rainfall patterns and climate.

Northern regions of Belize receive around 60-80 in (150-200 cm) of rain per year, on average. In this part of Belize there is also a distinct dry season from February through May. The chart below shows a typical seasonal rainfall pattern in northern Belize. The timing of the start and end

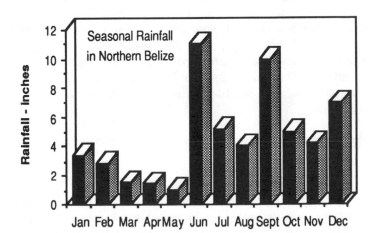

of the dry season are important cues for many forest species. One of the most conspicuous responses of northern Belizean forests to climate is that many tree species are deciduous (shed their leaves) for all or part of the dry season.

Leaves

Trees can lose large quantities of water under dry, sunlit conditions by evaporation through their leaves. When rainfall supplies diminish for a prolonged period, as occurs in the dry season, the loss of water cannot be adequately replenished and many trees shed their leaves to conserve water. Some common deciduous, dry season trees include the hogplum (*Spondias mombin*), mampola (*Luehea seemanii*), tubroos (*Enterolobium cyclocarpum*), quamwood (*Schizolobium parahybum*), cotton tree (*Ceiba pentandra*), mayflower (*Tabebuia rosea*), gumbolimbo (*Bursera simaruba*), dogwood (*Lonchocarpus guatemalensis*), and prickly yellow (*Zanthoxylum kellermanii*). While each of these species sheds its leaves during a portion of the dry, not all shed at the same time. When leaf shedding occurs depends on the ecology and physiology of the tree and its location in the forest. Many trees also flower in the dry season and leaf shedding may be a mechanism whereby the tree can reallocate water for developing flowers and fruits.

Some trees, however, do not shed all their leaves in the dry season and may be called semi-deciduous or evergreen. Examples of semi-deciduous trees in Northern Belize include the bri-bri (*Inga edulis*), cow okra (*Parmentiera asculeata*), many figs (*Ficus* spp.), and the wild grape (*Coccoloba belizensis*). New leaves are most often produced at the very beginning of the rainy season in late May or June. Often the timing of new leaf production is synchronous with the first heavy rains.

Flowering

There are several strategies as to when and how long a tree should produce flowers. Some trees will flower together in synchrony, others may produce flowers bit by bit all year (e.g. *Rhizophora mangle*). Some trees produce flowers for only a few days, others may produce flowers throughout the year. In northern Belize, there are two flowering peaks. The largest peak occurs during the dry season with a second smaller peak occuring about one month after the rainy season begins. There may be several explanations as to why dry season flowering is so common.

First, during the dry season, flowers are less likely to be damaged by bad weather and heavy rains. Second, flowers producing nectar are less susceptible to having their nectar washed away. Thirdly, there are generally more pollinators (mostly insects) available thereby increasing both rates of pollination and outcrossing potential. Fourth, deciduous trees are able to put more resources into flower and fruit production at a time which is least detrimental to vegetative competition. One, some, all or none of these factors may explain dry season flowering in any given species.

The following chart provides a small sample of different tree flowering phenology behavior. The chart is based on data collected by Fallet Young on several individuals of each species in the Community Baboon Sanctuary in 1988.

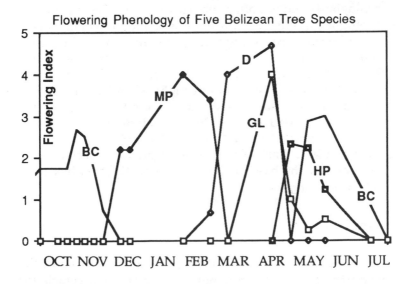

Graph showing seasonal flowering phenology of five tree species within the Baboon Sanctuary: BC - Bay Cedar (*Guazuma ulmifolia*); MP - Mampola (*Luehea seemanii*); D - Dogwood (*Lonchocarpus guatemalensis*); GL - Gumbolimbo (*Bursera simaruba*); HP - Hogplum (*Spondias mombin*).

Only five tree species are shown but they demonstrate differences in both the timing and duration of flowering. The bay cedar (BC) is of special interest because it flowers and sets fruit twice in the same year. Other species, like barley seed (*Andira inermis*), flower only once every two years.

Another common aspect of tree phenology is that individuals of the same species often flower at the same time, which is called synchronous flowering. Most tree species in northern Belize flower in synchrony. The main advantage of flowering together involves attracting pollinators; numerous trees in bloom encourage pollinator activity and increase the likliehood of cross-pollination and fertilization. Pollinators may include bees, wasps, moths, butterflies, birds or bats. The shape, color, and scent of the flower as well as the time of day of flowering are often linked to the type of pollinator the plant is trying to attract.

For example, many bright red or orange flowers attract hummingbirds and are often tubular in shape. The most noted hummingbird pollinated flowers are of the understory herbs the *Heliconias*. Hummingbird pollinated trees in Belize include *Quassia amara* and *Hamelia patens*. Many bat pollinated plants flower in the dry season. Bat pollinated flowers also commonly bloom at night when bats are active. Some bat-flowers also have strong, dank odors to attract the bats. Bat pollinated trees in Belize include the cotton tree (*Ceiba pentandra*), bri-bri (*Inga edulis*), and the calabash (*Cresentia cujete*). Each of these species produces nectar which accumulates at the base of the flower and the bats lick it up with their long tongues.

Fruiting

The phenology of fruiting plays a critical role in the functioning of the forest community. Fruits are a vehicle for seed dispersal for the plant and are important and often critical seasonal food sources for many animals. Hence, the availability of fruits and patterns of fruiting phenology can have a major impact on both the plants and animals of the rain forest. In northern Belize rain forests, there are at any one time, at least some tree species producing fruit. Some species like the gumbolimbo, bucut, and tubroos have fruits that persist on the tree for many months. Other species such as dogwood and the bullet tree fruit for only a very short period.

Seasonally, there are two fruiting peaks: near the end of the dry season and a month or so after the start of the rainy season. Like the flowering phenology pattern, most individuals of a given species produce fruits in synchrony. Some of the potential advantages of synchronous fruit production include increased disperser activity and decreased likelihood that seed predators will be able to eat or destroy all the seeds. It should also be noted that flowering and fruiting are closely linked behaviors and the fruiting phenology may be constrained by the seasonality of flower production.

Most species of figs (*Ficus* spp.) are exceptions to the synchronous patterns described above. Many figs are asynchronous and produce small numbers of fruits at various times throughout the year. For example, the amate fig in the center of Bermudian Landing produces fruits from three to four times per year. Because figs are one of the few asynchronous fruit producers, they undoubtably provide a very important source of food for many animals including the black howler.

FOREST SUCCESSION

*A*ny given expanse of forest is unlikely to be similar in structure or history. Most forests are a patchwork of different stages and ages of forest growth. The patterns of occurence and abundance of different forest species over time are complex and vary from site to site. The term forest *succession* is used to describe the series of forest regenerative processes which occur after a disturbance. Succession can be defined as a directional and continuous pattern of change in species composition, abundance, and importance over time. In the rain forests of Belize and elsewhere in the tropics, four basic phases of forest succession and regeneration can be identified and used to help describe and clarify the complex ecological patterns of succession.

The first phase of succession begins immediately after some form of disturbance in the forest. The disturbance results is some type of "gap" being created in the forest canopy. In the case of most Belizean forests, this disturbance gap is usually the result of slash-and-burn agriculture or clearing land for livestock pasture. However, natural disturbances can also form gaps. One type of smaller disturbance occurs when a tree falls in the forest creating a "tree-fall gap". Larger scale disturbances often result from severe storms and/or hurricanes.

Within the newly created gap, whatever its origin, sunlight suddenly becomes abundant. Temperature and humidity also change in gaps and tend to fluctuate more than in the closed forest. As a result of these micro-climate changes, many "pioneer" species are able to become established from seeds blown or carried by animals from other areas or seeds already in the soil. Seeds already in the soil form what is called the *seed bank*. There may be thousands of dormant seeds in a single square yard of soil and some seeds may be able to survive for 30 years or more. Pioneer species are adapted to gap growth and often require full sunlight for their seeds to germinate. Many pioneer species also grow very rapidly to

PHASES OF FOREST SUCCESSION

Height

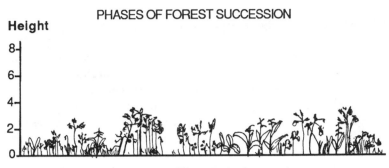

Gap-pioneer Phase   (1-2 years)

Secondary Thicket   (2-8 years)

Young Secondary Forest   (10-20 years)

Secondary Forest   (50 years+)

take advantage of the temporary sunlit conditions.

Some of the more common pioneer herbs are the heliconias (*Heliconia* spp.), bamboo (*Guadua spinosa*), plantanillo (*Canna* spp.), sensible weed (*Mimosa pigra*), and sour cane (*Costus* spp.). Other common pioneer herbs are members of genera such as *Panicum, Momordica, Centrosema, Paullinia, Melothria, Vitis,* and *Mucunia.* Some of the common pioneer trees include the trumpet tree (*Cercropia palmata*), capulin (*Trema micrantha*), wild papaya (*Carica papaya*) and *Piper* spp.. This early successional growth often forms a dense tangle of vegetation which is difficult to get through without a machete. Most of the plants reach a height no greater than 5-15 ft (1.5-5 m), although the capulin and trumpet sometimes grow up to 20 ft (6 m) in the first year alone.

Within a disturbance gap, many stumps may also resprout and grow. The survival of the sprouts can be extremely important in the regenerative process. Stump resprouts often have a great advantage over other newly established plants because they already have an extensive root system. In many cases in northern Belize, the resprouts regrow and become part of the developing forest. The root systems of stumped trees also help prevent erosion by keeping soil stabilized.

The second general phase of succession involves the establishment of secondary shrub and trees which grow large enough to shade out the sun-dependent pioneers. This type of growth can be called a secondary thicket and forms generally 2-8 years after the gap is formed or in the case of agricultural lands, 2-8 years after the land has been abandoned. Secondary thicket species include bay cedar (*Guazuma ulmifolia*), maya (*Miconia* spp.), grande betty (*Vismia ferrigunosa*), *Piper* spp., capulin (*Trema micrantha*), and the trumpet tree (*Cecropia* spp.). The secondary thicket may also contain dense tangles of bamboo which may grow to 20 ft (6 m) in height and form near impenetrable barriers. In cohune forests, many young cohune seedlings are also common in the secondary thicket along with numerous other tree seedlings adapted to growth in the partial shade beneath the thicket. The secondary thicket vegetation is generally 10-25 ft (3-8 m) in height.

Within 10-20 years, the secondary thicket species are disappearing and being replaced and overrun by more and larger tree species. The early stages of a secondary forest begin to take shape and the third phase of succession is underway. In this phase, several species from earlier successional stages may still persist in the understory but these species are becoming less and less common, especially the herb species. The developing secondary forest contains many species which will occur in the more mature forest and which are better adapted to tolerate the well shaded conditions now present beneath the developing canopy. In cohune forest areas, many young cohune palms are commonly found at this stage and the understory is much less cluttered with other trees although it still may be difficult to walk through. It will take many more years before these secondary forest trees will attain the stature of mature forest trees.

If the regenerating forest is left undisturbed for 50 years or more, a well developed secondary forest may be re-established. This secondary forest will have a well developed canopy and contain a relatively high diversity of tree species. In addition, numerous vines and epiphytes will have had time to become established in the canopy. Many maturing tree species in the forest may also display buttressing. The understory may be quite open except along riverbanks and in wetter areas. In wet areas the bri bri, bamboo, bullet tree, logwood, tarpon, and pokenoboy palm are abundant. In addition, bamboo often forms dense impenetrable thickets along the riverbanks. Depending on location and chance, the developing forest may have an entirely different composition.

The ultimate structure and composition of the forest depends on the soil, geography, and climate of a given region. It also depends to some degree on chance. Those species that produce seeds at the time a gap is formed or after a clearing is abandoned are more likely to be sucessful than those that don't. Those species that are by chance represented in the seed bank are also likely to be more successful. Because of the high degree of uncertainty relating to what specific tree species may become established, it is difficult to predict exactly what the composition of the developing forest will be.

Forest regeneration and succession are complex processes and are not completely understood or predictable. In some instances regeneration may not be possible. If land is extensively overused through farming, the soil may be destroyed and rendered incapable of supporting forest vegetation. In many low fertility soils areas in northern South America, highly disturbed areas may regenerate only into scrubby savanna. In addition, in all tropical regions, if areas directly along riverbanks are cleared of forest, massive erosion may result; with no trees, there is nothing to stabilize the soil during rainy season and valuable farm land may be lost to the river and valuable soil nutrients may be lost through leaching. Leaving strips of forest along riverbanks and allowing cleared areas to regenerate back to forest via the natural patterns of succession, will save both the forest and the valuable forest soil for the future and for future utilization.

LAND USE IN THE SANCTUARY

*L*and use depends to a great extent on the cultural heritage and economic status of the people who are using the land. The villages within the Community Baboon Sanctuary have been predominantly Creole for generations. Local farmers have practiced and continue to practice slash-and-burn agriculture and animal husbandry. Much of the current land use is steeped in traditional Creole techniques such that much of today's agricultural activity has been carried on in the same manner for generations.

Land use also is linked with the climatalogical and physical constraints of a region. The sanctuary is located in the lower Belize River valley. Most of the riverine and cohune ridge forests occur on alluvial soils of the *Bermudian Landing Series* (USDA: Vertic Europept). These soils are found extensively on flat areas of old floodplain alluvium in the lower Belize River Valley. This type of soil suffers a drainage impedence during part of the rainy season but is relatively fertile. Pine ridge soils in the Sanctuary are of the *Santos Pine Ridge Series* (USDA: Typic Tropaqualf). These soils are acidic, sandy loams of low fertility.

Slash - and - Burn Agriculture

Most land holders in the Community Baboon Sanctuary are practicing some level of slash-and-burn agriculture. The agricultural plots are known locally as "plantations" or milpas. Where a plantation will be located depends of the type of crop(s) being planted. Most farmers clear their plantations in cohune ridge, high ridge or riverine forests because of the fertile soils found there. Pine ridge areas are usually only used to plant occasional fruit crops such as cashew, mango, sour sop, custard apple, guava, and coconut. The average portion of forest cleared each year for a plantation is a little over one acre (0.4 ha). In many cases, an acre plot is cleared adjacent to the previous years' clearing, creating 2,3, and 4 acre clearings over the same number of years.

Clearing forest for plantations is done almost exclusively in the dry season. Forests are cleared anytime from February to as late a mid-May. All but a few acres of plantations within the sanctuary are cleared by hand with machetes and axes. On these hand-cleared plots, larger trees and cohune palms are often left standing because of the labor required to fell them. Other trees may also be left standing for various reasons including shade, timber value, erosion protection, and wildlife habitat .

The burning of a felled and dried plot is timed in anticipation of the first rains of the rainy season. Depending on the planting system, some farmers may burn in March and others in May. Burning the plot gets rid of the plant debris, kills most of the weeds, and the resulting ash acts as a short-term fertilizer for the first crops. Each plantation usually contains a variety of seasonal crops including rice, corn, beans, cassava, cocoa yams, sweet potatoes, and peppers. Often plantains and/or bananas will be planted on leaf-cutter ant nests which act as raised beds with adequate drainage and high nutrient value. The timing of planting specific crops is inextricably linked with seasonal rainfall patterns.

CORN (*Zea mays*): Three different corn crops may be planted. The first is planted in March and is known as the *San Jose* crop. This is a risky venture because planting occurs in the middle of the dry season and depends on sufficient dry season rainfall. Because of the risks, few farmers plant a San Jose crop. The advantages of the San Jose crop are that corn can be reaped as early as June and weed competition is less severe in the dry season. The most common corn planting season, however, is from mid-April into May. This crop is planted in anticipation of the first rains of the rainy season. This second crop is reaped in late July or early August. A third corn planting may occur in September and is known as the *Matambra* crop, which derives its name from the Spanish meaning to kill hunger. The matambra crop is traditionally intercropped with red kidney beans. Reaping occurs in late December. Because of the frequent over-abundance of rains during this cropping period, few farmers plant a Matmabra crop.

RICE (*Oryza sativa*):   Rice is planted almost exclusively from mid-May through June when rainfall is abundant during the first part of the rainy season.   Rice is commonly planted in the lower, wetter portions of the plantation.

BEANS (*Phaseolus vulgaris*):   Red kidney beans are planted in September after the second peak in the rainy season. Beans produce better under the cooler temperatures and decreasing rainfall in the latter portion of the rainy season.   As mentioned earlier, beans are also sometimes intercropped with the matambra corn crop.

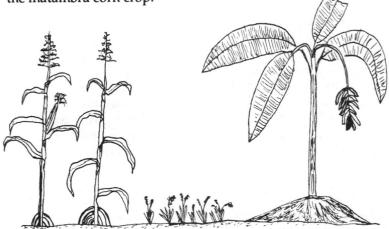

Because many of the nutrients in the tropical forest are contained in the living trees and many tropical soils are prone to erosion and leaching, the yield from the plantation steadily declines after the first season.   In addition, weeds and insect pests can decrease agricultural yields.   As a result, many farmers only use a plantation from 2 to 5 years and then it is abandoned or left *fallow*.   Successful slash-and-burn agriculture requires fallow periods between cropping sequences to avoid destroying the soil.   The farmers in the Community Baboon Sanctuary are fortunate to be farming very fertile river soils. In addition, the population pressure in the sanctuary is not increasing at an appreciable rate.   One result of these factors is that most farmers allow their plantations to fallow for an average of 15 years or more, thus allowing the forests and soils to regenerate.

Animal Husbandry

The trend over the past 30 years in the sanctuary has been away from plantation agriculture and towards livestock rearing. Brahmin beef cattle are the most commonly raised animal along with a few pigs and horses. Within the Community Baboon Sanctuary there are about 900 acres (365 ha) of pasture and around 10 large herds of cattle. Farmers without large herds often raise just a few animals on small pasture plots. About 95% of the pasture has been cleared by hand from mixed, cohune, and riverine forest. The use of chain saws for clearing forests, however, is on the rise.

The average pasture covers about 25 acres (10 ha) but often the larger pastures have been cleared one section at a time over several years to attain their present size. Cohune palms and other trees are also commonly left scattered in pastures as a source of shade and in the case of some tree species, as a source of fodder. Most pastures are also cleared to the banks of the Belize River to provide cattle with access to a water source. This practice has caused some severe erosion problems in certain areas and should not be continued. Leaving forest strips along rivers is an excellent erosion control practice.

Pastures within the sanctuary are not purposely fallowed. Some pastures will be let fallow if improper management results in the pasture being overrun by weeds, shrubs, and trees. Only a handful of farmers convert plantations to pasture and as such, plantation tending and livestock rearing are two separate and distinct activities. Most pasture land is also unimproved, meaning no seeding of pastures forbs or grasses has been undertaken. The most common improved grasses are Para grass, Carib grass, Pangola grass, African Star and Improved Star. Unfortunately, most farmers do not have the resources to acquire and develop improved pastures using these grasses.

TREE USE IN A TRADITIONAL CREOLE HOUSEHOLD

*A*s important as tropical rain forests have become to the modern world through foods, drugs, and the innumerable goods now produced for our modern technology, the forest was much more important in historical times for local people who depended on it for their basic needs and for survival. Although the direct uses of the forest by local people is rapidly declining, some people in Belize are still making use of it.

The Creole people now residing in the Community Baboon Sanctuary and other villages throughout Belize in past times depended on the rain forest for construction of their houses, boats, tools, rope, and a wide variety of other items. House construction in particular, involved the use of many forest trees and plants. Today, however, as a result of hurricane Hattie in 1961, most of the traditional dwellings in the area were destroyed and no longer remain. They were rebuilt using non-traditional methods and materials including mill-sawn lumber and galvanized, zinc roofing.

House Construction

The old style Creole buildings, now often called "trash houses", were and are still constructed of wild tree and plant materials. Many of the building methods came from a blending of the African and Mayan cultures. The traditional house is thus a blend of many different plant species and plant parts as well as cultures.

The house corner posts need to be strong and resist decay. The most prized woods for corner posts and framing include: pine (*Pinus caribaea*), ironwood (*Dialium guianense*), logwood (*Haematoxylon campechianum*), madre cacao (*Gliricidia sepium*), mylady (*Aspidosperma megalocarpon*), bullet tree (*Bucida buceras*), fiddlewood (*Vitex gaumeri*), silly young (*Lucuma belizensis*) and if living near the coast, white mangrove (*Laguncularia racemosa*). Lesser quality rafter trees include the pimenta palm (*Paurotis wrightii*), polewood (*Xylopia frutescens*), and grande betty (*Cupania* spp.). If none of the better trees are available, old William (*Vismia ferruginea*) can be used. This tree also goes by the name "can't-be-helped" in reference to its use only as a last resort.

The beams and rafters are tied tightly together and to the posts with either strips of bark, vines or aerial roots. Trees stripped for their fibrous bark include the narrowleaf moho (*Belotia campbelii*), capulin (*Trema micrantha*), cowfoot (*Bauhinia divaricata*), moho (*Hampea* spp.), bay cedar (*Guazuma ulmifolia*) and blue moho (*Hibiscus tiliaceus*). Vines and aerial roots used for rope are called "tie-tie's" in Creole. Many vines or tie-tie's can be used but the most common and durable include bellyfull tie-tie, quana tie-tie, and many members of the Bignonia Family (Bignoniaceae) including the genera *Arrabidea, Cydista,* and *Pithecoctenium.* The genus *Paullinia* in the family Sapindaceae also contains many vines used for cordage. The long, strong aerial roots of the common house plant philodendrons, *Monstera* spp., are also used for cordage. Fine bast fibers from the herbaceous wire or broom weed plant (*Sida acuta*) and the wild pineapple (*Ananas magdalenae*) can also be made into cordage or even cloth.

The house walls may be made of a variety of materials including cohune (*Orbigyna cohune*), pimenta (*Paurotis wrightii*) and cabbage palm stalks or slats cut from the trunk of the tree. The roof is thatched using palm fronds. Many species of palms can be used for thatch but the most desirable thatch comes from the bayleaf palm (*Sabal morrisiana*) also known as the botan palm, and the silver thatch palm (*Thrinax radiata*). The strong, fan-shaped fronds of these palms make for a tight and long-lasting thatch. The palmate leaf is clumped in thirds and arranged on either side of the rafters. Cohune palm leaves can also be used. The cohune fronds are long and linear and are split in half and laid so that the leaflets create a tight cross hatching. While the bayleaf palm is preferred for thatching, it is mostly found in the high bush (mature tropical rain forest) on limestone soils so alternative palm species are often used.

House Tools

A wide variety of trees are used for tool making. Mahogany (*Swietenia macrophylla*) and cedar (*Cedrela mexicana*) are hard but workable woods and are the preferred wood for making many household articles. However, many other trees can be used. Different portions of a tree are used for different purposes.

Bread boards, washing tubs, and large flat dishes are hand hewn from the spur or buttress of a tree. The common mortar, used for hulling rice resembles similar African tools, and is commonly made from tree trunks of mahogany or tubroos (*Enterolobium cyclocarpum*). The mortar stick, which must be heavy for pounding grains, is carved from stronger woods such as billy webb (*Acosmium panamense*), sapodilla (*Manilkara zapote*), calabash (*Cresentia cujute*), cashew (*Anacardium occidentale*), fustic (*Chlorophora tinctoria*), swamp kaway (*Pterocarpus officinalis*) or caimito (*Rheedia edulis*). These same strong woods are also used for making wooden tools and tool handles.

A sweeping broom is made of leaves of the give-and-take palm (*Chrysophila argentea*). A fly brush, used to brush off flies, is made from the fruiting stalk of the cohune palm. To make a brush, first the many nuts are cut off the stalk, and then it is beaten on one end until it separates into a fibrous brush.

Basket tie-tie (*Desmoncus schipii*), a long, spiny palm vine is used to weave baskets. After the spines are shaved off, the outer vine parts are split off and kept moist for weaving. Similar palm rattans are used in west Africa for baskets.

The pokenoboy or pork-and-dough-boy palm (*Bactris major*), is used to make tongs for removing coals or food from the cooking fire which is known as a "kis-kis". A kis-kis is made first by removing the many spines from the stem and then the outer stalk is split off. The center of a long, thin piece of stem is then rubbed with fat or oil and heated to soften and bend it. It is finally tied closed and remains so for use as tongs.

The large gourd-like fruits of the calabash tree or tuc-tuc can be hollowed out and dried to hold water or for storage vessels. Sometimes the fruits are set in ant nests to assist the process.

The dory or wooden canoe, historically important for travel on the Belize River, is still used today. Dories are cut from the trunks of large trees which are often left standing in milpas and pastures for that purpose. The preferred tree for dory making is the tubroos. Other less durable and workable trees, however, such as the cedar, cotton tree (*Ceiba pentandra*), santa maria (*Calophyllum brasiliense*), yemeri (*Vochysia hondurensis*), and barba jolote (*Pithecellobium arborea*) can also be used. The dories are carved by adze and ax and the center is hollowed and then tempered with burning coals. Today chain saws are used for some of the work. The narrow paddles are preferably carved from cedar or mahogany.

Bush beds were originally used in traditional Creole households and then became important furniture in seasonal logging, chiclero, and hunting camps. They were made of posts and frames of any wood, tied together by strips of white moho or other available cordage. The mattress was composed of cohune or bay leaf palm fronds.

Other curious household items include corks made from bobwood (*Annona glabra*), whistles made from wild physic nut stems (*Jatropha gaumeri*), sandpaper using the leaves of yaha (*Curatella americana*), and glues made from the resins of the gumbolimbo (*Bursera simaruba*), cashaw (*Acacia farnesiana*), and cojotone (*Stemmadenia donnell-smithii*). Charcoal can be made from many trees including buttonwood (*Conocarpus erecta*), yaha, nargusta (*Terminalia amazonia*), bastard logwood (*Gymnopodium floribundum*), craboo (*Byrsonima crassifolia*), and bay cedar.

THE IMPORTANCE OF TROPICAL RAIN FORESTS

Characteristics of Tropical Rain Forests

*T*ropical rain forests occur in three main areas of the world: the Neotropics, Asia, and Africa. Over half of the rain forests are in the neotropics, centered in the Brazilian Amazon region with a strip extending on the Atlantic coast of Central America into central Mexico. The Asian forests are centered in the Malaysian archipelago with some in mainland Asia, while the African forests center in Zaire and the Congo basin, extending west to Guinea.

Distribution of the Tropical Rain Forest

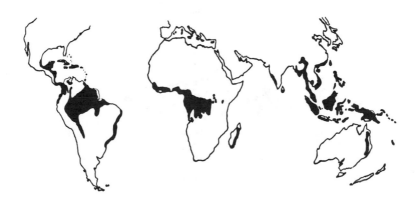

On first impression, one is struck by the incredible luxuriance of the tropical rain forest and its overwhelming sense of life; and it is one of the most complex systems of life on this earth but the complexity deceives. People think that land which supports this forest is so rich and fertile that anything, including crops, will grow there. This deceptive impression is causing the destruction of the rain forest. In reality, many tropical rain forest soils have a low fertility and the richness of nutrients and minerals lies in the vegetation and living forms themselves. Dead organic matter is the only significant source of nutrients for recycling. Constant high temperatures and humidity, cause rapid decomposition of the organic materials and the constant release of nutrients into the shallow topsoil. Complex surface root networks rapidly absorb the nutrients and carry them into the vegetation before the rains can leach them into the deep subsoils or wash them into the surface waters. Dead plant and animal material is rapidly decomposed and recycled back into the living plants. Thus, most nutrients are in the vegetation while the tropical soils have a low fertility.

Most of the Nutrients Are in the Living Forest

Tropical rain forests are extremely ancient plant formations, having evolved over 30 million years ago. Their complexity and their integrated nutrient cycling, if not catastrophically altered, permits them to recycle and maintain themselves. However, tropical rain forests, being destroyed at the extremely rapid rate of about 27,000 sq miles (70,000 sq km) every year, will be gone by the end of this century. Most of this destruction is for agriculture and timber exploitation, often for foreign export.

Cutting the rain forest exposes the topsoil, making it vulnerable to the constant rain which washes away the nutrients and leaves the poorer clay or sandy subsoil. Clear felling for timber or exploitive farming practices will soon exhaust the soil resources and in some cases the forest may never regenerate and will be lost forever.

Valuable rain forest in Belize is being cleared for agriculture, logging, and grazing lands. Slow sustainable use of safeguarded forests can provide long term economic gains. However, extensive and indiscriminate clearing of rain forest will only destroy the resource and render it unusable in the future.

Slash - and - Burn Agriculture

Farmers in the Community Baboon Sanctuary utilize traditional slash-and-burn agricultural methods. This farming has a seasonal cycle based on the rainfall pattern of the area. One or two acres (0.4-0.8 ha) are cleared by hand with machetes. Large trees may be left. This milpa or cleared area may be used for 1-4 years before allowing it to go fallow. Clearing must be done before the beginning rains in June. The resulting slash is burned before planting during the rainy season. Planting is often done by hand using a pointed planting stick to dig holes in which a few seeds of corn or rice are dropped.

After clearing and pruning for agriculture, the nutrient content of the topsoil goes up, temporarily enriched and consolidated by the ashes, which enhance crop growth. If cleared too often, the plant nutrients will be depleted and eventually the soil will harden and compact, the soil fauna will disappear and regeneration will no longer be possible. With proper management, the needs of tropical countries such as Belize can be met without totally destroying the forests. Selective logging or farming practices which cut small sections of the forest at a time and allow the forest enough time to regenerate, can make the forest a renewable resource for now and for the future.

Long Fallow - If farmers observe the necessary fallow time, nutrients lost during clearing will be replaced and the soil will regain its fertility and can be reused.

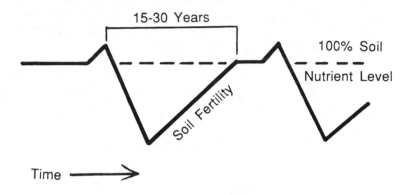

Short Fallow - If land is cleared too often, the soil nutrients are not fully replaced and the soil fertility declines. If overuse is continued, it can permanently damage or destroy the soil.

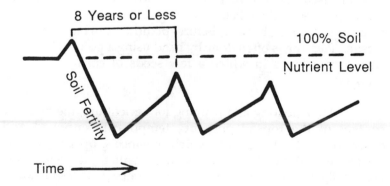

Shifting slash-and-burn agriculture can be an efficient sustainable land use if farmers observe the minimum fallow time required to replace the nutrients lost during the clearing, burning, cultivation, and harvest. In many areas, 8-10 years fallow replaces 70-90% of the nutrients but 30 years is a much safer time with 15 years being the lower limit.

Layers in a Tropical Rain Forest and Effects on Their Environment

The tropical rain forest is arranged in a series of levels or layers based on the height and the ecology of plants which are found in a given region. Specific tree and plant species are adapted to live in specific layers. Each layer forms a distinct microhabitat which is affected differently by various environmental factors. Sunlight, for example, the basis of photosynthesis, affects the upper layers most strongly with little light reaching the forest floor. Temperature, regulated also by the sun, follows a similar pattern. The force of rain and wind is also hardest on the exposed upper levels with only soft drippings and broken breezes reaching the forest floor.

Stratification of the Tropical Rain Forest

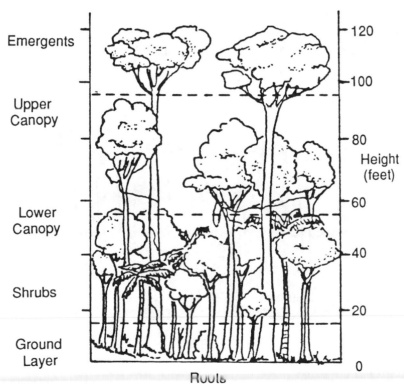

Emergents

Upper Canopy

Lower Canopy

Shrubs

Ground Layer

Roots

Height (feet)

120

100

80

60

40

20

0

Humidity shows a reversed effect, the various shrub and tree layers trapping the humidity at the lower levels. Thus, the forest floor is very humid while the upper canopy is dry. In general, the lower layers encompassed by the shrubs, maintain a much more stable and constant environment.

Emergent Layer - This level is composed of very tall trees which are able to rise above the main canopy. Trees at this level get the brunt of sunlight, heat, rainfall, and wind. They must sustain the most weather variability. Because the Community Baboon Sanctuary is composed mainly of young, disturbed semi-deciduous forests with many species removed, a well-developed emergent layer is not seen in the sanctuary.

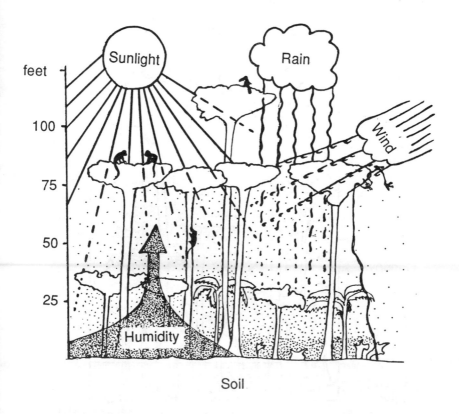

Layered Environmental Effects in the Tropical Rain Forest

Canopy Layer - This is a continuous layer of tree tops which receive roughly the same high temperatures, light intensity, wind, and rain and together they form a continuous top to the forest. As seedlings, however, the many trees making up the canopy layer developed in a much different environment, on the forest floor. Most canopy trees are adapted to start life in the shade or partial shade of the understory and then grow to compete with other trees in the canopy. Canopy trees also are support structures for epiphytes and climbing vines and lianas.

Understory - This layer is composed of shrubs which receive lower intensities of heat, light, rainfall, and wind due to the protective canopy above. Understory plants are adapted to live and grow in partial shade.

Forest Floor - Very little sunlight reaches the forest floor level, making it hard for plants dependent on light for chlorophyll, to live. Shade loving herbs and mosses can survive here where humidity is trapped by the understory and canopy. At this level, saprophytes rot fallen leaves, fruit, and other dead materials.

Animals, most which are more mobile than plants, respond to the microhabitats created by the environmental height gradient. In general, the upper layers have a greater number of species dependent on them. A study of a Central American forest found that 16 species of birds fed and inhabited the floor level, 75 lived mainly in the understory, while 130 species were found in the canopy. Although birds are primarily tree dwellers, mammal species show the same kind of distribution. Recent studies of insects in the canopy have shown an incredible number of species which scientists never knew existed.

Values of the Tropical Rain Forest

The most important aspect of the tropical rain forest relating to its antiquity and contributing to its complexity and fragility, is the incredible variety of species, types, and forms of life. One half of all animal and plant species occur in the tropics and many of the forms are highly specialized. They have provided the basis for many foods, drugs, and technological products. The destruction of the tropical rain forests, with the consequent loss of undiscovered plants and animals is already responsible for unforetold losses of potential usable products for the modern world.

Additionally, the most important aspect of the forests locally is the climatic and economic stability they provide for the host countries themselves. Agriculturally and economically, they are the life blood of these tropical countries and must be safeguarded for this reason. Although the desire for immediate economic growth through foreign capital is understandable, the slow sustainable use of the forests will benefit tropical countries such as Belize, much more in the long run. Already, the tropical rain forests are disappearing at an alarming rate due to the immediate gains from rapid conversion of the forest for quick profit from clear timbering or clearcutting for farming or cattle rearing. Without replanting or forest regeneration, these practices will soon result in barren useless land. However, traditional agricultural communities similar to those along the Belize River, practice a shifting cultivation which is sustainable. These communities are also able to supplement their agriculture with natural forest products such as wood for building and native food and drugs.

Tropical rain forests also have an important climatic and preservative function. They protect fragile soils from degradation through run-off or leaching, they protect the watershed and river systems by preventing soil erosion and flooding by equalizing the water flow, and they maintain a more even temperature and humidity through evapotransporation (water evaporation back into the air through the soil and plant surfaces) within the forests themselves. This maintenance of a steady climate has vast regional effects and may affect the climate globally as well. The riverine forests such as those within the Community Baboon Sanctuary are particularly important in preserving the rivers and their life systems. Clearcutting riverine forests could eventually lead to silting of the river, changes in the fish and other animal life, flood damage, and even lowering the water tables of village wells as happened in areas of Asia.

Belize is unique among the nations of Central America in that it still has large areas of rain forest land available. Wise use and management of these forests as is occurring in the Community Baboon Sanctuary will ensure their survival. However, rapid, indiscriminate deforestation will undermine this valuable and fragile resource, leaving only barren lands which will be unable to provide resources for future generations. To protect the rain forest of Belize is to protect Belize's future.

RIVERS AND WATER RESOURCES

The esssence of rivers is their flow. Without input from the rains and output of the oceans they would cease to exist. Through their eternal flow, they rework the face of the land. The force of the water flow moving abrasive materials like sand constantly wears down its banks. Rivers create canyons, flood plains, waterfalls, marshes, and estuaries by their flow from the mountains to the ocean. Because many rivers follow a gentle downward gradient, they don't flow in a straight line but rather follow lines of least resistance. They meander. When a river encounters an obstruction on one bank, the flow is deflected, swerving back to the other bank. Here erosion continues until new resistence is met, deflecting the flow back once again to the other side, resulting in the serpentine meandering commonly found across flat landscapes.

Oxbows

Rivers are constantly meandering across the flood plains, with some loops growing more tightly curved, almost pinching the land. During floods and high water flow, the river may break through the narrowed neck of the oxbow, flowing straight across. An island will initially be created. With time, the oxbow loop will become isolated from the main river flow, forming a small stillwater pond. This lake or pond gets its name from the U-shaped piece of wood placed under and around the neck of an ox, the upper ends forming the bar of the yoke. Without an outlet or inlet, the oxbow lake often becomes a marsh or swamp. Eventually through evaporation, filling in, and vegetation growth, it disappears. Some of the moist marsh or "pond" areas in the Community Baboon Sanctuary were once oxbows. The old ferry crossing at Bermudian Landing was located on an oxbow, which was one reason the new bridge was not built on the same road. Eventually the river would pinch through, creating an island, and a second bridge would have had to been built.

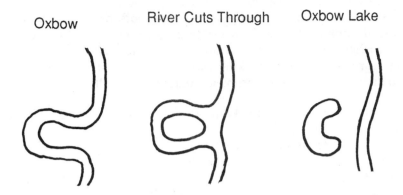

Oxbow   River Cuts Through   Oxbow Lake

Water's Source

Only a small percentage of rainwater runs off the surface into river and streams. Most of the water percolates down through the soil. Much of it is picked up by the extensive root system of the tropical rain forest. The remainder continues until it reaches a point of complete saturation. Above this level, known as the water table, the soil is filled with air. The shape of the water table somewhat follows the shape of the land. Flat land has an even water table while in hilly land the water table flows out from the river level but may rise beneath the hill top. Water tables fluctuate seasonally and according to the amount of water received. Some soils such as the tightly packed clay retain water for long periods and may percolate it as slow as several inches per year. In others like loosely arranged sand, the water moves as rapidly as several feet per day. The ground water, below the water table, flows downhill as river water does, attracted by the gravitational pull. It flows sometimes great distances but it doesn't flow in the form of an underground river but more like water travelling through a sponge.

Ground water is where we get most of our drinking water from through the digging of wells. It is a myth to think that ground water cannot be polluted. If substances such as disease producing bacteria from latrines, pesticides and other toxins from farms, oil and gasoline, are indiscriminantly used and dumped, especially in sandy areas, they will ultimately find their way into the ground water and may eventually appear in the village drinking water. Thus care must be taken to dispose and use such problem materials carefully.

Forests - Keepers of the Water

Water is our most recyclable resource. Although it changes in space and time, the total amount of water in the world remains relatively constant. When clouds form and release rain, it either flows on the earth's surface to the river or streams as run-off, it evaporates immediately, it trickles into the ground to be absorbed by plants or it trickles through the unsaturated substrate (soil) until it eventually reaches a saturation point which is the level of the water table. The water which is taken in by the tree root systems is recycled by being carried back through the plants and is lost through evapotranspiration. This evaporated humidity re-forms into small clouds causing local rains which then begin the water cycle again. Tree cover is especially important during the dry season when water loss through tree leaves can be returned to the atmosphere for occasional showers during the dry season. The rains recycle with some going into rivers, some back to the forest root system, and the rest into the ground water supply.

When large areas of the forest are cleared, a number of effects are felt. In dry periods, surface soils dry quickly due to direct sunlight and lack of wind protection. Because the upper soil horizons can hold little water against the force of gravity, roots can experience severe drought periods. Many soil nutrients can also be leached downward and out of the root zone. During rainy periods, direct erosion occurs on the unprotected land due to the heavy force of the falling rain drops. Since the root system has been largely removed, little water is resorbed by the plants, and most of the water moves directly away as surface run-off into streams and rivers causing increased flow rates, sedimentation, and potential flooding. Without forests in the water cycle, no evapotranspiration can occur through the trees so the dry season becomes more severe and the water table is lowered.

Controlling the Effects of Deforestation

If an area of forest by or near a river has been highly disturbed by clearing or logging, there are steps which can be taken to combat the potential serious problems of a disturbed watershed. The primary focus must be to re-vegetate the cleared or disturbed area. This can be accomplished by seeding or replanting areas before prolonged exposure seriously degrades the soil. Pitting, furrowing and fence building across degraded sites before planting can reduce surface run-off velocity and aid in more normal drainage. The planting of living fence posts is one short cut to faster re-vegetation.

The best way to avoid creating watershed problems is by taking preventative action. By leaving belts of forest along waterways, leaving thin strips of trees across large clearings, planning logging and vehicle road construction in areas least prone to erosion, using herbicides and pesticides only during proper seasons, disposing of dangerous chemicals properly, and discouraging large, damaging clearcuts, future deforestation and watershed problems can be greatly reduced and the forests, soil, and water will remain usable and viable resources.

EPIPHYTES

One of the more conspicuous aspects of Neotropical forests is the variety of epiphytes that occur. Epiphytes are plants that grow on other plants without being parasitic. Epiphytes are commonly called "air plants" and the plant they live on is called the host. Larger epiphytes such as the bromeliads, ferns, cacti, and orchids are the most visible. There are, however, many smaller epiphytes such as mosses, liverworts, and lichens. The many species of epiphytes found in rain forests are one reason for the high overall diversity of plant species in the tropics.

Why so many plants in the treetops? One reason is that there's much more light in the canopy compared to the dark and shadowy understory and plants living in the canopy are adapted to well-lit conditions. A second advantage is that canopy plants are the first to receive water during rainy periods. This is especially advantageous during the dry season when showers are far and few between. A third benefit of canopy life is that when plants produce flowers there is a greater chance that pollinators (usually insects) will be available to pollinate. Fourthly, most epiphytes produce tiny, easily blown seeds and there is a better chance that the seeds will be dispersed by winds in the canopy rather than on the calm forest floor.

Epiphtic Zones

Where epiphytes grow on the host tree is very important for the success of the epiphyte. Many epiphytes are adapted to living in a specific part of the canopy. A mature tree can be viewed as having five epiphytic zones as noted in the illustration on the next page. The lowest zone (1) is on the wet base of the tree which often supports mosses, especially on buttressed trees or trees with rough bark. The next zone (2) is on the lower trunk and this area is also relatively moist and often supports both mosses and lichens. Zone 3 is in a drier area of the trunk and often has crustaceous lichens growing in circular patches. The next zone (4) is where most epiphytes are found either in crotches of branches or on top of branches . In these areas, the plants can collect falling plant debris and epiphyte roots can absorb badly needed nutrients from the decaying plant materials just like they would collect nutrients from soils on the ground.   The host tree may send roots up off the branches to

Epiphytic Zones

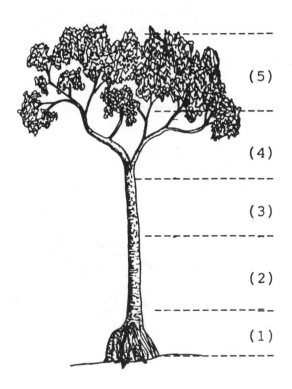

(5)

(4)

(3)

(2)

(1)

mine the nutrients from decaying plant materials caught in the crotches of branches or even send roots into the roots of epiphytes. The upper zone (5) is fully exposed and supports mostly small epiphytes known as microepiphytes.   One interesting group of microepiphytes are the *epiphylls*. Epiphylls, mostly lichens, algae, and liverworts,   are tiny plants which grow on the surface of other living leaves.

Dry Season Adaptations

Because the forests in much of Belize experience an extensive dry season from February through May, epiphytes are not as numerous or species rich as in forests where it is wet year-round. However, many epiphyte species have adapted to the seasonally dry conditions in the Belizean forests. One adaptation is the development of waxy, bulbous stems which can store water during dry periods. This is most pronounced in the cacti and the orchids. Another adaptation for obtaining moisture in dry periods is the development of a dense mat of roots which capture both rainwater and bits of leaves and decaying plant and animal material. These types of roots are often basket shaped and are most common in the orchids although they occur in other epiphytes.

Examples of Epiphytic Bromeliads

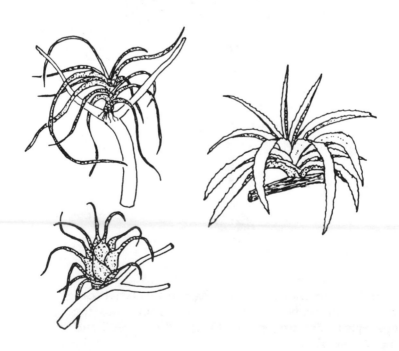

Another approach to collecting both water and nutrients is found in the tank bromeliads. These bromeliads have evolved long trough-like leaves which funnel rain water into a central stem storage tank. Some tanks may store up to 2 gallons (7.5 liters) of water. These storage tanks often support a whole little world of life. The tanks of water attract not only falling litter but also insects and small animals. The wastes and by-products of these animals are absorbed into the bromeliad so it gains needed nutrients. The tanks are important homes for many species and some species of tropical mosquitoes breed only in certain species of bromeliad tanks.

Epiphytic Loads

Epiphytes may not always be harmless to their hosts. Large numbers of water-laden epiphytes, creating what is known as an epiphytic load, may weigh hundreds of pounds and can cause large branches of trees to break off. This phenomenon is more common on rough barked trees which provide a better support for epiphytic roots. This might help explain the large number of smooth barked trees in the tropics. Epiphytes may also rob nutrients that were destined for the floor of the forest and limit the nutrients available for the host tree. In areas where a large number of epiphytes are present, many trees have adapted strategies of shedding epiphytes. Smooth bark is one adaptation, another is constantly peeling bark found on trees like the gumbolimbo (*Buresera simaruba*) and nargusta (*Terminalia obovata*).

Belizean Epiphytes

Belizean forests support a wide range of epiphytes. The most visible epiphytes are often the orchids, bromeliads, cacti, and ferns. Bromeliad epiphytes include members of the genera *Aechmea, Ananas, Billbergia, Catopsis, Tillandsia* and *Vriesa*. Most cacti (family Cactaceae) in Belize are epiphytic and include members of the genera *Acanthocereus, Deamia, Discocactus, Epiphyllum, Rhipsalis, Selencereus,* and *Wilmattea*.   It should be noted that some of the epiphytes mentioned can also live rooted on the ground and may be found in the wild living non-epiphytic lives.

The Orchid family (Orchidaceae) is a huge family of

plants containing several hundred genera and many thousands of species. Orchids are best known for their stunning flowers which are often both bizarre and beautiful. Most orchids also produce vast quantities of extremely small seeds. Some species, like *Cycnoches chlorochilon* which is found in Belize, produce nearly 4 million seeds in a single small fruit capsule. Readers further interested in Belizean orchids should acquire the book "Orchids of Guatemala and Belize" by Ames and Correll.

The following is a list of the epiphytic orchids reported for Belize. It should be noted that some of the species listed may also occasionally be terrestrial.

EPIPHYTIC ORCHIDACEAE OF BELIZE

Brassavola nodosa
Campylocentrum micranthum
C. sullivannii
Catasetum integerrimum
Cattleya skinneri
Chysis bractescens
Coryanthes picturata
C. speciosa
Cycnoches chlorochilon
C. warscewiczii
Diacrium bidentatum
Dichaea tuerckheimii
Elleanthus linifolius
Epidendrum belizense
Galeandra batemanii
Mormodes buccinator
M. ringens
Notylia barkeri
N. trisepala
Oncidium ascendens
O. carthagenense
O. cebolleta
O. ensatum
O. luridum
O. pusillum
O. sphacelatum
Ornithocephalus inflexus
O. pottsiae
Pleurothatlis Blaisdellii

G. baueri
Gongora maculata
G. quinquenervis
Ionopsis utriculariodes
Laelia digbyana
L. tibicinis
Macradenia brassavolae
Masdevallia tubuliflora
Maxillaria crassifolia
M. densa
M. friedrichsthalii
M. macleei
M. ringens
M. tenuifolia
M. uncata
P. marginata
P. racemiflora
P. yucatanensis
Polystachya cerea
P. clavata
P. luteola
P. masayensis
P. minor
Ponera striata
Rhyncholaelia digbyana
Scaphyglottis behrii
S. cuneata
S. wereklei
Trigonidium egertonianum

VINES AND LIANAS: *TIE - TIE's*

*O*ne of the more visible aspects of mature tropical forest is the high number of vine and liana species found on the forest floor, climbing up tree trunks, and sprawled out in the canopy. The differences between lianas and vines are often loosely defined but in general, vines have flexible stems and climb on other plants, depending on them for mechanical support; lianas are usually woody and high-climbing. Most vines and lianas start on the forest floor either as shrubs or vines and grow their way up into the canopy. Many shrub-lianas will begin growing upward as strict lianas when a canopy gap is formed by either a natural or human disturbance.

In Belize, there are many dozens of liana species found in many plant families, but they are especially common in the Bignoniaceae, Apocynaceae, Combretaceae, Dillenaceae, Sapindaceae, Vitaceae, and Leguminosae. Many Belizean vines and lianas are called *tie-tie's* reflecting their usage as cordage for tying and fastening. The local Creole names for the vines and lianas are often descriptive of the vine's appearance. For example, mahogany tie-tie has mahogany like bark; barracouta tie-tie (*Liabium* sp.) is long, rounded and tapering at both ends; water tie-tie (*Vitis tilifolia*) contains a clear tasteless sap; basket tie-tie (*Desmoncus schippii*) is used in making baskets; and iguana tie-tie (*Bignonia dasyonyx*) has sharp tendrils shaped like iguana claws.

Vine Adaptations For Climbing: a) down-curved spines; b) sucker-like pads for adhesion; c) tendrils; d) twining stem; e) modified roots.

Often the only evidence of vines and lianas in the canopy are flowers or fruits that have dropped down to the forest floor; because most vines/lianas have both leaves and flowers only in the canopy, the sole part of the vines one sees walking in the forest are the woody stems twisting and spiralling upward into the hidden canopy above.

Like other rain forest plants, vines and lianas are in an intense competition for sunlight and the only way to find light in a closed canopy forest is by growing upward. It is crucial for vines and lianas to find a tall tree to grow up otherwise the trip may be fruitless if the vine does not make it into the sunlight of the upper canopy. Some vines and lianas have adapted to this requirement by growing horizontally into very shaded regions before they grow up in an attempt to find the base of a tall, shade throwing tree.

Vines and lianas come in many shapes and sizes. Some are large and woody reaching a diameter of over 8 in (20 cm); others may be only a few mm in diameter and very fragile. Many vines, like the common houseplant philodendrons, produce no or only very small leaves in the shaded understory (2-3 inches [5-7 cm] across) but the portion of the vine which reaches the sunlight may produce leaves over three feet (1 m) across. Many vines and lianas, upon reaching the full light of the canopy, shed their lower leaves leaving only bare twisting stems below. In the full sunlight, such as along river banks, there are often a dense tangle of leafy vines draping over the forest canopy and giving the impression of an impenetrable thicket. In the dark understory on the other side of the river bank, however, the forest floor is often relatively clear and all that is seen are bare vine stems reaching up into the canopy.

Non-woody vine growth is most common in secondary growth areas that receive a lot of sunlight such as grown over milpa clearings or abandoned pastures. These clearings tend to support non-climbing vines adapted to high-light conditions which flower and set seed quickly while light is still available. Common vine species genera include *Solanum*, *Cissus*, *Commelina*, and *Corchorus*. Over time, however, many of these short-lived, light-gap dependent vines are choked out by the shade from growing trees. With trees established and as the young forest matures, a new group of longer-lived climbing lianas begins to grow and many of these lianas may be as long-lived as any tree in the forest.

Lianas have adopted several strategies for climbing. Many lianas have clasping tendrils (thin, coiling modified leaf structures) that attach on to tree trunks and branches as the liana moves upward . Many lianas also produce glues on the outside of their stems which fasten onto tree bark and enable the plant to climb upward. In general, more lianas are found on rough-barked trees than smooth barked trees because the lianas can get a better grip on the rougher bark. Many lianas grow in spirals or twist around tree trunks to help support their weight or to avoid kinking.

One of the more incredible lianas in the neotropics is found in Belize. The vine is locally called basket tie-tie (*Desmoncus schipii*) and is actually a species of palm. This large, climbing palm (known as a rattan palm) is densely armed on the stem and leaves with slender needle-like spines and is one of the longest vines in the tropical world, reaching lengths of well over 1,000 ft (310 m). Other tropical vines have been reported up to 3,000 ft (930 m) long. Long vines such as these frequently cross between tree crowns and provide a travel route for other lianas and many animals. In some forests there may be up to 600 lianas per acre (0.4 ha). Often in forests that are heavily infested with vines, a single tree may be supporting lianas which weigh thousands of pounds, and if one tree falls it can carry one or more liana-connected trees down with it at the same time. Logging operations can cause the same type of damage.

In addition to weight problems, numerous vines and lianas on a tree may completely choke off the sunlight to the host tree's leaves and essentially starve the tree to death. An extreme example of this can be found in the strangler figs. Strangler figs, often called *matapalo*, frequently start off as epiphytes in the canopy of a host tree and then send down roots that wrap around the trunk of the host analagous to tendrils. Eventually the roots reach ground and and develop their own soil root system. Meanwhile the hanging roots fuse and slowly crush the host tree by constriction. The epiphyte/strangling fig species in Belize include *Ficus colubrinae, F. costaricana, F. hemsleyana, F. lapathifolia, F. oerstediana, F. padifolia, F. panamensis, F. popenoei,* and *F. schippii.*

Life Cycle of a Typical Strangler Fig

RAIN FOREST ADAPTATIONS

Buttresses

*M*any tropical trees have buttresses. There has been much debate as to the function(s) of buttresses and why some trees have them and others do not.   Their main function is to provide support and stability for the tree. Buttressed trees are common in both wet areas and in windy regions. Other buttress benefits have been suggested including protection against vine and liana growth   and   a compensating structure for   an unbalanced canopy. Buttresses come in many shapes and forms.

The most common buttress is an outgrowth of the trunk called a plank buttress. Plank buttresses are variable in shape ranging from very thin to very thick. A common misconception is that   timber is wasted when many tropical trees are cut above their plank buttresses.   In reality, however, the lower

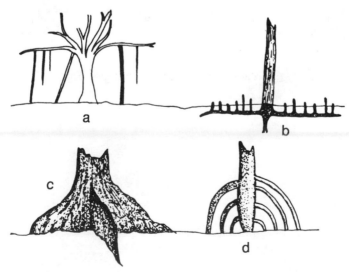

Buttress Types: a) adventitious roots; b) breathing roots (pneumataphores); c) plank buttress, d) stilt roots

trunks of most buttressed trees are hollow. Within the sanctuary the most common plank-buttressed tree is the mampola (*Luehea seemanii*). Mahogany, cedar, and banak also commonly have plank buttresses.

Roots may also act as support structures. Root supports come in the form of stilt roots, adventitous roots, or breathing roots (pneumataphores). Stilt roots grow from above ground, sometimes as much as 15 or 20 ft (5-6 m) up on the trunk of the tree. Stilt roots are very common on the red mangrove (*Rhizophora mangle*) and trumpet tree (*Cecropia* spp.). An adventitious root is any root arising from an unusual place such as a bud, branch or leaf. Adventitious roots are common on hemi epiphytic species which send down aerial roots from branches or stems to the ground for nutrients and support. Many fallen trees also sprout adventitous roots on parts of the tree that touch the ground. Breathing roots grow from beneath wet ground or water to get needed oxygen for the plant. Breathing roots are common in the black mangrove (*Avicennia nitida*).

Leaf Drip - Tips

Tropical rain forests typically receive lots of rain and many plants have adapted to tolerate very wet conditions. Buttressing is one such adaptation found on the stem. On the leaves, a very common adaptation is the development of the drip-tip. A drip-tip is simply a leaf tip that tapers to a slender point. This tip allows water to quickly run off the leaf after a shower. Some leaves with drip-tips dry over four times faster than leaves without drip-tips. Why is this so common in tropical wet forest trees?

The answer may involve several issues. First, with drip tips more water reaches the ground and is available for the plants roots; second, drip-tips actually reduce the size of rain drops such that the tips may help reduce soil erosion to some degree; third, the faster a leaf drys the more quickly it can photosynthsize again; fourth, having quick drying leaves may help reduce the number of little plants able to grow on the surface of the leaves, known as epiphylls. Epiphylls, such as

115

moss, algae, and lichens require a wet environment and once established, can completely cover the surface of leaves choking out sunlight and damaging the host plant.

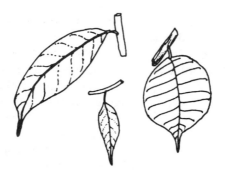

Leaf Drip Tips

In the dark understory of the forest, many leaves have adapted to the low light conditions by developing purple or dark undersides to their leaves. The purple or dark underside reflects light back into the leaf rather than letting it pass through the leaf. This adaptation helps the plant capture more sunlight in the dimly lit forest. In many plants, the young plants growing in the shade have dark undersides on the leaves while adult plants which reach the full sunlight do not.

Thigmonasty

Another adaptation leaves have developed is movement when they are touched. This touch response movement is called thigmonasty. Tendrils which wrap around any object they come in contact to are responding to touch. Touch response is most spectacular in the sensitive plant (*Mimosa pudica*) which is common in Belize. The sensitive plant when touched appears to droop and wilt almost immediately. Only a single tiny leaflet needs to be touched and the entire leaf will "wilt". This response is a result of a sudden change in water pressure within the leaf.

There may be several reasons why plants have developed such a mechanism. Often on hot or windy days compound leaves will "close" or fold-up to prevent from drying out. Some plants may droop when touched to fool hungry herbivores into thinking the plant is dying or diseased. In other plants, like the Venus flytrap (*Dionaea muscipula*), the touch response is used to imprison prey.

PLANT DEFENSES

*I*n order to survive, plants must protect themselves from being eaten or damaged by insects and larger animals. Plants also face the threat of damage by other plants such as strangling figs and sap-sucking epiphytes. In response to these dangers, plants have developed defenses to protect their vulnerable plant parts from the perils around them. There are many plant defenses a plant can employ and numerous examples of different defense strategies can be found in the plants of the Belizean forest. Plant defenses can be grouped into two main categories: Structural Defenses and Chemical Defenses.

Structural Defenses

Protective plant parts located on the exposed surface of the plant can be classified as structural defenses. Structural defenses include sharp spines, thorns, prickles, and sticky hairs, which can be on the stems, trunk, leaves or even roots of the plant. These sharp and often dangerous structures can limit or prevent browsing animals from eating the plant. For example, spiny leaf edges on some trees have been shown to limit insect damage. Various structural defenses such as dense spine clusters may also prevent or inhibit climbing-vines from moving up the plant and choking out sunlight. The figures on the following page illustrate some of the different structural defenses found on Belizean plants.

Sticky hairs are produced by many plants including some *Solanum* spp. , locally known as tear-coats, which are found in pastures and in secondary growth areas. On these plants, sticky hairs cover the entire leaf surface and when a hungry insect lands or crawls across the leaf to eat, its legs get stuck to the glue-like liquid and it eventually starves to death. Some species of tear-coats are especially nasty in that they also have stout, recurved prickles which indeed can tear ones clothing.

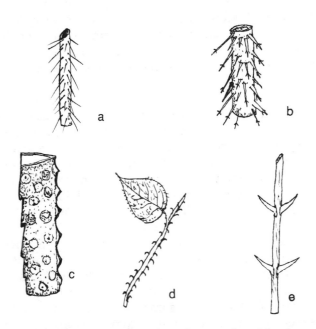

Structural Defenses: a) pokenoboy palm; b) give-and-take palm; c) ceiba tree; d) tear-coat [*Solanum*]; e) spiny bamboo

Chemical Defenses

The other category of plant defenses involve activity within the plant and are classified as chemical defenses. There are literally thousands of different chemicals that plants produce to protect them from being burrowed into, eaten or attacked by herbivores, fungi and bacteria. However, most chemicals are produced for protection against hungry insects mainly due to the huge number of potentially harmful insects occuring in tropical regions.

Defensive chemicals come in many different forms. Some plants have distasteful or poisonous sap, resin or latex which leaks out of the stem, trunk and/or leaves when the plant is cut or bitten into. Examples of saps and resins can be found in the fig, papaya, poisonwood, gumbolimbo, pine, and chicle. In the fig, for example, if you cut any part of the trunk or any branch with a machete, a white milky latex leaks out almost immediately. The same thing happens if you break off a leaf. For many insects and larger animals this milky latex is horrible tasting or poisonous and thus prevents them from eating or digging into the fig tree. Many of these saps also act to quickly cover and heal scars and wounds thus preventing infection.

Another form of chemical defense is not so easily seen as the saps and resins. These chemicals are produced inside plant leaves or stems and cannot be seen. These chemicals are called "secondary compounds" and most are toxic to few, some or many potential herbivores. There are thousands of secondary compounds produced by plants including alkaloids, phenolics, tannins, and terpenoids. These chemicals are released whenever the plant is bitten or burrowed into. The ability of plants to produce these unseen toxic chemicals gives them a competitive advantage which is similar to the advantages gained by plants with thorns and spines; those plants with good defenses are more likely to survive and reproduce. Nearly all tropical plants have some type of chemical defense system, especially in their leaves. Many plants also have nutrient poor and/or tough leaves which further limit herbivore damage.

Chemical defenses are the most developed in long-lived plants such as forest trees, mangroves, dry forest species and desert plants. In addition, young leaves are generally grazed more heavily than older leaves and gap colonizing trees like the *Cecropia* are grazed more than deep forest trees. However, some mature forest trees such as the cow okra (*Parmentiera aesculata*) and cotton tree (*Ceiba pentandra*) commonly suffer from leaf herbivory.

Hungry insects and other animals, however, have not been completely deterred by the huge variety of plant structural and chemical defenses. Some species of leaf cutter ants, for example, avoid the toxic saps in some plants by "blood letting" the leaves of their harmful chemicals. The ants cut the main veins in the leaf to drain out the dangerous saps before they use the leaf. Other animals, over time, may build up immunity to many chemicals so plants must constantly adapt by producing new chemicals or different combinations of chemicals to prevent from being eaten. Those plants that are able to produce effective secondary compounds will be the plants which survive and be able to produce healthy seeds for the next generation.

Many resins and saps, however, are useful to people such as rubber latex produced from the rubber trees of South America (*Hevea brasiliensis*). Some saps even taste good. The latex or "milk" from the chicle tree (*Manilkara chicle*), for example, although it is poisonous to many insects, can be tapped by chicleros and boiled down to make chicle and ultimately chewing gum. Nearly every plant sap, resin or chemical of use to people are actually adapted to prevent insect, animal, or fungal attack. Other examples of chemical defense compounds produced by plants used by humans include caffeine, morphine and cocaine.

Despite the the presence of plants poisonous to humans, the many chemicals produced by plants to defend themselves can be of enormous benefit to people. Plants found in Belize whose chemicals have been of great importance include logwood dye from the logwood tree, chicle from the sapodilla tree, and strychnine from *Strychnos* spp. plants. Many hundreds more plant chemicals have been used as traditional medicines for many generations by both Mayans and Creoles in treatment of a wide range of diseases. Knowledge of these chemical-bearing plants is the basis of "bush medicine". It is most unfortunate that bush medicine and "bush doctors" are vanishing from the nation of Belize and around the world.

Bush medicine gives us a glimpse of the huge potential of tropical plants to yield new medicines and treatments for all types of disease. Tropical forest plants are the great untapped pharmacy of the world. They have already yielded numerous famous medicines including quinine (from *Cinchona* spp.), birth control pills, cortisone and strychnine. To protect and learn from the forests is to protect and learn about ourselves. All living things have a place in our world and most we have not even begun to study or understand.

FRUITS

*B*ecause plants are rooted in the ground, fruits, and the seeds they contain, are the primary vehicle by which plants are dispersed. Fruits can be large and tasty like the mammee apple or tiny and dust-like as in many orchids. Why fruits are so variable in shape, size and form depends on how they are dispersed. There are two general strategies a plant may follow to distribute its seeds: Wind Dispersal or Animal Disperal.

Wind Dispersal

Wind dispersed seeds are often very light or have structures which catch the wind. Tiny wind blown seeds are common among epiphytes and some canopy liana species. Most orchid seeds are so small they're microscopic and blow about like dust. Some orchid seeds may only weigh one-millionith of an ounce. Other larger seeds have structures specially designed to catch or ride the wind. Some seeds have cotton-like hairs such as the ceiba or cotton tree. The cotton tree produces "kapok" attached to its seeds which is easily blown by the wind. The mahogany tree and other members of the Meliaceae produce seeds shaped like an airplane wing (called a *samara*) which twirls like a helicopter when it is released from the fruit. Other trees with fruits designed for wind dispersal include leguminous trees with thin, flat pods, the yemeri tree with small winged seeds, and members of the Bombaceae and Bignoniaceae.

Another curious dispersal mechanism is by water. Some species produce fruits and seeds which can float. Many palms including the coconut and cabbage palms have floating seeds as well as many legumes including the genera *Pithecellobium*, *Dalbergia*, and *Cynometra*. Many of these fruits are spongy or water-tight. One of the most interesting water dispersed trees is the provision tree (*Pachira aquatica*), a member of the Bombaceae. The provision tree produces large fruits up to a foot (30 cm) in diameter which may weigh six pounds (3 kg) or more. The fruit is filled with white flesh surrounding many large seeds about the size of a chicken egg. When the fruit opens at maturity, the brown seeds fall in the water and germinate immediately. The germinating seeds may float for days until they land somewhere on shore and the developing roots take hold.

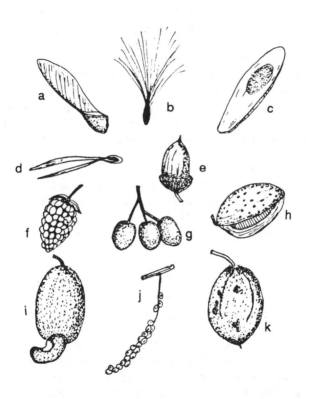

Fruit Types: *Wind Dispersed Fruits* - a) samara, disperses by twirling flight; b) achene, small seeds with light seed filaments that are carried by the wind; c) flat thin-pod with large surface to catch wind; d) silique, usually contains many light, fluffy seeds; *Animal Dispersed Fruits* - e) acorn, frequently buried in the soil; f) aggregate, many small seeds in the fruit are dispersed in animal feces; g & j) drupe, edible fruit with single seed carried by many mammals; h & k) large edible fruit with small seeds dispersed in feces, l) fruit with an engorged hypocarp, animals eat hypocarp but often leave seeds

Animal Dispersal

Animal dispersed fruits and seeds are extremely variable in shape and size depending on the type of animal disperser. The animals are not interested in dispersal whatsoever, but only in eating the often delicious and nutritious fruits and seeds. Many bird, bat, monkey, rodent, and even large insect species, travel throughout the forest canopy in search of edible fruits. As a result of this plant-animal interaction, rain forest trees have exploited the many mammal, bird and other animal species in the forest to disperse their seeds. Many fruits and seeds are specially adapted to attract a specific animal or group of animal dispersers. These animals are called specialized fruit eaters or specialized frugivores. Other dispersers may eat many different types of fruit and are known as generalized or unspecialized frugivores.

Why put so much work into developing tasty and showy fruits? The main purpose of the fruit is for the animal disperser to eat or carry the seeds away from the host tree and deposit them somewhere else where they might have a chance to germinate and grow. Many fruits provide a tasty and often nutritious pulp which surrounds the seeds, but many seeds themselves are not palatable or digestable. Some seeds have evolved to survive passage through mammal and bird guts thereby increasing the likliehood that seeds will be dispersed and likely away from the parent tree.

Most animals have different sensory perceptions and trees use different signals to attract potential dispersers. Birds have a weak sense of smell but good vision and as a result, many bird dispersed fruits are smaller and brightly colored. The most common colors being bright red or orange. Many understory shrubs and trees have these types of fruits including many members of the Melastomaceae and Rubiaceae. Bats are nocturnal and color-blind but have a good sense of smell so many bat dipsersed trees produce strong scented fruits that hang outside the trees canopy. The barley seed tree (*Andira inermis*) has bat-dispersed fruits (the tree is named after the brazilian word "andira" which means bat). Other bat dispersed trees include some members of the genera *Calophyllum, Couepia, Licania,* and *Spondias*.

Many larger fruits are dispersed by monkeys or rodents. Trees producing large animal dispersed fruits include the tubroos (*Enterolobium cyclocarpum*), mammey apple (*Pouteria* spp.), chicle tree (*Manilkara chicle*), some figs (*Ficus* spp.), craboo (*Byrsonima crassifolia*), and cojotone (*Stemmadenia donnell-smithii*). Many primate dispersed fruits are light green or yellow-colored. Many fruits that fall to the forest floor are often dispersed by rodents such as agoutis. While many rodents can destroy seeds with their powerful teeth and jaws, many also scatter hoard fruit and can carry undamaged seeds far from the parent tree.

Agouti Caches Seed

ORCHIDS

*F*or many, orchids have a mysterious attraction owing to their many beautiful flower forms, colors, and fragrances. There are over 20,000 wild species of orchids which all have a single structure which includes both male and female reproductive organs (ovaries, pistils, stamens) called a column, capped by a single anther. All orchid flowers are composed of 3 petals and 3 sepals. One petal forms a lip (labellum) on which insects are induced to land through various attractive forms and colors.

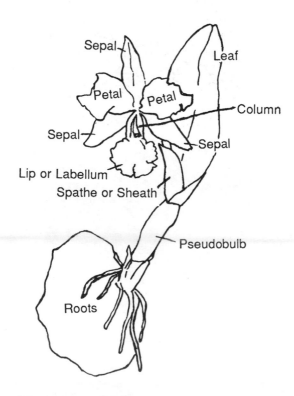

Parts of an Orchid

Sex and Mimicry

The name orchid comes from the ancient Greek word "orkhis" meaning testes. A student of Aristotle described a Mediterranean orchid based on its tuberous root which resembled testicles. Due to this myth, orchids were thought to influence fertility and virility and were used as aphrodisiacs to stimulate sexual desire.

Despite this myth, orchids are in reality linked to a more fascinating sex story which involves insects and a strange way of inducing pollination. The flowers of orchids range from 1/32 of an inch (0.08 cm) to a foot (30 cm) in size. Orchids have adapted fascinating mechanisms to deceive insects, often specifically one insect species, to act as their pollinator. This specialization functions to reduce hybridization in the wild. Able to cross this special barrier, humans are able to hand-pollinate orchids and have produced over 30,000 hybrid orchid types.

The orchid's intricate flower structures show intriguing yet efficient methods of propagation. The lip or labellum is the most conspicuous part of the flower. Although it varies from species to species, its function is always to assist in flower fertilization. The lip structures and smells emanating from the flower are attractive to specific insects. The lips often mimic a female insect's form and smell, to attract the males. Deceived males attempt to clasp and mate with the female decoy. In the process, the male may trip mechanical devices of the flower or be projected or directed onto the anther area where he will pick up or exchange pollen for cross fertilization. In some cases, the attracted insect may be temporarily trapped by the flower, dunked into a pool in the flower or enticed to become drunk by the flower. All of these deceptions result in bringing the male into contact with the pollen which attaches to his body and is later transferred to another flower.

Bee orchids are an example of this specialized case of deception. They are visited by a specific species of bee or wasp male who clasps the orchid decoy with its legs as though it were a female and begins copulating motions. In the process, pollen clings to the head or abdomen of their body. They are additionally attracted to the flower smell which duplicates the smell of a sexually ready female which acts as an aphrodisiac for the male.

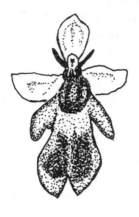

Bee Orchid

Epiphyte Lifestyle

Epiphytes are plants which live on trees. Over half the orchid species are epiphytes. Despite contrary myths, orchids are not carnivorous nor parasitic. As epiphytes they cling to trees for support with their roots but get nutrients only from rain water, decaying leaf litter and sloughed bark. The epiphytic plant experiences a wide variability in temperature and water availability. Orchids have structures which help them contend with this situation. Their roots are covered with a layer of dead cells with small holes into which rain water easily flows. Their thick cyclindrical leaves are modified to conserve water. The bulk of the leaf consists of cells that can fill with water to act as a reservoir during drought. The leaf surface is covered by a thick waxy layer to resist water loss except through small pores on the underside, which open and close in response to light. Some orchids may even dispense with leaves altogether, having only a short stem with tiny vestiges of leaves and extensive living roots. Some orchids also have a pseudobulb as part of the lower stem which stores water for the orchid's future use.

Seeds

Orchids bloom once a year and may maintain the bloom for only minutes or as long as 9 months. Bloom period is usually dependent on fertilization. Fertilization sets off a chain reaction causing the production of a substance toxic to the flower and causing it to degenerate. Then a seed pod forms which may require as long as 9-14 months to develop and may have hundreds, thousands or even millions of seeds which are dispersed by wind or water. These seeds have no nutrient reserves around them and will die unless they contact tiny micro-fungi which can provide nutrients for their growth.

Vanilla is the one orchid product other than the flowers which is commonly grown for profit. It was cultivated by the Aztecs in Mexico as a flavor for their chocolate. Pollination is by hummingbirds or by hand if the hummingbirds are not available. The white blossom ripens into slender, hanging, green seed pods. They are picked by hand, dropped in boiling water, fermented, and dried until they turn black. Then the bean may be used directly or the flavor may be extracted using alcohol.

Vanilla Orchid

PASSIONFLOWERS

Religious Symbolism

*W*hen the Jesuits arrived with the Spanish conquistadores to South America, they were amazed to find what they thought to be the same flower which according to Christian legend was seen growing upon the cross in the visions of St. Francis of Assisi. The flower was thus named *Flor Passionis* (passionflower) or *Flor de las Cinco Llagas* (flower of the five wounds).

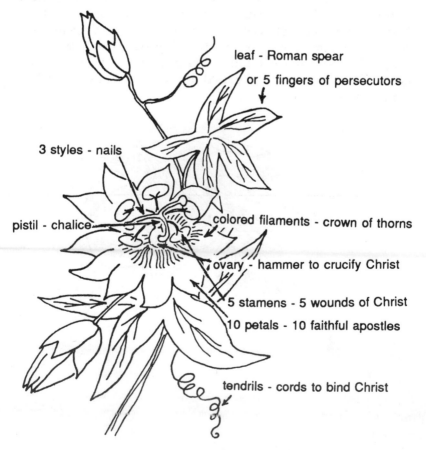

leaf - Roman spear
or 5 fingers of persecutors

3 styles - nails

pistil - chalice

colored filaments - crown of thorns

ovary - hammer to crucify Christ

5 stamens - 5 wounds of Christ

10 petals - 10 faithful apostles

tendrils - cords to bind Christ

The floral organs of the passionflower, *Passiflora* spp., which are found in Belize and throughout Central America, represent symbols of the passion of Christ on the cross. The 10 petals represent the 10 faithful apostles, excluding Judas who betrayed Jesus and Peter who denied him. The corona, whose inside has a showy crown of colored filaments which are nectaries, symbolizes the crown of thorns and the 5 stamens represents the 5 wounds. The ovary signifies the hammer used to impale Christ and the 3 styles symbolize the nails used while the pistil is the chalice. The leaf is shaped like the spears of the Roman soldiers. They are 5 fingered which is suggestive of the hands of Christ's persecutors or the prongs of the lance which according to a 17th century Jesuit " *pierced the side of the Savior, whilst they are marked beneath with round spots signifying the 30 pieces of silver*". The tendrils signify the cords used to bind Jesus. The central column represents the pillar before the Praetorium. A white variety of the species has been seen as a symbol of Christ's innocence while the petals of the blue variety are said to take the color from the Virgin Mary's sky blue cloak.

Native peoples in South America were cultivating passionflowers to eat the yellow egg shaped fruits. The Jesuits thus interpreted this as a divine sign that the Indians were hungering for Christianity. This encouraged them to religious zeal and to convert the Indians to Christianity amazingly rapidly.

Species Diversity

Passifloraceae is a medium-sized family of vines, trees, shrubs, and herbs which are mainly native to the Neotropics. There are between 400-500 species of the genus *Passiflora* most of which occur in Central and South America with some species in Asia, Australia, and a single species in Madagascar. There are 25 species of Passiflora reported in Belize. They are vigorous annual climbers which are found in a variety of tropical forest habitats including regenerating forests, as well as mature forest canopies. Fifty to 60 species of the genus have edible fruit but only a few are commercially cultivated. The fruit is sweet tasting and is either eaten raw or crushed to make a drink. Another 20 species are cultivated for their attractive and unusual flowers.

These brillant and complex flowers advertise to hummingbirds, bees and wasps which come to feed off the sizeable reservoir of nectar deep within the flower. These feeders also help to pollinate the plant. Some bees which are equally attracted to the passionflowers get a free ride. They are the wrong shape and size to pollinate the species. The corona is shaped in a stiff collar to block the bees and allow only the long thin bill of the hummingbird. The stingless bees instead go to the rear of the flower and chew holes directly into the nectary. This same species has adapted a defense for the bees by developing tiny nectar producing cups built into the leaves. These cups feed ants and wasps which in return protect the plant against the bees.

Whereas some lianas climb by twisting the stems around any suitable support, the passionflower, like peas and cucumbers, uses tendrils, which are modified stems or leaf stalks which coil themselves around any available support. In such climbers, the tendril is known as a branch-tendril, since it grows directly from the stem. Once it has a hold, the tendril coils up on itself pulling the plant up so that new tendrils can reach even higher.

Members of the genus*Passiflora* are mostly climbing plants with palmate leaves, tendrils and the unusual flower structure. Flowering occurs between July to August and in some species the flower lasts for only a day.

Passionflowers and Butterflies

One of the most interesting aspects of passionflowers are their constant evolutionary struggle and interaction with insects. This struggle has evolved over millions of years mainly in order to protect themselves from a family of butterflies, Heliconidae. The passionflower has evolved to synthesize new chemicals which are poisonous to most insects; but certain butterfly species of the genus *Heliconus*, have evolved to detoxify and thus tolerate these poisons so that their larvae can feed on the passionflower foliage. Usually these are specific relationships such that specific butterfly species larvae have evolved to tolerate the poisons of a specific passionflower species and are restricted to feed only on the one passionflower species. Passionflowers, in turn, develop different toxins in this evolutionary battle which has led to the evolution of a large number of passionflower species.

Heliconid butterflies can live for 6 months, a long time for butterflies because they can extract hard to get pollen by squirting a mixture of nectar and enzymes onto the pollen and then gathering up the pollen-rich solution which forms on the surface. These extra nutrients allow the females to lay large numbers of eggs on the passionflower. The larvae then feed on the plant. Although they can tolerate the poisons, they acquire them in their body tissues and pass them into the adult stage. This turns out to be advantageous since they are thus unpalatable to bird predators. This property is advertized by brilliant colors and distinctive patterns of black, with red, orange, yellow, and blue in a variety of displays.

Passionflowers have evolved other protections against these butterflies. Beside producing nectar deep in the flower for pollinating bees and hummingbirds, one species produces additional nectaries on petioles, stems, and leaves which attracts aggressive ants and wasps to protect the plants against the butterfly's larvae.

Passionflowers have evolved other techniques to change their leaf shapes in response to herbivore pressure. Some species of *Passiflora* actually mimic the leaves of trees in the canopy in order to make their leaves less recognizable to the butterflies. Some species have evolved structures on the leaves which resemble heliconid eggs. When landing on the plant, the heliconid butterfly tests the quality of the vine's leaves by drumming on the surface with its specially sensitive front legs. Satisfied it has found the correct passionflower species, it searches for an egg laying site. Young leaves and growing shoots are the best sites, being least poisonous and most tender for the larvae. Females will rarely lay eggs where eggs are already laid, so these egg imitations fool females who look for areas which have no eggs laid on them. If eggs are present,

false butterfly eggs

Mock Butterfly Eggs on Passionflower Leaf Tips

the first laid will hatch earlier and cannabalize the unhatched eggs. Some vines also produce tendrils which attract females to lay their eggs on them. These specific tendrils then drop off shortly, sending the undeveloped eggs to their demise.

Another protective mechanism evolved by *Passiflora foetida* are protective hairs on the plant's surface which trap and puncture the larvae causing their death by starvation and bleeding. These glandular hairs are tipped with a sticky droplet which traps the insects.

The family Heliconidae comprises about 70 species which are characterized by a narrow wing shape, long antennae and a thin elongated abdomen. They are extremely uniform in size varying only between 2.25-4 in (60-100 mm). They are lazy fliers which often congregate in large numbers in open clearings and at night in sleeping assemblies, hanging in clusters from low shrubs, from the same place each night.

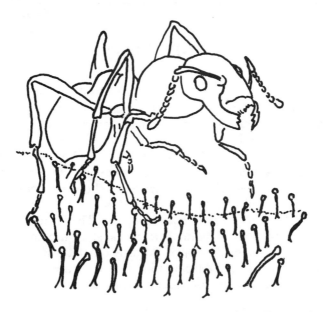

Passionflower Sticky Glandular Hairs Trap Enemy Insects

If the butterfly-passionflower interrelationship isn't complex enough, butterfly evolution additionally revolves around the unpalatability of the heliconid butterflies due to their poison intake.   Since birds learn of the heliconid butterfly's distaste and associate it with a warning coloration, experienced predators usually then leave the species alone. Thus other butterfly species evolve to camouflage themselves like the poisonous butterfly.   There are 3 main ways this happens.   1) More than one species which have poisons evolve to appear similar.   In this example called Batesian mimicry, predators only have to learn one color pattern to beware of. 2) Other non-poisonous species evolve to look like the unpalatable butterfly and take advantage of their warning coloration.   In this Mullerian mimicry, the non-poisonous species cannot become too numerous.   In some cases a number of unrelated species in an area share a common mimetic pattern and appearance.   3) Some species show sexual dimorphism.   If other species evolve to mimic them, then the sexes have their own mimic. Generally heliconid butterflies show a combination of black, yellow, and orange as a warning coloration.

FIGS AND WASPS

The lives of plants and animals of tropical rain forests are based on interrelationships. One is just the simple process of howlers feeding on fig fruits, which are an important food source for the monkeys. Other interrelationships are so complex that one species cannot live without the other. This is the case between fig trees and fig wasps. Fig trees show an incredible interdependency on specific wasp species. The wasps pollinate the fig flowers and the figs donate 50% of their fruits as nurseries for the wasp larvae to develop in. The "fruits" of fig trees as we know them are actually a special structure known as a "synconium" which encloses and protects the male and female flowers of the fig tree. Also within this structure, the tiny fruits develop and a very fascinating life-cycle of the fig wasp also unfolds.

Female wasps which have been fertilized by the male and have just hatched are attracted to female fig flowers by their scent. The female wasp enters the fig "fruit" by pushing the scales over the opening away with her wedged shaped head. She bores into the tiny flowers with her ovipositor, seeking to lay eggs. At this time she also pushes pollen out of her pollen sacs onto the flowers. Some of the female flowers have short styles (entrance to the fruit ovary) and she lays eggs in the ovary of these gall flowers. The others are too long for her ovipositor to reach and these instead become pollinated and fertilized and develop into fig fruits (stage 1).

The wasp larvae develop in these gall flowers and produce a substance which slows the other fig fruits from developing. This prevents animals from eating the fruits before the wasps can complete their cycle (stage 2).

The male wasps emerge first and fertilize the females. Then they bore a tunnel to the outside of the fig releasing the build up of the carbon dioxide gas which has slowed the female development. This stimulates the females to hatch (stage 3).

The female on leaving the fig , walks over the male flower and is coated with pollen which she stuffs into sacs on her abdomen and legs. With the help of the males , the females chew away the scales at the opening and leave to seek new fig flowers to lay their eggs in. The wingless males die in the fruit (stage 4).

The remaining fruit then develops and ripens and is eaten by the howlers and other animals. The tiny seeds pass through the howlers digestive tract and are distributed in the feces of the monkey. The feces may even help the seeds to germinate into another fig tree (stage 5).

Fig Wasp Cycle

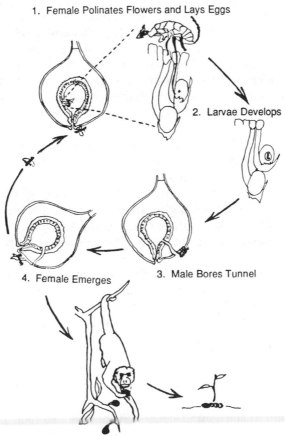

1. Female Polinates Flowers and Lays Eggs

2. Larvae Develops

3. Male Bores Tunnel

4. Female Emerges

5. Howler Eats Figs And Disperses Seeds

AMAZING ANTS

*A*nts exist in all parts of the world in varied habitats except for the frozen Arctic and Antartica, high mountains, and deserts.   They evolved 30 million years ago, but ants found embedded in amber petrified from the Oligocene period (25 million years ago) are identical to some species existing today. They are very successful, perhaps too successful since they have become such a pest to humans.

Ants are related to bees and wasps as part of the Order Hymenoptera a group of highly evolved social insects which characteristically have 2 pairs of thin transparent wings and a body with a tiny waist.   Usually only the queens and males maintain wings for a short while during mating.   Except for termites which are relatives of the cockroach, all other social insects are found in this order. Although some hymenopterans are solitary, most lead a highly organized complex social life.

The family Formicidae which includes the ants, has more species than all other species of social insects put together.   Part of the ants' success lies in their adaptability. Whereas bees and wasps construct rigid nests in rigid patterns, ants are more flexible changing their nesting according to sites and materials available rather than having to conform to rigid instinctual plans.   Ants can learn a great deal by experience.

They are also long lived.   Whereas wasps and wild bee hives may last a season or two, ant nests can survive for 10-30 or more years.   The queen can live up to 15 years and some of the workers   may live 5-6 years which all contributes to a stable community.

Although all insects have a jointed body, it is very noticeable in ants.   They have 3 main body sections.   They have a large head with "elbowed" feelers or antennae with well developed compound eyes.   Since they use their jaws for eating and as tools they have 2 pairs.   The larger upper pair are mobile and used for grasping, digging, tearing and biting. The lower pair are smaller and used for chewing food.   Other mouth parts include a highly developed tongue for licking and ingesting liquid food and large salivary glands at the base of the lower lip.

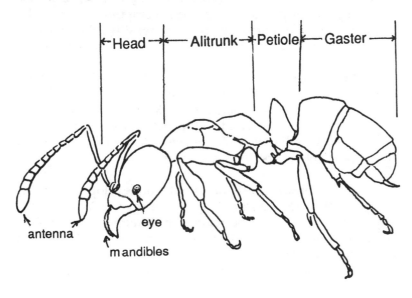

Generalized Ant Showing Body Parts

The thorax has 3 separate joints with a pair of legs attached to each. The legs have 4 main joints with claws at the end.   The front pair additionally have small combs for body grooming.

The abdomen or hind body has several segments.   The first two segments are very narrow, forming a waist which joins the thorax to the large rounded hind body called the gaster. The segments give the ant great mobility in moving and bending in all directions. The gaster contains the crop, digestive organs, reproductive organs, and poison glands.   The poison glands secrete formic acid and other poisons which the ants can either inject with a sting-like organ similar to bees, spray or inflict it in wounds through biting.

Caste System

The social system of ants is a caste system with 3 main colony members.   The queen is the largest. After initiating a colony, her main function is to produce eggs; she is the mother of the whole colony.   The queen is a fully developed female with fully developed sexual organs, compound eyes and 3 simple eyes.   Her antennae are more sensitive than those of the workers and she retains wings during the breeding swarm.

Males are larger than workers but smaller than the queen. They have a limited role in mating with queens during the swarm and die soon thereafter.   Males have small heads and brains but large eyes and well developed antennae used in locating and breeding with the queen.   Their life is brief and they appear only at specific seasons for mating.

The workers are females with undeveloped ovaries. They do not mate and rarely lay viable eggs.   Workers can vary in size which may be related to different development. Some colonies such as the leaf cutters produce soldiers which have abnormally large heads and powerful jaws.   They are not particularly aggressive but rather are slower and more sluggish.   Their development depends on a different diet. During a defense of the nest, it is usually the normal workers who respond first then the soldiers come out to grasp and hold the invaders.

The sense of smell is very important to ants. They use it to recognize friends and enemies, to follow trails to and from the nest, and to locate their food.   The smell organs are situated in the tips of the antennae, having over 200 olfactory cones.   Hearing and visual senses are not so important but ants are sensitive to vibrations.   Touch in the feelers is also important.   Taste organs are situated in the lower jaws which are used for chewing.   Ants are able to distinguish flavors and they like aromatic liquids.

Ants go through a complete metamorphosis from small eggs to larvae, pupae, and adult forms.   The small eggs have a sticky coating causing them to adhere to each other.   The egg sex is determined when laid.   Males develop from unfertilized

140

eggs determined by the queen when laying. Females come from fertilized eggs; queens are additionally determined by being fed different and better food and by the queen's nutrition. Larvae hatch in about 13 days into helpless, legless larvae which are totally dependent on the nurse workers who carry them, groom them, and feed them. They remain larvae for 8 days after which they enter the pupae stage for about 15 days. Adults emerge weakened but are aided for 3 days until they can begin work in the colony.

The cycle of the new colony forms with swarming of newly emerged queens and males. Since swarming occurs synchronously in colonies throughout the area, specific environmental factors trigger it. The winged queens and males fly in the air where mating takes place. Males die soon after, while the queens seek a place to begin the new colony. Many die in the process. After fertilization, often by many males, the queen tears, bites, and rubs off her wings. Guided by instinct she seeks a hidden chamber where she secludes herself and begins to raise a family. She lays eggs but usually fasts, obtaining nourishment to sustain her during this time from reabsorbing her flying muscles and by eating some of her first eggs. She feeds her first young on her saliva and some of the first eggs as well. Since this is a lean time, only about 10-20% of the eggs survive and they become small adults. These young begin to take over foraging and begin the colony. Later ant colony members choose different jobs depending on their age as adults and their general disposition.

Incredible Tiny Farmers

There are about 200 species of tiny farmer ants which live mainly in Central and South America. In Belize they are called wee-wee's but are generally called leaf cutting ants or parasol ants. They belong to the genus *Atta*. Their large underground nests, identified by a huge dome of dug soil sometimes as large as 150 ft (50 m), caps a tiny air conditioned city of millions who live 9-18 ft (3-6 m) underground. This city is composed of casts of different sized and shaped ants. These include tiny minima ants only 1/16 in (2 mm) long, a large number of workers, and large 3/4 in (20 mm) long soldier ants. Each of these groups have specific duties to maintain the ant community and they are all genetic sisters with a common mother, the queen.

The city starts with a new queen who hatches from a large hill and with other virgin winged queens, performs her nuptial flight. She is followed by newly hatched winged males who follow her up. As many as 3-8 males fertilize her, giving her enough stored sperm to last her whole life span of about 10 years. Before she takes this flight she packs her buccal cavity behind her mouth parts with a special fungal mycelia which she will use to begin a new farming community.

If she is one of the lucky 10% to survive, she begins her new home by excavating a narrow tunnel which descends about a foot under the ground ending in a small chamber. Here she

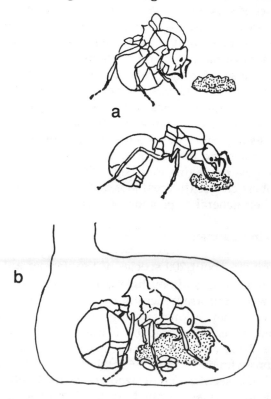

a) New queen anoints her manure with fungus; b) New queen and her first eggs

spits out the fungal pack and allows it to grow for a few days. She then lays 3-6 eggs which will be the new farmers. She continues to lay eggs for a while. During this time she remains in the chamber both eating many of the ill formed eggs and using others to nourish her larvae. The ill formed eggs fuse together to form 'omelettes' which she deposits directly into the mouths of the larvae. She never consumes the fungus at this time but mainly exists on the eggs and her resorbed fat and wing muscles. She helps replenish the fungus with her manure and fecal fluids. After 40-60 days, the first workers emerge and feed on the small, swelled spherical bodies of the fungus called gongylidia. These are also fed to the larvae. A week after hatching, the new workers dig out of the clogged tunnel and begin foraging for bits of leaves to bring back for their fungal garden. These leaf sections are chewed into small bits and kneaded into a mass which is deposited in the garden, which appears like a spongy breadlike structure, after being innoculated with bits of the living fungus.

The queen now stops caring for the larvae leaving their care and other tasks, including grooming her, to the workers while she becomes an egg-laying machine until her death. The colony grows rapidly during the first year and tapers off after 2-3 years yet remains a large size. Instead of growing larger, however, the colony then begins to produce new winged queens and males who will continue the cycle of new communities. The workers dig and build other interconnecting galleries and chambers to begin new gardens. It can be dangerous work but the worker ants have an alarm signal they use if caught under a dirtslide. They rub one part of their abdomen against another in a stridulating vibration on the soil which causes their sisters to dig them out and rescue them.

The Farming Community

A mature community may have as many as 1-2,000 chambers of which 10-25% maintain fungal gardens. As many as 5 million ants may live in this community which is well laid out to maintain the proper environment for the ants and their fungal crops. In the center of the mound, the air is warmest from the body metabolic heat of the ants and it rises out of the central entrances drawing in the cool air from the peripheral entrances. This helps to maintain a steady environment particularly maintaining a steady moderate temperature and humidity during extremes of the day.

Despite their farming nature, wee-wees are not welcome by human farmers since they attack most kinds of vegetation including crops and are considered serious pests in some areas. They are, however, valuable to the tropical rain forest and are major movers of nutrients within the forest ecosystem. During the 6 years of one colony study, the workers gathered almost 13,000 lbs (6,000 kg) of leaves. Their lifestyle is very intricate and interesting. The ants begin their foraging at dawn responding to the light. When going out on gathering foreys, the ants leave chemical trails for others to follow. Over time, these trails are cleared and become spotless, wide, highways between the nest and the needed vegetation. The workers cut large sections of leaves showing incredible balance until they have cut a leaf area considerably larger than their own body. They carry this back and give it over to the minima workers who cut them into small pieces which they chew around the edges, clearing it of its cuticle and foreign fungi. They may add a drop of clear anal fluid, placed with their forelegs. Finally, they pluck tufts of the fungal mycelia from the garden and plant them on the newly formed chewed mass in the garden.

These minima workers additionally have another function. They accompany the medium-sized workers and ride on the cut leaf sections but do not participate in the leaf cutting. Instead they protect the large workers from parasitic phorid flies by snapping their mandibles and "fencing" with their hind legs. As the workers cut pieces of leaves and carry them back to their nest, they are guarded by the minima. When holding leaves in their jaws the large workers are defenseless against parasitic flies (family-Phoridae) which lay their eggs on the neck of an ant. The emerging larvae burrow into the ant and kill it. The small workers fend off these flies.

The farming process shows a delicate interrelationship of survival between the ants and the fungi. Because the ants have been feeding on the growth of the fungi for so long historically, the fungi are no longer able to make fruiting

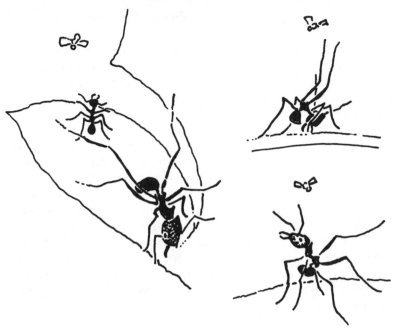

bodies or spores to replenish themselves.   Instead, the fungi depend on the ants to replant their mycelium in other areas of the community or to start new ant farms.   The fungi are deficient in other ways, lacking the necessary enzymes to break down leaves and provide enough nitrogen for healthy growth. The manure and anal fluids of the ants provide the fungi with these nutrients for their growth.   The ants also seem to "weed" the garden, ridding it of foreign fungi for once abandoned the ant hill is easily invaded by foreign fungi.   The ant-fungi relationship has evolved so far that the species of fungi have become totally domesticated and can no longer survive in the wild except within ant colonies.

Army Ants

A very exciting spectacle for visitors to the tropics is a run in with a colony of army ants on a march bringing disaster to almost all animals in their path failing to escape.   Species of the genus *Eciton* which occur in Central and South America, are the most studied of the army ants which occur in Belize. *Eciton burchelli* occurs in the lowland humid forests from southern Mexico to Brazil and Peru.   These have been called foraging ants, army ants, legionary ants, soldier ants or visiting ants.

Army ants have no permanent home but proceed through a regular cycle of a stationary state (Statary) and a moving phase (Nomadic phase).   These phases change, based on the reproductive and developmental periods of the colony. The statary phase revolves around a temporary encampment of 2-3 weeks in a sheltered area usually between tree buttresses, in fallen logs or in sheltered areas along trunks and main branches of trees to about 60 ft (20 m) above ground.   The "nest" which protects the laying queen and her immatures is provided by the bodies of the worker ants themselves.   As the workers gather to form the bivouac, they lock legs and bodies together with their strong tarsal claws and thus form chains and nets that accumulate into interlocking layers of workers. The entire worker force ultimately comprises a solid cylinderal or ellipsoidal mass, as large as 3 ft (1 m) across containing 150,000- 700,000 ants which also exudes a musky fetid odor.   The queen and immature ants are in the center.

With the beginning of the nomadic phase, at dawn the nest dissolves and begins flowing in all directions until a raiding column grows along the path of least resistance in one direction.   There are no leaders but all workers press forward short distances laying down a chemical trail from their abdomen tips and return being supplanted immediately by others who extend the trail a little farther.   The others press forward behind them.   Their movement seems chaotic but the column formation and movement seems to respond to 2 factors. First, they respond to the pressure moving away from very tight places.   Secondly, they respond to drainage or vacation of space by filling in the gap spaces.   Thus it seems as though they are responding to a medium-level of spacing between colony members.   The columns take on a specific order with small and medium-sized workers moving along the trails extending it and the larger soldiers travelling more slowly on either side of the trail.   The colony travels 300-600 ft (100-200 m) every day.

As with other ants and social insects, army ants have a

caste system. Males and new virgin queens only appear seasonally in the early part of the dry season. There are different sizes of workers, minimas and medias, all who are generalist workers. They capture and transport prey, choose the bivouac sites, and care for the queen and larvae. Their long, strong legs enable them to travel rapidly with larvae slung beneath them. Workers characteristically change their work preference with age. Soldiers have large heads and long sickle-shaped mandibles and only function in defense.

The bivouac is controlled by an internal rhythm connected to the stages of the immature development which is somewhat connected to food supply. During the statary phase, the queen feeds a great deal in the early stages as she develops and lays eggs. This begins the synchrony of the colony rhythm. Within a week of the statary phase the queen's abdomen swells with 55,000-66,000 eggs. She lays 100-300,000 eggs in several days which hatch synchronously within a few days of each other. As the labial glands of the larvae become fully functional at the 8th or 9th nomadic day, it is thought that they produce a pheremone or communicatory smell which excites the workers. A few days later, the new workers emerge from their cocoons. Due to the sudden appearance of these new workers, the older workers increase their level of activity, increase the intensity of their hunting raids, and begin emigrating each night, starting the nomadic phase. As the larvae pupate, the intensity of the raids diminishes and the colony passes again into the next statary phase. As they pupate, they reduce feeding, creating a food surplus, and the queen begins to feed voraciously.

With the hatchings, sudden complex behavioral changes occur. At dusk, the workers stop carrying food into the old nest area and begin carrying the larvae away from the bivouac. After most of the larvae have been removed the queen begins to move about 8-10 pm. She is escorted by a thick column of workers with a high number of soldiers for protection. The workers push her along, enveloping her. She is guided to the temporary bivouac by the odor trail.

While this cycle occurs regularly throughout the year, a change occurs early in the dry season. At this time a sexual brood is produced.   The queen, instead of producing workers, produces a brood of 1500 winged males and about 6 virgin queens. When one of the queens has successfully bred, the colony which has already begun to divide in their work orientation, splits. The older workers who have been attending the old queen in a brood-free environment, move off in one direction with her while the other group of workers moves off with the new queen. Unsuccessful queens are sealed off from progressing to form a new colony.   In some cases the old queen is sealed off and the colony splits between two virgin queens.

Ants and Plants

Within the Community Baboon Sanctuary there are two other ant types whose colony life is intertwined with a plant species in a symbiotic relationship in which both ant and plant species benefit.   Throughout the tropics such plant species have evolved an amazing array of special structures adapted for the use of ant colonies. In both cases within the sanctuary, the plant provides the ants with a home and food while the ants protect the plants from herbivorous animals and light-choking vines.

The bull horn acacia or cockspur found in the sanctuary develops large thorns filled with spongy tissue.   The ants of the genus *Pseudomyrmex*, chew their way in near the sharp thorny tips and live in the thorn interiors.   The trees sprout detachable Beltian bodies from the tips of leaflets which are eaten by the ants.   In turn the ants attack invading insects. Plants that sprout nearby the acacia trunks are chewed by the ants until they die.   Plants which touch the acacia canopy are also attacked.   If the tree is 'attacked' by humans or cows, the ants swarm out and counter-attack.   Their stings are very painful and dissuade foragers.

The *Pseudomyrmex* life cycle conforms to the basic ant pattern.   After the nuptial flight, the queen alights, sheds her wings, and searches for a nest site, which may only be an unoccupied acacia thorn.   The queen gnaws a circular hole near the thorn tip and enters it.   She then lays 15-20 eggs and rears her first brood in seclusion in the thorn cavity.   The worker

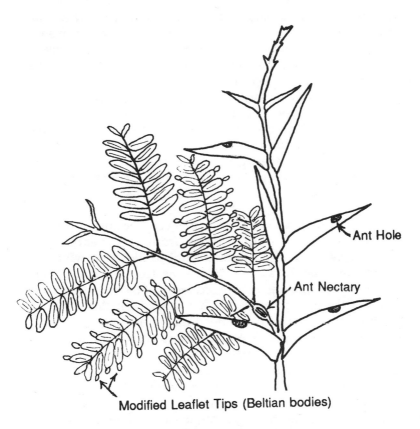

Ant Hole

Ant Nectary

Modified Leaflet Tips (Beltian bodies)

Bull Horn Acacia Showing Ant Colony Openings
and Ant Food Sources

population increases rapidly, with 150 workers in 7 months which then doubles by 10 months.   In younger colonies the workers leave their thorn home long enough only to gather nectar and Beltian bodies.   When their numbers reach 50-100 they begin patrolling the plant surfaces near their nest thorns. At 200-400 they become aggressive, attacking and destroying other smaller colonies in nearby thorns.   In old colonies the queen female does nothing but lay eggs and is heavily attended by workers who take care of her and the eggs and larvae. Finally the dominant colony takes possession of the entire tree, wiping out all competitors. Production of males and virgin queens begins in the second year and continues thereafter.

The ant colonies subsist primarily on Beltian bodies and foliar nectar from the host tree. The larvae are fed on the Beltian bodies in a peculiar manner. The nurse worker pushes the fragment of food deep within the trophothylax, a special food pouch found on the lower thorax behind the head. The larvae then rotates its head in and out of the pouch, chewing and swallowing its contents. Simultaneously it ejects a clear fluid droplet possibly containing a digestive enzyme, into the pouch. If the Beltian body fragment is too large the nurse will remove it cut it up and put it back. Workers will also force open the pouch and regurgitate fluid droplets into it. The workers may also on occasion catch insects which they then feed to the larvae.

The *Cecropia* is an early pioneer tree that begins to colonize vacated milpa areas from 1-6 years after abandonment. It is a jointed, bamboo-like tree which is divided into chambers . When the tree is small, 2-6 ft (.75-2 m), it is sought out by winged forms of the recently mated females of the genus *Azteca*. The winged females leave the old colony and mate with a winged male from another colony. Single females then go off on their own to seek out a young, actively growing *Cecropia* tree. She searches the trunk to find a small depression, called a prostoma, or internodal pit, which is located just above the base of the leaves emerging on the main trunk. This is a thin area in the trunk wall which the queen can easily chew through and make an entrance hole into the hollow trunk. She enters one chamber and begins raising a brood. She feeds the larvae to maturity who will then take over in maintaining the colony. The offspring then expand the nest and bounds of the colony by boring holes in the septa between walls in the trunk . When the *Cecropia* reaches 10-15 ft (3-5 m) it has a well developed colony.

By eating out the internal tissue of the trunk, the trunk wall becomes weakened and under the pressure of the weight of the crown of the tree, it bulges out to form a larger chamber than normal. The ants feed on certain superficial gland-likebodies which grow in the velvety triangular base of the *Cecropia* leaves. These small red or yellow elliptical corpuscles embedded in dense mats of hair at the base of eachleaf petiole are called Mullerian bodies. They are rich in oil and proteins and can be detached and carried off for consumption. The ants also gather honey dew, sweet secretions from mealy bugs and other homopterous insects which live on the *Cecropia* tree.

When an animal touches the tree, the ants go into a frenzy and come out of their hole in the tree chamber. Some emerge and drop off, biting whatever they land on. Additionally, if vines touch the tree, the ants bite them and may inject a chemical exudate which is poisonous to the vine.

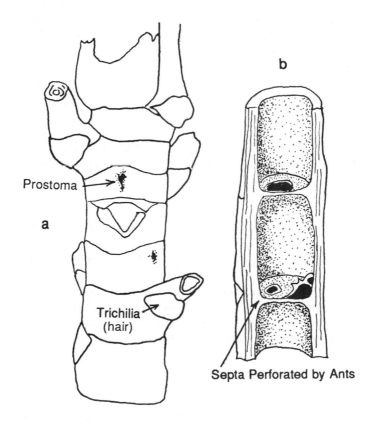

a) Cecropia Stem Section Showing Prostoma Area With Ant Colony Opening; b) Cut Away View of Stem Showing Hollow Chambers and Ant Openings

ENDANGERED SPECIES IN BELIZE

*N*ature has produced an incredible array of plant and animal species and the tropical rain forest is a center for the greatest number of species, many of which have valuable uses for human kind. The failure to preserve this rich variety of life for future generations is outright and irrevocable theft from our children because once lost, a plant or animal species cannot be reconstructed. All life, especially in a complex environment such as a tropical rain forest, is part of a web of interrelationships and each species depends on others in specific and complex ways. To ensure the survival of endangered species, we must conserve their environment as well.

Conservation is the ensuring that nothing in the existing natural order be allowed to become permanently lost (extinct) as a result of human activities unless all foreseeable consequences of the loss have been thought out.

As human activities become more and more prominent in Belize, they will begin to infringe upon the natural environment. The beginnings of plans for large agricultural operations are starting the cycle of rapid change in the natural environment of Belize. Yet with proper planning, Belize can maintain these species and their habitats while still encouraging sensible development. But all precautions must be taken because when humans alter the environment, the results are frequently unforeseen and unpleasant.

Although we often concentrate on saving endangered species because they are more visible and have more appeal, in trying to preserve them, we must look at the broader picture. We must look at saving their environment, because what would a species be, and how long could it survive without the necessary food and habitat which the environment provides. In saving any species, we must look at how it interrelates with other species and the environment. For example, to protect the baboon or howler monkey, we must ensure that the food trees which they depend on, are protected. Many of them are fig trees, and fig trees depend on specific wasps for their pollination and thus their continuation as a species. So we must ensure that these tiny wasps are protected as well or the figs will die and the baboons will go with them.

What Makes a Species Endangered?

1. <u>Major alteration of its environment such as for agriculture or logging</u>. Howlers and other monkeys are species most hurt by rain forest clearing because they depend on it for their food.

    Solutions - a) use the land at a slow enough rate to allow regeneration of the forest needed for the howler; b) selective logging will utilize economic hardwoods yet still maintain a usable forest for some species; c) some forest crops such as chicle or cacao utilize the forest while still maintaining much of it for other plant and animal species.

2. <u>Pet trade, zoos, and medical laboratories</u>. The yellow headed parrot and scarlet macaw are endangered due to the pet trade. The capture of young parrots often entails destruction of the hollow tree nest site, a valuable resource for the species. For every 4 parrots taken and shipped out for the pet trade, only 1 will survive. Monkey infants are captured by killing the mother. As with parrots, only a small percentage of these will survive to be purchased as pets.

    Solution - create laws and restrictions on the pet trade and develop breeding colonies as a resource for medical research. Don't maintain wild animals as pets.

3. <u>Hunting animals for their products</u>. The hickatee and sea turtles are examples of how hunting can endanger a species.

    Solution - regulate the taking of the species especially at critical times in their life history when they are most vulnerable. In sea turtles, restricting the hunting of fertile females and eggs, as well as protecting the beaches where eggs are laid, is helping in their protection. The hawksbill turtle shell is prized for use in decorative objects. Not buying, selling, or using these products in Belize will decrease the market for them and help save the species.

4. Predator control. Humans may perceive themselves to be in direct competition with predators such as jaguars, mountain lions, and ocelots for game or livestock.
   Solution - regulate the hunting of predators such as jaguars to include only problem animals, since it is known that such livestock killers are the main problems and many may only become problems due to wounding by hunters.

5. Superstitions or misinformation. In Belize, common harmless snakes are often killed when found because they are mistaken for the deadly fer-de-lance or tommygoff.
   Solution - educate yourself and others as to which are harmful species and do not kill others for no reason.

What Makes a Species Susceptible to Extinction?

1. Large size - Large animals such as the jaguar or tapir require a large home range to get the food they need and they are most susceptible to habitat destruction.

2. Predators - Predators such as any cat species are most threatened due to their perceived incompatibility with humans.

3. Narrow habitat tolerance - Howlers or baboons which are restricted to low altitude and often river forests suffer when these forests are cut. The hickatee river turtle is limited to deep, clear rivers and lagoons.

4. Valued for hides or other reasons - The hawksbill turtle is valued for its shell for jewelry and the ocelot's skin is valued as a stylish fur.

5. Hunted for food - Sea turtles, hickatees, curassows, and ocellated turkeys are all hunted for food.

6. Restricted distribution - The black howler, the hickatee, and the ocellated turkey are found only in the Yucatan

peninsula area of southern Mexico, northern Guatemala, and Belize.

7. Species which are migrants across international boundaries - Migratory birds which breed in the USA and Canada may be well protected in the north but they depend on the tropics for their winter survival.

8. Intolerance of humans - A species such as the jabiru stork seems to need a great deal of space around its nest, away from populated areas, for its breeding and survival.

9. Species which produce in large colonies - Colony breeders such as the booby need areas set aside for breeding. Destruction of breeding areas areas can lead to eventual extinction of the species.

10. Long gestation periods and limited young - Baird's tapir, the mountain cow of Belize, produces only a single young, from a long gestation period, causing a very slow build up of its population numbers.

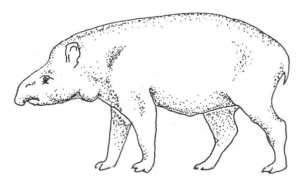

This table shows 15 Belizean species which share a number of characteristics which make them vulnerable to extinction.

	howler monkey	spider monkey	jaguar	tapir	turkey	curassow	hickatee	green turtle	hawksbill turtle	yellow headed parrot	scarlet macaw	ocelot	booby	jabiru stork	warblers
1. large size	x	x	x	x	x	x	x	x	x		x				
2. predator			x									x			
3. narrow habitat	x						x						x		
4. hunted for parts			x							x		x			
5. hunted for food	x	x		x	x	x	x	x						x	
6. small distribution	x					x	x								
7. migrants								x	x						x
8. intolerant of humans											x			x	
9. colony breeders								x	x				x		
10. long gestation limited young				x						x	x			x	

EDENTATES - TOOTHLESS, NOT QUITE

The order Edentata includes 6 living families and 33 species which exist entirely in the new world, inhabiting areas from the southeastern U.S. through Mexico and Central America to southern South America. They evolved in South America 60 million years ago. When the Panamanian land bridge connecting Central and South America rose up from the sea 2.5 million years ago, edentates were able to cross into Central America and parts of North America. They were more diverse long ago having 10 times the numbers of species than are now living. Such early edentates included huge ground sloths and giant armadillos.

Three Toed Sloth

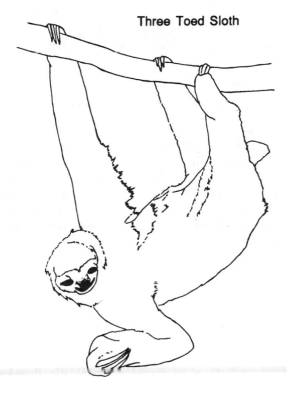

Three main groups, tree sloths, anteaters, and armadillos make up the order. The one character which distinguishes edentates from all other mammalian orders are *xenarthrales* which are extra articulations between the lumbar vertebrae. These lend support particularly to the hips which aid armadillos in digging. Another characteristic which separates these groups from others is the presence of a double post vena cava in the blood system that returns blood to the heart from the hind quarters. Most mammals have but one.

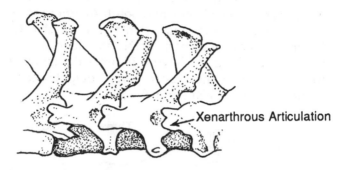

Armadillo Lumbar Vertebrae Showing
"Xenarthrous" Articulations

All edentates share some general characteristics, such as having 2 or 3 digits on the hand which are much larger than the others. All the fingers have long sharp claws. The foot usually has 5 toes. While the upper arm bones are separated, those of the leg may be joined at the ankle or at both ends. The mammae are located near the armpit, on the chest, or less frequently on the abdomen. Living edentates also differ from other mammals in having simple skulls with no canines, incisors, or premolars. Females have a primitive divided womb only a step removed from the double womb of marsupials and a common urinary and genital duct while males have internal testes and a small penis with no glans. Armadillos are the most primitive edentates with a very small neocortex in the brain but with a well developed olfactory brain.

The extinct edentates were huge unspecialized herbivores of scrubby savannas. They were probably outcompeted by northern invaders with the opening of the Panamanian land bridge. In contrast, the living edentates are successful due to their narrow niches. Anteaters and sloths have very specialized diets. To cope with the low energy of their diets they evolved low metabolic rates (33-60% of other mammals) and low temperatures (91-95°F) to burn fewer calories. Armadillos have a wider range of food choices but are specialized for a burrowing way of life. They also have lower metabolism and temperatures. Sloths and anteaters are thus slower in movement. The social life of edentates are dominated by smell. All species produce odoriferous secretions from anal glands, to mark paths, trees or conspicuous objects.

Although their name, edentata, means toothless, only the anteaters are actually toothless. Armadillos have primitive, undifferentiated, rootless, peg-like teeth which

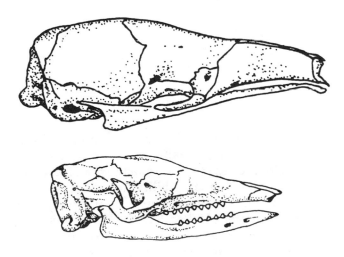

Tamandua Skull Showing Lack of Teeth (top)
Armadillo Skull With Peg-like Teeth (bottom)

grow throughout their life. The giant armadillo has 100 teeth which is the most teeth of any mammal, but the teeth are small and vestigial. None of the edentates have incisors or canines and the cheek teeth are uniform and lack dentine a condition conducive to continuous tooth growth.

9-Banded Armadillo
(*Dasypus novemcinctus*)

Range

There are 20 species of armadillos which range from the southern United States to the Strait of Magellan in South America. The 9-banded armadillo is the only species of armadillo found in Belize. Its genus name *Dasypus* was an attempt by scientists to Latinize the Aztec name "azotochtli" which means turtle-rabbit. The species is the most successful of all armadillos, adapting to a wider range of habitats than any other species. It ranges from the southeastern United States to Peru and northern Argentina in South America. It is also found on some Caribbean islands in between.

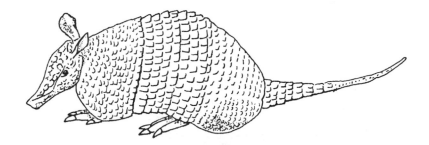

The 9-banded armadillo has shown one of the most rapid expansions in mammalian history in the last half century. In 1880 it crossed the Rio Grande from Mexico into the United States. Showing an ability to adapt to changing environments and thrive close to humans, it rapidly colonized most of the southeastern United States. The species appears limited now by long-term arid areas and extended periods of cold. Whereas it could probably survive colder areas, it depends on insects which cannot. Armadillos can also endure extreme heat as found in Belize and other tropical areas. During hot periods their breathing quickens, they pant, and lie on their side to facilitate heat loss. They roll into a ball and become inactive during drops in temperature.

Their incredible swimming traits have aided in their range expansion. They can cross rivers despite their heavy armor by inflating their stomach and intestine by gulping air for buoyancy . They can also hold their breath for as long as 6 minutes and literally walk across the bottoms of small streams.

Their success is due to their flexible diet and reproductive behavior which allows them to exploit all but the most arid habitats. Having weak dentition the armadillo detects small vertebrates and invertebrates with keen smell and then rapidly digs them out. To keep the scent, it places its snout in soil and holds its breath for up to 6 minutes to avoid inhaling dust.

Armor

Its striking and unusual shell gives it its name armadillo which in Spanish means little armored one. The armor develops from the skin which is remarkably modified to provide a double-layered covering of strong bony plates or scutes, overlaid by a layer of horny epidermis. The shell lacks any surface hair. The scutes cover most of the upper surface and sides of the animal, with some protection afforded to the head and limbs. The armor is arranged in bands or plates connected by flexible skin, making the shell flexible in the living animal. There are broad rigid shields over the shoulder and hips with varying numbers of bands over the middle, connected to flexible underlying skin. The limbs are covered by exposed margins of the horny shields, the top of the head is covered by tough scales, and the tail is protected by 12-15 rings.

The shell is composed of three parts, a scapular shield over the shoulder, a pelvic shield over the hips, and 8-11 transverse bands joining the two shields. The underside is soft and sparsely haired. Armor makes the body heavy, weighing 16% of body weight, but protects the armadillo in two ways. First, it is protected from thorny shrubs as it plunges away from predators. Second, the armor protects it from some predators although the teeth of large predators can pierce the armor and kill the animal. They are a favorite prey of jaguars.

Armadillos usually depend on bursts of speed or frantic burrowing to escape enemies. Although they can defend themselves with their powerful claws they usually run on the claw tips of the hands and soles of the feet and can move very fast when chased. If possible they will burrow into the ground and then anchor themselves in the burrow. But when overtaken on the ground they will draw the feet within the armor, which is in direct contact with the ground. A few species can roll up into a ball, their head and tail plates making them completely protected.

Although many of the armadillos natural predators have been removed in North America, they succumb to the ravages of the automobile. When startled, armadillos have a curious jump reflex which can be effective against natural predators but is deadly when confronted by a car. As a car approaches and roars over them, instead of fleeing they bound straight up almost vertically, hitting the car's underside.

Diggers

The 9-banded armadillo is built for digging. The body is broad and depressed with short legs and a soft belly sparsely covered with yellow hair. The forefeet have 4 toes of which the middle two are largest. They have powerful curved claws for digging. The lower leg bones are united at both ends and the

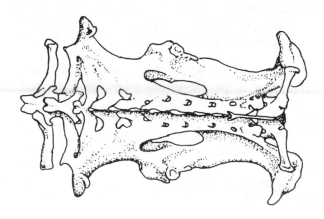

Upper View of Armadillo Skeleton Showing Fusion of the Vertebrae with the Ilium and Ischium Bones of the Pelvic Girdle

hind feet have 5 toes. Another skeletal modification which strengthens the armadillo's body for digging is the fusion of the pelvic girdle with the adjacent vertebrae.

They are powerful diggers and construct burrows 3-5 ft (1-1.75 m) underground and as long as 4-15 ft (1-5 m) with nests at the end lined with leaves and grass. In nest building the armadillo bunches the leaves under its body and inclines on its hind legs. With its forepaws clutching the material, it hops, usually backwards to the nest. The active dens have about a 7 in (18 cm) entrance which faces south. It digs, loosening the soil with nose and forefeet, piling dirt up under it. It then balances on its forefeet and tail and kicks reflexively with hindfeet simultaneously to scatter soil behind it. The burrow is often located in the banks of streams or at the base of trees. They also maintain short 12-18 in (30-45 cm) burrows for safety. Armadillos are mainly nocturnal, solitary, and terrestrial where they can ply their powerful digging traits. During the day they rest in their underground burrows.

They have an average home range of 2.5-35 acres (1-14 ha) but most are only several acres. Although they omit a musky odor from scent glands located near the base of the tail, they don't have territories and seem to share home ranges without antagonism. They may share their burrows with others of the same sex and they are known to share burrows with other species of animals including snakes, rabbits, and opossums.

Foraging

Armadillos have a long snout with a long tongue that can thrust outward. Small, peg-like and ever growing teeth are arranged 7-9 in each half jaw of the elongated skull. The giant armadillo has a total of 80-100 small vestigial teeth, having more than other mammal. They have a good sense of smell, sight , and hearing. The 9-banded armadillo weighs around 14 lbs (6.5 kg) but is dwarfed by its South American relative the giant armadillo which weighs 130 lbs (59 kg). They forage in a jerky fashion poking into holes, crevices and leaf piles, grunting continuously. Their diet consists of 78% insects, 1.2% reptiles and amphibians, and the remainder spiders, millipedes, earthworms, slugs, other invertebrates, and a slight bit of plant material, and carrion. They'll also eat fungi, tubers, and fallen fruits. They may also eat a good number of ants. They have been accused of taking birds eggs but do so rarely. They also seem to need to ingest soil to prevent gastro-intestinal problems.

Breeding

Its sex life is eccentric. In contrast to most mammals the armadillo mates belly to belly with the female on her back. Mating occurs in July-August when the female is two years of age but implantation of the embryo is delayed until November. Gestation is 4-5 months but with delayed implantation the full gestation can be 20 months.

Mammae are usually located in the chest region but abdominal pairs are occasionally present. The normal litter is four but curiously they are 4 identical twins from the same fertilized egg. Interestingly these quadruplets sometimes show major differences. The young are born with their eyes open and move around within a few hours. Their pinkish shell is leathery and pliable at first. In a few days it turns gray-brown and begins to harden although it doesn't complete the process until it is full grown. By the next breeding season the yearlings are on their own. They can live about 12-15 years.

Females show the strongest tendency to maintain exclusive home range areas. Males overlap freely and may encompass ranges of several females. Males ranges are 50% larger than female ranges, from 4-26 acres (1.5-10.5 ha). Home ranges of both sexes include up to 12 different den sites which are usually used by single individuals on different nights. Sociality in nests is usually a mother and an all male or all female litter. Spacing is probably regulated by smell. They have glands on the ears, eye-lids, and soles of their feet, as well as bean-shaped pair of anal glands which produce a yellow nauseous secretion. Adults often sniff anally on meeting. Spacing may be due to the depositing of urine or feces. Armadillos sometimes resolve territorial disputes by kicking, chasing, and fighting.

Leprosy

Armadillos have been especially useful to humans in the fight against leprosy, a bacterial disease found in the tropics. Although the leprosy organism was identified in 1873, research on it was difficult because scientists were unable to grow it in a test tube. Leprosy attacks the cooler parts of the human body such as the nose and ears. Armadillos proved to be a good experimental host because of their low body temperature which ranges between 82-91° F (28-33° C) as compared to 98.6 ° F (37° C) in humans. Scientists found that they could produce the disease by innoculating armadillos with bacilli from infected persons. Later they discovered armadillos with the disease naturally in the wild. How the disease is actually contracted is unknown. Because of their lower body temperatures armadillos develop much more serious symptoms which are fatal. This is because the disease affects their brain, spinal cord , and lung tissues which are not affected in humans. The armadillos main use in disease investigations is to produce bacilli in making Lepromin, a reagent used in the prognosis to tell if an inflicted person has a serious or benign type of the disease which in turn dictates how the leprosy can be treated. Further research is leading to the production of a vaccine to prevent the disease.

Anteaters

Anteaters are the only fully toothless members of the order Edentata. Thus, they depend almost exclusively on the soft-bodied ants and termites as denoted by their Latin family name Myrmecophagidae which means anteater: "myre" meaning ant and "phag" meaning to eat. Three species of anteaters are thought to occur in Belize. In addition to the silky anteater (*Cyclopes didactylus*) and the tamandua (*Tamandua mexicana*), the giant anteater (*Myrmecophaga tridactyla*) has formerly been reported in southern Belize, which is the northern most part of giant anteater's range.

All anteaters have elongated, tapered snouts in a hard bony skull with tubular mouths. Their long tongue, with minute posteriorly directed spines, when licked out is covered with a sticky fluid secreted from large saliva glands in the neck when the animal is feeding.   Both the silky anteater and tamandua have a prehensile tail which is very useful in their arboreal life.   The giant anteater, on the other hand, is strictly terrestrial and its tail is flag-like and modified both for conserving heat and for camouflage when sleeping.

Anteaters have 5 fingers and 4-5 toes but the fifth finger of the giant anteater and the first, fourth, and fifth fingers of the silky or two-toed anteater are much reduced and not visible externally.   The 3 middle fingers of the tamandua and second and third of the giant and silky, bear sharp powerful claws.   Long sharp claws on the forelegs are both powerful defense weapons and tools used for opening ant and termite nests.   The giant anteater has a remarkable sense of smell but poor sight and hearing. Its smell has been measured to be 40 times more sensitive than humans sense of smell. Both sexes repond to the smell of their saliva and produce secretions from the anal gland.   They have slow metabolism and low body temperatures (91°F - 33° C). They do not dig burrows but rather dig shallow depressions and sleep for 14-15 hours per day. They walk on the knuckles of the front feet.

Tamandua

The tamandua, a medium-sized animal weighing 8-13 lbs (4-6 kg), is common in the Community Baboon Sanctuary as it is in other humid, low elevation habitats throughout Central America. It is replaced by a related species in the southeastern Andes in South America. The tamandua is clothed in dense bristly hair with a naked prehensile tail. It lives arboreally, attacking tree termite mounds with its powerful claws.   The third claw of its four digits is curved and enlarged for ripping. To compensate for its lack of teeth, its stomach is a muscular gizzard comparable to the gizzard of a chicken.

It tears holes in the tough walls of the termite nests, pushing in its long muzzle as its tongue probes the galleries of the nest, trapping insects on its sticky saliva. Its tongue can extend 16 inches (40 cm). Individuals differ in how arboreal or terrestrial they are.   Arboreal individuals eat more ants and

Feeding Tamandua with Young

those which are more terrestrial eat more termites.   Their diets may change seasonally as well.   Certain ants are not as palatable; ponerine ants have a severe and painful sting, army ants also sting and bite, and leafcutters are spiny and unpalatable.   The tamanduas skin is remarkably thick and tough with wiry fur but it is not a complete protection from ants.   When attacked by ants, however, they often don't pay much attention to them.

Tamanduas have a strong set of foreclaws for opening up wood and nests of ants and termites, and rarely bees.   They are specialized feeders with long saliva-covered tongues with microscopic backwards pointing projections, a thick walled muscular stomach for crushing the hard chitonous exoskeletons of the ants, and a prehensile tail for balance and arboreal movement.   The tamandua specializes in eating termites and ants and detects them by scent.   It is repelled by leaf eating ants, army ants, and others with chemical defenses.   It eats more termites, avoiding the soldiers and eating the vulnerable workers and reproductive castes.   It especially eats arboreal termites.   Tamanduas also eat bees and their larvae.

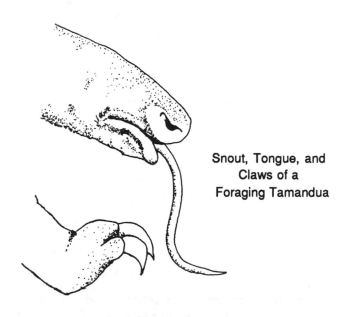

Snout, Tongue, and
Claws of a
Foraging Tamandua

The tamandua inhabits savanna, thorn scrub and wet and dry forests, spending half its time in trees. Walking on the outside of its hand to avoid forcing tips of its large claws into its hand, it ranges from 125-345 acres (50-140 ha) with some overlap between home ranges.   When it moves, it uses distinct pathways both arboreal and terrestrial.   Although mainly nocturnal it may be seen during the day, usually settling in a curled sitting posture in a tree crotch to sleep out the day.   It may also sleep in tree hollows during the day. Tamanduas are solitary and communicate by hissing and using an unpleasant odor from the anal gland. If attacked, it assumes a tripod posture on 2 feet and its tail. It outstretches its arms and bears its claws at the predator.

Tamanduas mate in fall and give birth to a single young in spring after a 130-150 day gestation. Young vary in color from white to black. The female carries the young by setting it down or letting it get off her to feed when she feeds. The young rides the mothers back until half the mothers size.

Silky Anteater

The squirrel-sized silky anteater is the smallest anteater, about 6 in (15 cm) long and weighing 1/2 lb (223 grams). It ranges from southern Mexico into Bolivia and Brazil. It is completely arboreal with a long prehensile tail with a naked underside. It has a soft, silky pelage, buffy-gray to golden-yellow in color, darker above with a dark line along top of the head, neck, and back. Its nose tip is pink, the soles of its feet are reddish, and it has black eyes. The claws of the second and third fingers are large, curved, and sharp. Its lifestyle is highly dependent on its long hind feet which have a heel pad and peculiar "joint" in the sole that permits the claws to be turned back under the foot to give a good grip on branches. It is completely nocturnal, arboreal, and solitary and found only in the tropical rain forests. It rests in the day among shaded vines in or below tree crowns, curled in a ball to conserve heat while lowering its temperature during the day. It often rests in clumps of small diameter lianas. It almost never descends to the ground but can walk on flat surfaces by placing the sides of its forefeet, turning the claws inward.

The silky anteater's front foot has a large pointed claw for defense and for opening holes in the stems of lianas through which it feeds on ants inside. Ants comprise the main part of their diet, eating termites only rarely. Once they feed in one area they move to another area. Males establish a relatively large territory from which they exclude other males. However, a male's territory may include as many as 3 adult females. Females exclude other females from their areas although the male moves freely through the females areas.

It has been seen frequenting the cotton tree (*Ceiba*) which has seed pods that are a massive ball of soft, silverish fibers. The silky anteater's hair looks like the pod hairs and may be protective coloration against predators. Like the tamandua, in defense it raises up on its hind legs, its feet grasping opposite sides of a limb and its tail wrapped around a twig. Its forefeet are held close to its face to strike swiftly and forcibly. It is quite inconspicuous and few people know it is found in their area. Thus there is a good chance that it may be found in the Community Baboon Sanctuary.

It has a single young which it places in a tree hole nest made of dry leaves. The young nurses for 6 weeks until it is about 1/3 of its mother's size. During these 6 weeks the mother leaves the young to forage, although it forages only near the nest site. Each day the mother returns and carries the young to a new location The young are raised by both parents who regurgitate semi-digested insects to feed it. Sometimes the male carries the baby on his back. When it is about half adult size and the female is pregnant again the young disperses from the female's territory. Females produce one young per year.

Giant Anteater

The giant anteater, weighing up to 65 lbs (30kg), ranges from southern Belize to northern Argentina. Despite its large range it is not common and is endangered. The giant anteater inhabits swamps, humid forests, and savannas during the day. Although a powerful digger, it doesn't dig burrows. It has a rapid, effective defense reaction whereby it uses its strong claws and forelegs. It lives a solitary life with overlaping home ranges indicating a lack of territoriality. Densities are from 1.2 sq acres (0.5 sq km) or sometimes 1/10th as sparse. It forages only on the ground using its powerful claws to rip apart termite and ant mounds and then feeds with a saliva coated tongue on ant eggs, cocoons, and adults. It may consume as many as 30,000 ants or termites in a day. But it stays only a minute at each nest taking as few as 140 ants from the colony after which it is driven away by the biting ants. It usually ignores termites, leafcutters, army ants, and others with large jaws. It specializes in large ground dwelling ants such as the carpenter ant. It revisits the same colony at regular intervals and so avoids overexploitating it.

Giant Anteater

Its tongue can be extruded 24 in (60 cm) and up to 150 times a minute. The sheath containing the tongue and tongue retracting muscles is anchored on the breast bone. Salivary glands secrete enormous quantities of viscous saliva onto the tongue. Trapped ants are drawn back and chewed and ground first by horny papillae on the roof of the mouth and sides of cheeks and then by the muscular stomach.

Breeding occurs in the fall in the southern part of its range. After a 190 day gestation period, one young is born in the spring. It gives birth standing upright using the tail as a third leg and licks its young after it crawls onto her back. The mother carries the young on her back until it is half her size. The newborn will remain with the female until the mother is pregnant again. The young are camouflaged when clinging to the mother by aligning its exposed lateral stripe with the mother's stripe. They do not feed independently until full grown at 2 years.

CATS

*T*here are 5 cat species in Belize, all which occur in the Community Baboon Sanctuary. The largest, the jaguar, has lived in the sanctuary area in the recent past and on occasion signs of jaguars have been seen in outlying sanctuary areas. The jaguar, however, no longer commonly resides here probably due to lack of game species and human habitation.

Jaguar

The cat family (Felidae) is a very uniform family which includes 4 genera and 37 species which are found throughout the world. Most of the species have been lumped into 2 main genera although some scientists dispute this grouping. The 2 groups are basically distinguished from each other by size and the ability to roar. *Panthera* includes the tiger, leopard, lion, and the jaguar. These four cats are generally larger, have pupils which close to a circle instead of a vertical slit, and have the ability to roar but not purr. The

(left to right) Wide Open Pupil; Small Cat Closed Slit; Large Cat Closed Circle

ability to roar is due to the replacement of a fully ossified hyoid bone at the base of the tongue with a pliable cartilage in the large cats which allows greater freedom of movement. It is this same hyoid bone which is modified in the howler monkey to amplify their roaring sounds.

Most cats are uniform in having similar characteristics which adapt them for a highly predatory life, feeding almost exclusively on vertebrate prey. Despite size differences, all have lithe, muscular, compact, deep-chested bodies for quick, sudden rushes at prey. Their forefeet have 5 toes and hindfeet have 4, which they are able to walk on due to elongated foot bones. This equips them with speed when running. In addition, the forepaws can rotate flexibly to aid in clutching and grappling with prey. Each toe has a large, sharp, compressed, and strongly curved retractible claw for snagging and holding prey. Only the cheetah is an exception. Since they are built more for long distance running down of prey they have lost partial claw retractibility to allow for a fleeter gait.

The cat tongue, with its sharp, pointed, recurved horny papillae, is well suited for lacerating food in the mouth. The most highly predatory characteristics can be seen in the cat skull, especially in the reduced complement of teeth which are used for seizing and cutting, rather than for grinding. The shortened skull has powerful jaw muscles and long canine teeth used in killing prey. Although their incisors are small and ineffective, their rear carnaissal teeth are highly adapted for cutting and chewing meat. They thus chew from the side.

Cats stalk prey slowly with their body close to the ground, crouching and watching, until they can seize the prey by making a short rush at it. They rely mainly on hearing and sight in this form of hunting. They have large eyes set forward in the skull giving them binocular vision. They can also see colors. At night, their vision is 6 times more acute than ours, having an extra reflecting layer outside of the receptor layer of cells. This reflects light back to the receptor cells, enhancing light collection. It is this reflecting layer you see when a light is shined into the eyes of a cat or other nocturnal animal having this eye characteristic. Their hearing is also acute often being very sensitive to high frequencies since many small mammals use high frequencies in communication.

Small Cats of Belize

There are 3 small cats found in the sanctuary which are becoming increasingly endangered due to the loss of their habitat. These are the closely related ocelot (*Felis pardalis*) and margay (*Felis wiedii*) and the jaguarundi (*Felis yagouaroundi*). All 3 have a similar overlapping ranges from northern Mexico throughout Central America and most of South America. The ocelot and jaguarundi occur a bit farther north ranging into areas of the southwestern United States. These small cats have different niches or lifestyles based on their different sizes and specific adaptations.

Small Spotted Cats

The margay and ocelot, both called tiger cat in Belize, are very closely related and look very much alike except for their size. The ocelot gets its name from the Mexican Aztec word "tlalocelotl" meaning field tiger. The margay is the size of a domestic cat and weighs 6-13 lbs (3-6 kg). The ocelot is a

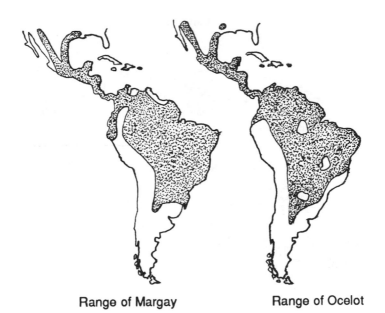

Range of Margay   Range of Ocelot

medium-sized cat which may grow to 4 ft (1.3 m) long with a
15 in (35 cm) tail and weigh 24-35 lbs (11-16 kg).   The ocelot's
fur is very beautiful and has been long sought for fur coats, thus
endangering the species.   In 1972 the U.S. banned their
importation as pets or for skins which has aided their plight
considerably.   Their fur has a yellowish to light gray
background with dark spots and streaks.   Two black stripes
adorn each cheek with one or two stripes on the inside of the
legs and a ringed tail.   The margay has a yellowish-brown
ground color with white below.   It has long rows of dark brown
spots with paler centers. Both spotted cats have open spots
outlined in black but in the ocelot lateral spots tend to be joined
to form long bands a few centimeters wide.   On occasion, as
with many cats, one may find a melanistic dark form.

       The margay resembles the ocelot but is smaller, more
slender and with a longer tail, over half the body length.
Because of its small pelt, the margay has not been hunted as
intensely as other cats but it is now rare because of the
destruction of its forest habitat for agricultural use.   In the
bush a margay track is 1.5 2 in (35 50 mm) measured across the
toes. The fore and hind feet are of equal size.

Ocelot

The margay is the most arboreal of all cats and is a agile climber. Its hind limbs have broad soft feet with mobile metatarsals allowing them to supinate (rotate) 180° so that when descending a tree head first they can strongly grasp the tree trunk. Although all 3 small cat species eat a somewhat similar diet of small mammals, birds, reptiles, and amphibians, the margay forages more in trees and concentrates on the smaller more arboreal prey. The margay is thus tied ecologically to forested watershed areas and especially tropical rain forests, shunning open country as its home.

The ocelot, which lives in a great variety of habitats from dry scrub to tropical rain forest, hunts mainly on the forest floor. It also can swim and is suited for climbing. Ocelots seem to concentrate on taking birds, specifically ground-dwelling birds. Ocelots show 3 behaviors which indicate their specific prey choices. First, they show less patient stalking behaviors than other cats. They instead have a tendency to make instant rushes with skillful acrobatic leaps in the air which are most advantageous in the hunting of birds. When stalking small mammals, such as rodents, it is advantageous to wait cautiously until the rodent is away from its burrow. With birds, however, a quick response is necessary or the birds will flee unharmed. Second, they show a tendency to hold onto struggling prey rather than releasing it to attack it again. This is probably an adaptation to bird or fish killing for either of those prey, once released, can easily escape into the air or water. Third, whereas other cats show an incidental plucking of birds to get to the flesh, the ocelot plucks even small birds so neatly that it appears to be a pattern in its own right and is clearly a desirable adaptation for a bird-eating specialist. Ocelots however, do hunt a variety of other animals including rodents, rabbits, young deer, peccaries, snakes and fish.

Both spotted cats are mainly nocturnal with the margay being more strictly so. They rest in the day in hollow logs or on tree branches. Breeding is thought to occur twice a year although it is not known if the same female breeds twice in the same year. They become sexually mature at 2 years. Breeding occurs in June-July and December-January with births in March-June. Gestation is 10-12 weeks. Ocelots have litters of 2-4 in grass-lined nests situated in hollow logs, rock crevices or under bushes. Margays have only one pair of mammaries and usually have only 1 or 2 kittens. Although not much is known of their social behavior, both species seem to maintain territories. Ocelots are thought to be more social, sometimes hunting in pairs, mewing to keep in contact. Males of both species mark their territories as do many cat species by directing urine backwards onto a specific object.

Jaguarundi

The jaguarundi is a very different looking cat having a slender, elongated body with short legs and small flattened ears. It is about 4 ft (1.3 m) long with a 21 in (53 cm) tail but is only about a foot (30 cm) in height at the shoulder. They weigh from 10-20 lbs (4.5-9 kg). They are uncat-like, resembling weasels, and have been called otter cats owing to their shape. In Belize they are also called tiger cats. The name jaguarundi is derived from the Tupi Indians indigenous of Brazil. Jaguarundis are polymorphic in color being either uniformly rusty-red or gray in color. Their habits differ from the spotted tiger cats, they inhabit more open savanna, lowland forest edges or dense brush, especially near water.

They are shy and secretive being crepuscular, often active in the daytime. They can swim and climb but instead of stalking they pursue prey by running them down, often sprinting for a mile after rodents or ground birds. They have also been seen climbing trees to feed on fruits including figs in the presence of howler monkeys. They live solitary or in pairs. Young are born in March and August after an extraordinarily long gestation period of 9 months. Litters are 2-4 in number.

Puma

Of all the cats, the puma is perhaps the most ambiguous to people. Puma, cougar, mountain lion, panther, painter, catamount or red tiger as it is called in Belize, are a few of its many names. Amerigo Vespucci first called the species "lion" since it resembled the female lioness of Africa. The name puma comes from the Quechua language of Peru while cougar comes from the "sussuarana" of the Tupi Indians. It has been called red lion or red tiger in Belize due to the red coloration of the subspecies *Felis concolor mayanensis*, which is found in the Yucatan Peninsula. This subspecies is also the smallest of all the races of the species. The Mayan name is "ah coh" which has also been spelled cah coh and interpreted as referring to its red color.

It is an animal of many names, perhaps due to its many images to people. Although it rarely attacks humans, it has a mixed image. On one hand, attacks on humans, particularly towards children, have been recorded. However, as in jaguars in Belize which may take domestic animals on occasion, such attacks are rare. In both cases attacking stock or humans is more often done by weakened or injured animals. Despite many reports of attacks, confirmed reports are rare and have been attributed to mistaken identity and weakened or injured individuals who were hungry. In Belize, the puma is referred to as being "very upstart" indicating its behavior of standing its ground when confronted by humans. In contrast, the puma is prominent in many Amerindian cultures and is respected for its cunning and strength and is often revered as a protector and source of power. In the southern part of its range, this red lion in Brazil has been called "friend of Christians". This name is attributed to a legendary woman who supposedly was cared for by a wild family of pumas.

Although classified with the small cats due to its round eye pupils, inability to roar, and its ossified hyoid giving it the ability to purr, the mountain lion is the second largest plain-colored cat and the fourth largest of all cats.   In the Americas it is second in size only to the jaguar, yet some pumas may be larger than some jaguars.   The largest puma recorded is 9.5 ft (3 m) in body length and 276 lbs (125 kg), although they are generally 6-8 ft (2-2.5 m) in length and weigh 100-200 lbs (45-90 kg).   The Belizean subspecies falls within the lower size range and some adults may be even smaller.   Females are smaller than males.

Pumas are generally a plain colored tannish-brown and may show a darker central line with whitish under parts. Reddish forms predominate in tropical countries, with brown and gray forms in dryer habitats.   Rarely, black pumas have been found in South and Central America.   They have vertical stripes along the inside corner of the eyes and slight horizontal bars from the outside corner of the eyes.   The young however, are marked with blackish brown bars or spots with a ringed tail, causing one very old report to claim incorrectly that the spotted young were hybrid offspring of the mating between a jaguar and a puma.   The kittens lose their spotted coat at 6-8 months but it may be faintly evident in some animals throughout life.   Pumas have a long tail and small head.

The puma's legs are fairly long with the larger front feet used in prey capture.   There are 4 toes on the hind feet and 5 on the forepaws.   The fifth toe, however, doesn't show up in their tracks being higher on the foot.   This fifth toe, also called the "dewclaw", is thus not subject to much wear and may grow to become a very formidable weapon in prey capture and can inflict heavy damage.   The dewclaw is sometimes also called the "killing claw" and has the capacity to hook, slit, and rasp as it grips the prey animal.   The puma's feet, except for the pads, are generally covered on the bottom with hair which enables the cat to walk and stalk prey silently.

The puma has the most extensive range of all the new world cats and other mammals, occurring throughout the

Americas from the Yukon of Canada to southern Argentina. It has thus adapted to a great variety of natural conditions and environments in wet or dry, hot or cold climates and from sea level to as high as 17,000 ft (5300 m) above sea level. Despite its wide range it is not plentiful anywhere and has been exterminated from much of its range in the United States and Canada. It is still fairly numerous in Belize and is often found in the same areas where jaguars are found.

Range of Jaguar   Range of Puma

Female pumas attain sexual maturity at 2.5-3 years when about 80 lbs (36 kg) in weight. Males have a wider range than females and mark their territory with urine or feces deposited on heaps of fallen leaves or ground litter. This marking establishes his territorial rights against other males and attracts females to his area. The female's heat period lasts 8-10 days and more than one male may compete for her.

Copulation is brief with the female raising her rump and placing her tail to the side. Both may scream during copulation.

After a 3 month gestation, usually 1-4 and sometimes as many as 6 kittens are born in a concealed nest in dense brush, a rock crevice or in the tropical rain forests of Central America in a hollow tree. The nest must afford vision and escape and is

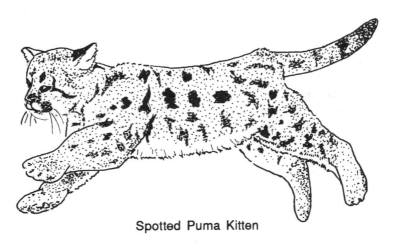

Spotted Puma Kitten

commonly lined with dry grass, leaves, feathers or even hair from the females abdomen. Young are born at all times of the year but a female probably has only one litter every other year, but sometimes may have as many as two litters within a year to year and a half. Born blind, pumas eyes open at 9-10 days and they cut their first teeth at 20 days. The mother doesn't go far from the nest for the first few weeks and purrs while tending her cubs. The kittens begin to eat solid food which the mother brings back at 6 weeks. They suckle for about 3-4 months or longer (until they are half grown) but they remain with their mother for over a year or longer until they are run off by their mother's new mate. At 3-4 months the mother will move the kittens to kills she has made that she covers with leaves or brush. There is mixed information on the role the male plays. Some males have been known to kill young while there are also instances of a male and a female defending young.

A puma's home range is determined by its food, water, and cover requirements. Males establish territories of about 15-30 square miles (38-75 sq km) with females establishing smaller 5-25 square mile (13-65 sq km) area. Males have fairly rigid boundaries with other males' territories which are maintained by scent markings. A male's range, however, may overlap with more than one female. Pumas move a great deal, covering sometimes 30-40 miles (45-65 km) in a night. They can maintain contact with one another using high pitched whistles. Scent marking can function both to bring animals together or to space them. They leave urine and feces on scent posts or scrapes of piled litter with feces inside. The anal scent gland leaves other smells in the pile. The piles are round and about 12 in (30 cm) wide and 5 in (13 cm) high. They also leave scratch marks on specific tree trunks or posts on the ground. These will consist of 2 parallel claw scrapes 8 in (20 cm) long.

A great deal of the puma's legends come from the scream it makes. It has been described as a scream, yowl, cry or wail and has been likened to a highly amplified housecat cry. It is often described as having a terrifying human quality. They make the scream with lips curled back along the jaws with teeth bared but close together or opened slightly. It is a very high pitched scream and may be given repeatedly. Some observers believe it is the female which makes this cry during the mating season. Captive observations seem to bear this out.

The puma is an extremely agile cat especially for its size. It is a rapid runner for short prey chases. It can swim well and is an extremely good climber-- the best climber of all the big cats. It hunts mainly during dawn and dusk. Its main prey are deer, a single puma taking perhaps 50-100 deer per year. In Guiana it is called a "deer tiger". Following its silent stalk, it jumps extremely well, landing fully on the deer's back, holding the deer with its front paws and using its dewclaws while raking the prey's flanks and sides with its hind feet and biting the prey's neck. The puma often breaks the deer's neck by quickly pulling its head to the side.

Besides deer, pumas in Belize also feed on small mammals including pacas, armadillos, coati, monkeys, tapirs, rabbits, agoutis, porcupines, and peccaries.   With larger prey they may remove the unfinished carcass to a secluded place and cover it with leaves, sticks or other debris.   They may return a number of times or they may abandon the cache. There are a host of stories about humans laying down to sleep in the forest and finding themselves covered with debris by a puma, who returned later, perhaps expecting to eat them or bring their cubs to the human cache.

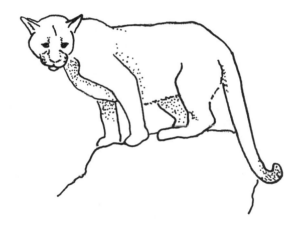

GRAY FOX (*Urocyon cinereoargentus*)

*T*he gray fox (*Urocyon cinereoargenteus*) is the only wild canid (member of the dog family) found in Belize. They inhabit shrublands and brushy forested areas from Canada throughout Central America into northern South America. They live in varied habitats but do well in dry areas and are thus often seen in the pine ridge. The best habitat for the gray fox is in mixed forest and cultivated areas where it benefits from the "edge effect" (interface between habitats) created by human disturbance. This may be why they are fairly common in the Community Baboon Sanctuary.

Its range excludes the central plains of North America since it is rarely found in areas totally devoid of trees. The gray fox is the most arboreal of all foxes and thus functions best where there are trees. It is sometimes called the tree fox because of its arboreal habits. Unusual for canids, the gray fox is adept at tree climbing. It can scale vertical tree trunks even as a pup. It climbs by grasping the trunk with its forepaws and pushes up with the hind paws. The hind paws have long claws for this purpose which act as climbing irons. The gray fox in Belize and other tropical areas is more arboreal than northern races and the hind claws are sharper and more recurved. It can climb as high as 15-20 ft (4-6 m) and then may run down head first or back down depending on the tree's steepness. Its laterally flattened tail is used in balance when climbing.

The gray fox, a small animal weighing about 15 lbs (7 kg), stands a bit over 2 ft (0.6 m) and has a 17 in (42 cm) tail. It is mottled gray with white underneath and a rusty tinge on the sides of the neck, flanks and undertail. A black stripe adorns its midback and black lines occur on the face. Some scientists consider them part of the genus *Vulpes* (red fox). However, they have oval eyes instead of the vulpine narrow slit and they have a longer supracaudal gland at the upper base of the tail. They also have an erectile band of hairs on the upper tail and they lack the red fox's musty smell.   They have larger toe pads than a red fox but a smaller overall foot and they don't show the tail drag on the ground.   They also have shorter canine teeth than most members of the genus *Vulpes*.   The genus *Vulpes* is mainly distinguished by the fact that "brows" formed by the frontal bones above and between the eyes are slightly indented (includes the gray fox) or dished rather than flat or convex.   Like other foxes, the gray fox has a pointed muzzle with a somewhat flattened slender skull.

The species has a fairly small home range of 0.4 sq mi (1 sq km).   Studies show that families of a mated pair and their young stay separate from each other, indicating that they maintain territories.   Like most foxes, they maintain scent posts where urine and feces are left on or next to prominent objects.   They cock the leg against a grass tuft or other object to urine mark just as a dog does. Scats are commonly seen along roadsides or trails, deposited directly on top of logs, rocks, stumps or elevated areas.   All foxes have paired anal glands on either side of their anus which can be evacuated at will or the secretions can be used to coat feces.   They also have skin glands on the dorsal surface of the tail near its base which is covered with bristles and appears as a black spot on the tail.   Additional glands are found between the toes. They can also communicate by sound with barks and howls.

The gray fox is an opportunistic feeder, foraging at night.   It mainly forages on the ground but will climb when pursued and to get fruits. Its diet is like most foxes, generalized and omnivorous.   Diet changes with the local and seasonal abundance of foods.   Although it eats a preponderance of meat, mainly mammals (40-70%), it also consumes a high percentage of plant material for a carnivore, feeding on from 15-35% plant material which includes fruits, nuts, and grains.   Seasonally, it will feed on what is most abundant.   Insects form a large part of the diet in some seasons.   Rabbits and rodents are the most important food in their diet and they will also eat carrion.   They use stealth and a dash-and-grab method of catching prey.   They use the typical fox pounce whereby they can spring 3 ft (1 m) off the ground, diving forepaws first onto the prey. This behavior may be a device to squash the vertical jump used by mice and other rodents to escape predators.

Gray foxes are monogamous and males will help care for the pups which are black at birth. The breeding season varies with the latitude but occurs between January and March. Nests are located in brush piles, rock crevices or hollow trees. They may pad their den with grass, leaves or shredded bark. Gestation is about 60 days. Having 6 mammae to nurse young, litter size is 2-6. They have only one litter a year. Young begin following the parents from the den at 4-6 weeks and they leave the parents to forage on their own when they reach adult weight at about 5-6 months.

Although they have a high fecundity they also have a very high yearly mortality. There is a high probability that a pup will die within its first year. Due to their high reproductive potential however, most foxes within a given area are young animals. Gray fox populations are essentially an annual crop. Females can breed within their first year. In the north they have few predators other than humans but they are susceptible to disease. Rabies appears to limit their numbers considerably.

HOOFED MAMMALS - UNGULATES

The word ungulate comes from the Latin word stem "ungul" which refers to a hoof.   There are two main groups of hoofed mammals which have replaced claws with hooves. These include the odd-toed hoofed ungulates like the horse and tapir, and the even-toed ungulates like the cow and deer or "antelope" (red-brocket deer).   The hooves are an adaptation to a terrestrial lifestyle which depends on rapid locomotion for escape from predators.   The hooves are also an adaptation for feeding on vegetation.   Both ungulate groups live similar lifestyles but in different ways.

Both groups have shown an evolutionary reduction in the number of toes which have become covered with thick hard edged keratinous hooves.   In horses, only the third toe is functional while tapirs use the center three toes.   The fourth toe on the front foot is used for support in soft or muddy terrain.

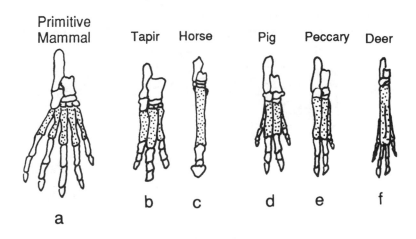

Hind Feet Exhibiting Extended Metapodial Bones (stippled): Primitive Mammal (a); Odd-Toed - tapir (b) & horse (c),   Even Toed - pig (d),   peccary (e) & deer (f).

They additionally show a lengthening of the long bones of the "hand" and foot (metapodials) which lifts the foot, shifting the weight onto the toe-tips. Fast moving ungulates such as horses and deer actually walk on the toe nail-- a mode of locomotion termed unguligrade. The odd- and even-toed description refers to the weight bearing toes on each foot. Even-toed ungulates have the weight bearing axis between the third and fourth toes while odd-toed ungulates bear their weight on the third toe. In the latter group, the first and fifth toes are often absent.

Evolution of the teeth and digestive system parallels the locomotion trends. Ungulates feed mainly on leaves and grass but since their feet are so specifically adapted for terrestrial locomotion, they are unable to manipulate food with them. They have hence evolved lips, tongue, and teeth to handle food. Plants are high in carbohydrates but low in fats and proteins. The carbohydrates are also locked in by the fibrous, cellulose cell walls. The large flat square molar teeth of ungulates function like a grinding mill to break down cell walls and release the digestible contents, reducing the plant matter to fine particles. In conjunction, the jaw musculature and the jaw joint configuration are modified such that the lower jaw can be moved across the upper teeth in a transverse grinding motion. This is in contrast to the more up-and-down motion of other mammals which simply cut and pulp the food.

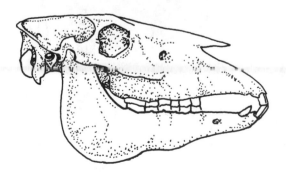

Horse Skull

The high crowned cheek teeth are made to last a lifetime of continual abrasion. Tapirs have complex, massive, low

188

crowned, grinding teeth with prominant transverse ridges and cusps.   Horse teeth, in contrast, have higher crowns with 4 main columns and various infoldings.   The ungulate mouth shows a typical gap between the grinding molars and the biting incisors. The canines are often absent unless they are used in defense or the lower canines have been modified like a lower incisor.

Ungulates have specific adaptations to their browsing and grazing lifestyle.   The strong incisors function in cutting grass and leaves.   However, other mouth parts have been developed for grasping the leaves. For example, the upper lips of the tapir have evolved into an extended trunk-like organ that curls itself against the palatine ridge for grasping and tearing leaves.   Even-toed ungulates like cows and deer have no upper incisors and instead use the mobile lip and upper palate for grasping and pulling in vegetation.

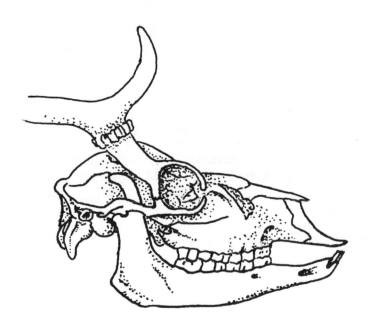

Deer Skull Showing No Upper Incisors

Even and odd-toed ungulates have unique digestive systems. Because it is hard to break down cellulose and gain access to plant nutrients and since mammals lack the enzymes to do this, ungulates have evolved special alimentary canals for this purpose. Both groups use microorganisms with cellulose-digesting enzymes to ferment and break down the cellulose. However, the even-toed ungulates have a complex multi-chambered stomach which allows food to be sorted and digested in two ways. First, the digested food passes through a sieve and goes to the posterior stomach and intestine. Undigested food is set aside to ferment so that it can be regurgitated to the mouth to be rechewed later. This process is called rumination or "chewing the cud". Even-toed ungulates can also recycle the nitrogen from urea (waste in urine), using it to feed the microorganisms which they later digest as well. Although this is a very efficient way to get maximum use of the cellulose, the food is retained for a very long time, sometimes as long as four days so there is a limit on the amount of vegetation which can be eaten and processed. Thus even-toed ungulates are more selective in choosing food and can afford to specialize on a limited range of plant species. They are at an advantage in areas with a limited quantity but higher quality of foods available.

In contrast, in the odd-toed ungulates fermentation occurs in the hind gut areas of the cecum and large intestine. This is less efficient than even-toed fermentation, the food being retained about half the time, and they can eat large quantities. Odd-toed ungulates are at an advantage in areas where food is of limited quality with high fiber. They can also make better use of fruits because nutrients are absorbed before fermentation in the stomach whereas the even-toed ruminants ferment the fruit in their complex stomach and lose much of the fruits' nutritional value.

Comparison of Two Ungulate Digestive Systems

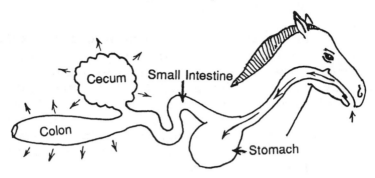

The horse (odd-toed ungulate) uses hindgut fermentation whereby food is digested directly in the stomach and passes to the large intestine and cecum where microorganisms ferment the cellulose.

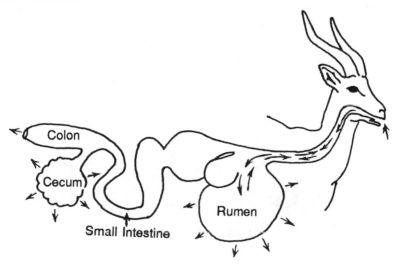

The antelope (even-toed ungulate) uses a more efficient rumination process in a complex digestive system whereby food is retained in the gut much longer than in hindgut fermentation. Food is fermented by microorganisms in the first stomach chamber then is regurgitated and re-chewed and passed to the second chamber. Digestion is completed in the third and fourth stomach chambers and nutrients are absorbed in the small intestine.

The Mountain Cow - A Horse

Tapirs are the most primitive of the odd-toed hoofed mammals being much closer to the general basic pattern of mammals. They are relatives of the horses and rhinoceros. The have been called "living fossils", having originated in the northern hemisphere with a group of animals from an ancient geological era when a large variety of similar tapir-like forms were distributed throughout the world. Tapirs and other odd-toed ungulates were once generally more common in the world but are now radically reduced in the numbers of species. Currently living species of this ancient grouping are included in three families: tapirs, rhinoceros, and horses. At this time, tapirs occur mainly in the American tropics with one species in the Asian tropics. This disjunct distribution reflects the remnant status of a once widespread group.

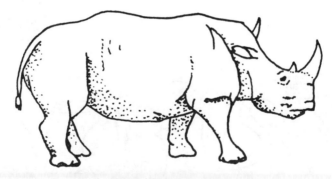

White Rhinocerous

Baird's tapir (*Tapirus bairdii*) or the mountain cow as it is known in Belizean Creole, is a rather large (500-700 lbs, 225-320 kg), round, dark to reddish-brown animal. The tapir's body tapers in front and their short powerful legs make them suited for rapid movement through thick underbrush. The tapir has a thick, coarse, leathery, skin 0.5-1.25 in (1-3 cm) thick which is sparsely haired with stiff bristles, white fringed ears, white lips and sometimes a white throat patch. It also has a low mane.

Its most interesting characteristic is its snout and upper lips which are projected into a short, extensible, fleshy proboscis with nostrils located at the tip. It can be imagined as the forerunner of the elephant-like trunk, with both organs

Tapir Using Trunk to Pull in Leaves

being used similarly although the tapirs snout is not as dexterous in plucking leaves and putting them in the mouth. The tapir's primitive trunk can be moved in all directions, stretched out and contracted. It also has hair-like tactile bristles giving it information by touch. It has a button shaped ridge under the lip against which a branch is pressed while the trunk and its tip grasp the branch on all sides. Then the trunk is contracted bringing in the leaves. If a leaf cannot be reached with the trunk, they will rise up on their hind legs against a tree to grasp the morsel. In grazing, the tapir bites off grass like a horse with its trunk contracted.

Tapirs are the less specialized forms from which other species evolved. With the evolutionary emergence of grasses, more specialized animals evolved to occupy the grassy savannas. Tapir s, however, inhabit the humid tropical rain forests emerging mostly at night to feed in grassy and shrubby areas. They seem to prefer early successional vegetation and riverine forest. Their feet have 3 or 4 toes in comparison with the more specialized   horse which is a much fleeter animal adapted to open plains and savannas.   Their teeth are less specialized not showing the high crowned grinding cheek teeth of the horse.   Tapirs are browsers of tree and shrub leaves, twigs, fruits, and seeds, which reflects a more primitive diet. Leaves are coarsely chewed between the strongly dentate molars while soft fruits are chewed against the strong, broadly ridged pallet and the molars.   Although their jaws are tremendously strong and can crack strong seeds like tubroos seeds, such seeds are generally spit out or swallowed whole. Unlike horses which pass tubroos seeds whole, tapirs can digest them by a delayed passage through their gut which also probably aids seed germination. Tapirs only digest about 70% of the seeds that they swallow and since they defecate in the water this is one way the tubroos is propagated along the river banks.   Tapirs also eat gumbolimbo, hog plum and fig fruits as well as red fowl seeds.

Despite their usual slow walk with snout to the ground in foraging, the mountain cow can trot or break into a rapid gallop when in flight. When walking in wet areas and withdrawing their feet from the mud, their flexible toes swing together allowing a silent withdrawal from the large track made by the splayed foot, allowing them to move quietly. Tapirs also have a primitive lying down process. Instead of supporting themselves on their wrists in lying down as horses do, they lie down by assuming a sitting posture characteristic of less advanced ungulates. They are also shy and will usually disappear into the vegetation or water to escape a potential predator. Shy mothers however, are known to defend their calves and can attack with their teeth or by rushing violently and knocking a threatening predator down and attempting to trample it. They can also climb well on steep slopes, swim, and dive.

Water is important to tapirs and they are excellent swimmers and feed on aquatic plants. They use water to cool off in hot weather.   They can dive, submerging for 15-30 seconds, and are known to walk on the bottom of streams with their snout, ears, and eyes protruding. They sometimes wear paths to the water. They also roll in mud to cover themselves with a protective film.   A mud wallow can be easily recognized by the three toe tracks and feces in the area. Tapirs seem to prefer defecating in water which may actually stimulate their defecation.   However, in captivity they drop feces in one place and show pawing motions afterward.   This may show the beginning of a marking behavior which is more developed in their close relative, the rhinocerous.   Rhinoceros deposit feces in piles to denote their territory and then they scatter the feces with a pawing motion of the rear feet which makes the feces very visible from a distance. Tapir dung resembles horse dung except it contains large woody twigs. Male tapirs do mark territories with urine.   In captivity, one may see an area covered with white urine crystals where the male accurately sprays urine with his penis arched backwards after sniffing the marked area.   He then paws the ground with his hind legs.

Otherwise, tapirs are unsociable, occurring only in mother-calf groupings or in pairs during the breeding season. Calves may stay with the mother for as long as a year when it is about 2/3 her size and has attained adult coloration. Adults may live as long as 30 years. Tapirs show a limited vocabulary of sounds used in communication. These include a short squeal used in contact while feeding, a pain squeal, a clicking sound produced by the tongue and palate used in greeting, and an alarm snort.

Females become capable of breeding at 3-4 years and may come into heat every 50-80 days which may last 2 days or longer.   The breeding pair approach each other in parallel, sniffing each other's rear and they may circle each other.   The somewhat smaller male pushes at the female's underside and snaps at her hind legs.   Prior to copulation they utter short wheezing sounds or shrill piercing whistles and the male may spray large quantities of urine.   The male may sniff the female's urine and give a lip curl like other ungulates to help project the smell over a small sensory organ in the upper palate.   He then rolls his tongue inside his mouth and around the trunk. Gestation lasts 13 months.

Females give birth in a squatting posture and the young, like most young , come out head first.   The mother licks it as it nibbles her, seeking the udder. As with other ungulates the two teats are located between the hind legs. The calf nudges the treats and will eventually push the mothers flank, causing her to lie down to offer the udder. The young in contrast to adults display protective coloration of dark-reddish brown marked with yellowish-white stripes and spots which is lost by 6-8 months.

All four tapir species are endangered due to the destruction of their tropical rain forest habitat and hunting pressures. Even though the meat is extremely fatty and not very tasty, tapirs are still hunted in Central America and as a result are very rare in Mexico. In Belize, they have been designated the national animal and their hunting is prohibited. Although not common in the sanctuary they do occur in Flowers Bank area and below Double Head Cabbage. They are common in nearby Mussel Creek and other areas of Belize. The Macal River is one such area and their tracks have also been found in Bladen Branch.

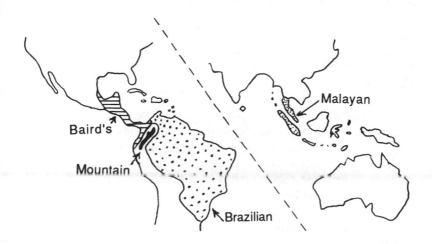

Ranges of the Four Tapir Species

Besides Baird's tapir there is the South American lowland tapir (*Tapirus terrestris*) which inhabits the lowlands of northern South America. They are hunted for their skin and meat by some indigenous peoples while others prohibit their hunting for religious purposes. The ancient Mayans may similarly have revered the Central American tapir as there are several temples which display a human figure with a trunk, presumably modeled after the tapir. The third neotropical tapir, the mountain tapir (*Tapirus pinchaque*), is a graceful animal with a dense, wooly fur for protection from the cold in the high Andes mountains of South America. The Malayan tapir (*Tapirus indicus*), found on the other side of the world, is distinctly colored in a tripartition, head and rear-gray and center-white, which protectively breaks up its body outline making it difficult to see in the shade of the forest.

Peccaries

Peccaries are most closely related to pigs but only superficially resemble them. In other characteristics such as their teeth, stomach and feet, they more closely resemble the even-toed ungulates, the ruminants of the same order Artiodactyla. Although they do not have a true ruminant stomach, their stomach is modified into three compartments. They assume the same niche in the American tropics as the pigs in the old world tropics.

The peccary family, Tayassuidae, includes only three living members, the collared peccary (*Tayassu tajaca*), the white lipped pecary (*Tayassu pecari*), and the Chacoan peccary (*Catagonus wagneri*). Only the collared (pecari), which is found in the Community Baboon Sanctuary, and the white lipped (wari) peccary are found in Belize. The collared peccary has the largest latitudinal range inhabiting a wide variety of habitats from the southern United States to southern South America. The white lipped peccary, which is commonly found west of the Community Baboon Sanctuary in the Hill Bank and Gallon Jug areas, has a wide range but due to its more narrow habitat restrictions it is mostly confined to tropical rain forests. Its range stretches from southern Mexico to southern South America. However, the two species mostly inhabit the same areas. In certain parts of Argentina, Paraguay, and Bolivia, both species are sympatric with the Chacoan peccary.

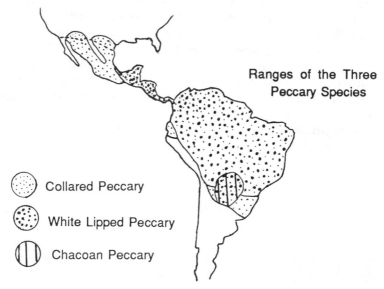

Ranges of the Three
Peccary Species

Collared Peccary

White Lipped Peccary

Chacoan Peccary

Besides being fairly restricted to the humid rain forest, white lipped peccaries differ from collared peccaries in a number of respects. The former are larger, weighing 60-85 lbs (25-40 kg) and are all dark black in color with a white area along the mouth and jaw giving them their name. Their young are reddish to dark tan in color. Both species have two hooves on their hind feet laterally placed which do not reach the ground. White lipped peccaries are also found in much larger herd sizes than the collared peccaries, sometimes reaching several hundred. White lipped peccaries thus have much larger home ranges and do not often return to the same area.

In general, peccaries are fast disappearing because their habitat is being destroyed and there has been a high demand, especially in Europe, for their pelts which are used in making leather goods. The Chacoan species with its small, limited geographic range is most vulnerable but the white lipped peccary with its dependence on tropical rain forests is also threatened. The collared peccary, which has been expanding its range in the arid areas of the United States partly due to managed hunting, has the best chance for survival.   This is particularly so because its generalist habits allow it to thrive in cultivated areas if it is not overhunted.

The collared peccary, called pecari in Creole, weighs on average about 35 lbs (16 kg) but can get up to 50 lbs (23 kg) and even to 78 lbs (35 kg).   As with most of the other large mammals which are found throughout the new world tropics, the peccaries are smaller in Belize and Central America. They have a pig-like appearance but with a larger head, more graceful legs and small feet.   They are blackish gray in color with a crest along their back of longer black hair.   Only a remnant tail exists. Their most distinctive characteristic is a large gland 6 in (15 cm) in front of the tail which is displayed when the crest is raised.

Collared peccaries can inhabit a wide variety of habitats from desert or semi-desert, oak woods, to the lowland tropical rain forests.   They thus can live in very wet to very dry areas.   This adaptable lifestyle also allows them to do well in the cutover areas such as occur in the regenerating forests of the Community Baboon Sanctuary.   Collared peccaries also have wide ranging behavioral adaptations which enable them to survive in a variety of habitats. Most of their activities are largely controlled by ambient temperatures. In hotter areas and during hotter seasons the peccaries feed early in the morning and later in the day and are primarily nocturnal. During cooler seasons they will continue foraging throughout the day.

Peccaries have teeth, jaws, and a digestive tract adapted to their omnivorous habits. They have a cartilaginous, bare, flexible snout for rooting out roots and tubers.   Although their incisors are well developed for cropping vegetation, their large interlocking canine teeth do not allow the transverse movements of the lower jaw in chewing which is common to other ungulates including pigs. They also have an unusual stomach consisting of a large gastric pouch with two blind sacs and and a glandular stomach. The pouched stomach probably allows them to utilize plant roughage by transforming cellulose to usable fatty acids. This is useful where they are forced to eat low quality foods in minimal habitats. Their food staples include fruits, tubers, rhizomes, bulbs, acorns, grasses, green shoots, and a variety of small animals. In each habitat a few species are preponderant in their diet.

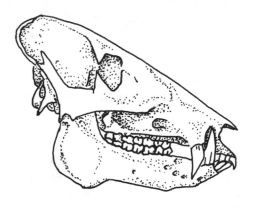

Peccary Skull Showing Generalized Tooth Pattern
and Enlarged Interlocking Canines

Collared peccaries seem to be able to breed all year long. Females are able to breed initally at about 11 months and they have an estrus cycle of 23-24 days with the period of heat lasting 4-5 days. After a gestation of 145 days they give birth to 1-2 young, usually twins. Following birth the mother rolls or tumbles the young with her nose to disconnect the afterbirth and stimulate the newborns. Newborns are tan to yellowish-gray with a dark back and yet darker vertebral stripe. The collared pattern shows at birth. Young nurse from the standing mother who has four pairs of teats but only the two posterior teats are functional. When very young, the piglets may freeze and hide on the ground when the herd flees from a predator. Usually the twins stay in close contact with the mother who will aggressively defend them against other herd members with growling and tooth chattering. Weaning occurs at about 6 weeks but often juveniles will establish a close relationship with others in the herd, a male or female, following them closely instead of their mother.

Collared peccaries are very social and live in small

groups of 1-21 averaging 7-9 which have a home range of between 150-495 acres (60-200 ha).   They have territories which overlap by 280-575 ft (90-180 m).   Only one herd at a time occupies the overlap zone.   The territories and group cohesion are maintained by the use of an unusual scent gland on their back. This gland is a raised area of bare skin about 2-3 in (5-8 cm) along the dorsal midline about 6 in (15 cm) in front of the tail.   It is a nipple-like protuberance with a central opening from which the scent fluid is emitted or even projected.   The gland is complex and composed of numerous sebaceous and sudiforous glands that empty their secretions into a common storage area.   They deposit the scent by rubbing the area against trees or other environmental posts and they apply it mutually to other herd members by rubbing a partner while positioned head to rump. They then synchronously rub the head area against the partners gland.   Herd members will also rub their cheeks against marking posts which they identify by sniffing.

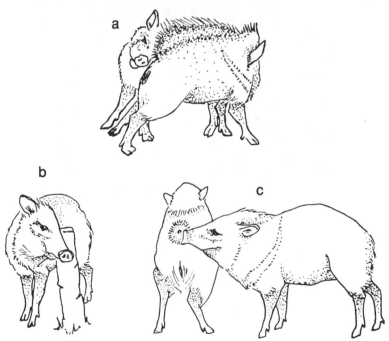

Scent Marking Behavior in Peccaries - a) mutual gland rubbing; b) rubbing against a marking post; c) sniffing an exposed gland

Peccaries have a number of vocal calls which are mainly used in communications within the herd.   These include a purring call of contentment often used to keep mothers and their young in contact, a grunting used similarly between adults, and a growling and tooth chattering used in aggressive encounters. During aggressive encounters two animals engage in a head to head face off often with the canines displayed which is followed by tooth chattering made by moving the canine teeth up and down grating against each other.   Despite these squabbles the peccaries are quite social and spend their resting time clumped together   against 2 or 3 others in the group.

White Lipped Peccary

THE MANATEE

The manatee was first recorded by Europeans when Christopher Columbus observed three manatees near Hispaniola in 1493. He thought they were the mythical mermaids, noting that they had a human face but were not as beautiful as they had been painted. The name of the order of manatees and their relatives, Sirenia, indicates this link. Even the common name manatee is rooted in the Garifuna language meaning woman's breast, a reference to the resemblance of the manatee mammae to human breasts and their position on the chest area.

Despite its unlikely link with mermaids and its common name, "sea cow " (a reference to its phlegmatic docility and herbivorous diet), the manatee is most closely related to the elephants. This common evolutionary link began 54-38

African Elephant

million years ago when a sea cow species closely related to ungulates took to the sea to feed on the vast sea grass meadows in the western Atlantic and Caribbean seas. The relationship has been determined by fossil and anatomical evidence and blood protein analysis. Today, the rounded hoof nails and location of the breasts between the forelegs are shared with elephants.   Sirenians and elephants additionally share a distinctive tooth pattern. Both have large cheek teeth used for grinding plant materials which are replaced from the rear as newly erupting teeth moving forward in the tooth row push out the anterior tooth, worn down from grinding the silica needles in water plants. Manatees have no front incisors except for four vestigial ones at birth which are later resorbed.   In elephants and to a lesser extent dugongs, these incisors have become specialized into tusks.

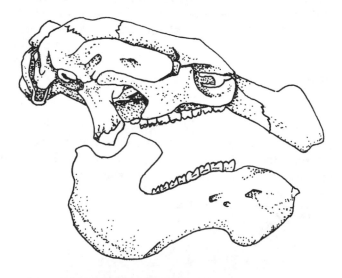

Manatee Skull Showing Replaceable Cheek Teeth
and the Absence of Incisors

The order Sirenia is composed of two living genera in the family Trichechidae, which share body form, flipper forelimbs, and a fluke-like tail. These are the only mammals with 6 (instead of 7) cervical neck vertebrae. These include three species of manatee: the West Indian manatee (*Trichecus manatus*) which occurs along the shores of Florida and the gulf coast in the U.S. throughout the Caribbean and along the coasts of Central America and northern South America; the West African manatee (*Trichechus senegalensis*) which lives along the coastal areas of West Africa; and the Amazon manatee (*Trichechus inunguis*) which is specific to the Amazon River in South America.   The one species of Dugong (*Dugong dugon*)

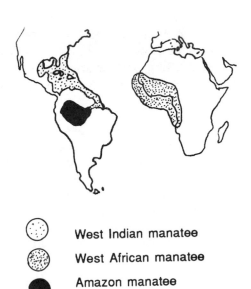

⦾ West Indian manatee

⦿ West African manatee

⬤ Amazon manatee

Ranges of the Three Manatee Species

lives along the coasts of East Africa, southern Asia , and Australia.   Steller's sea cow (*Hydrodamalis gigas*) which lived in the Bering Strait and reached gigantic proportions of 35 ft (11 m) long and up to 8,000 lbs (3600 kg) became extinct through hunting before 1800. All Sirenian species are threatened with extinction due to hunting, depletion of their environment, and modification of their environment from motor boats, herbicides, and other pollutants.   The Amazonian manatees number only in the thousands while the West Indian manatee population has been estimated at 5,000 to 10,000 within its complete range.

Conservation

Docility, their delicious flesh, and low reproductive capacity make manatees the most threatened of aquatic mammals.   Population numbers of manatees have decreased in recent times but the manatees have come under recent legislation for their conservation.   In the United States they are protected under the U.S. Marine Mammal Protection Act of 1972 and the Endangered Species Act of 1983.   Florida, their main home in the U.S., has 25 "Manatee Sanctuary" areas and the whole state has been designated as a manatee sanctuary by the 1978 Florida Manatee Sanctuary Act. These laws protect the species against hunting and regulate motor boating in specific areas of manatee congregation during specific times of the year.

Only about 1,000-1,200 manatees survive in Florida waters today, which is up from the 750-850 estimated in 1976. The overall population appears to be increasing due to proliferation of introduced aquatic vegetation and to recent legislation protection but they have not reached levels of former abundance. Hunting pressure has resulted in local extirpation producing semi-isolated populations within their range. Manatees are now listed as endangered by the U.S. Fish and Wildlife Service and as vulnerable to extinction by IUCN.

Manatees have been long exploited for their meat which tastes like tender veal. Soon after Columbus observed them, the Spanish declared manatees a fish so they could be eaten on friday. Even before European discovery, Mayans hunted manatee, killing them with flint headed lances, eating the meat and utilizing the hides in canoe making. Manatee bones have been found in middens (refuse heaps) of pre-Columbian Indian villages. Manatees have also been exploited for their dense, heavy skeleton, especially their ribs which are like fine ivory, oil for many purposes, and their thick hide as a tough leather.

Manatees were at one time brought regularly to the Belize City market but by 1931 only 1-2 animals were sold there. British Honduras soon thereafter passed a Manatee Protection Ordinance as early as 1935-6. Now the population is fully protected under the Wildlife Protection Act No. 4 of 1981. However, a low level of illegal take continues as noted from Ambergris Cay, Dangriga, Punta Gorda, Long Cay and Gales Point. They are still occasionally used for meat, accidentally taken in nets and killed, and their bones are used for pendants and scrimshaw due to the high density, ivory-like quality of the bones, especially the rib bones.

An aerial survey of 4 areas of high manatee usage

indicated a high population in Belize relative to other areas in the range surveyed. The greatest numbers were seen in Southern Lagoon. There has been no indication of a decline since a previous survey in 1977 and the proportion of calves noted in 1989 is on par with other surveys reported for healthy growing populations in Florida. This evidence indicated that Belize has a growing population of manatees.

An estimate for the country is 300-700 manatees indicating that Belize is one of the last stongholds for the species within its range. This appears to be due to the high quality of habitat and the low level of killing by humans. The areas between the reef and the mainland are well vegetated by sea grass beds for manatee forage. There is also good access to rivers, creeks, and lagoons. Indeed, there is a population which inhabits the Mussel Creek area adjacent to the Community Baboon Sanctuary lands. The manatees appear to seek out freshwater for drinking and are abundant where it is available. This may be why Southern Lagoon is important due to the spring which upwells from the bottom, northeast of Gales Point.

Today most of the threat to manatees comes from human threats to their environment. Despite conservation efforts in the U.S. , up to 30% of deaths are caused directly by humans. Half of these are from collisions with motorized boats due to propeller injuries or death from impact. In Belize this is not occurring as frequently as few manatees were seen to have propeller scars. Other threats are due to reduction of the habitat as well as to herbicides, pesticides, and other pollutants which result in silting and other adverse environmental changes detrimental to the manatee.

Natural History

Manatees inhabit rivers, estuaries, and coastal areas of tropical and subtropical regions of the northwest Atlantic Ocean from Florida to the northeast coast of Brazil. Their habitat is mainly defined by tepid 68°F (20°C) temperatures, shallow water plants, and shallow slow flowing rivers and lagoons. They occupy both fresh and salt water, clear or muddy, preferring a depth of 3-10 ft (1-3 m) below the surface with most manatees balking at channels less than 3 ft (1m) deep. The deepest manatee dive recorded was 32 ft (10 m).

Cool weather seems to be a nemesis for the manatee who seek warm water refuges in Florida (the northern part of their range). Only 6 of the 25 Florida refuges are produced by naturally occurring warm springs, the others are created by power plants and factories which discharge warm waste water into the rivers. Though protected by a tough skin and a fat layer they are susceptible to cold due to their low metabolic rates. Prolonged exposure to water below 60°F (16°C) can put them at a risk of disease or hypothermia.

They exhibit a number of adaptations which enhance life in their watery environment. Their large, hairless body, their valvular nostrils which can close under water, the absence of ear pinnae, and a protective nictitating eye membrane are all adaptations to an underwater lifestyle. The muscular alveolar sacs in the lungs are also modifications which seem to function to compress air in the lungs enabling the animal to sink without the use of flippers, tail or exhaling air.

Despite living underwater, the manatee's hearing is exceptional as suggested by their large ear ossicles. Females can respond to faint calf cries up to 190 ft (60m) away. Their eyesight is good and in clear water they use their binocular vision to investigate objects but they seem far-sighted sometimes bumping into close objects. They have adequate night vision and good smell abilities.

Adults are about 10-12 ft (3-4 m) long and weigh 1,000-2,000 lbs (450-900 kg). Their skin is finely wrinked with the young born with smoother skin, darker blackish-gray in color. Sometimes the skin is covered with algae, barnacles and other incrustations. Scar tissue created by propeller scars are pale in color and serve as individual markings in manatee studies in Florida where boat scars are unfortunately common.

Feeding

Sirenians are uniquely the only plant eating marine mammals alive today. They are non-ruminant herbivores with long intestines, a large mid-gut cecum, and without a chambered stomach. They are wholly herbivorous and follow an order of preference from submergents, natants, to emergents. They eat as much as 220 lbs (100 kg) of aquatic plants daily to maintain a size of up to 2,000 lbs (900 kg) and 13 ft (4 m) in length.

Since many sea and fresh water plants contain relatively few nutrients, sea cows have developed mechanisms to better utilize them. They ingest 5-10% of their body weight per day. They have extremely long intestines up to 120 ft (37 m) long and it may take over 5 days for food to pass through it. Microorganisms in the intestines and cecum help digest cellulose so the manatees can process large volumes of plants. Their slow metabolism also helps them utilize water plants. Hydrilla and water hyacynths are favorite foods and they also like ragwort and sea grass which is restricted to a highly saline environment. Their digestive process creates a huge quantity of gas which creates a buoyancy problem. Continued flatulence releases much of the gas but their heavy massive bones and the long , narrow lungs help to distribute the buoyancy. Their diet also consists of some incidentally ingested insect larvae, amphipods, molluscs, shrimp, and other invertebrates as well as manatee feces. Due to their diet they have been experimented with in maintaining clear channels in canals in Guyana.

Manatees feed 6-8 hours per day in 1-2 hour sessions at a depth of 3-10 ft (1-3 m). They are generally arhythmic feeding day or night. Fleshy, muscular upper lip pads hang laterally over the sides of mouth covered with coarse bristles. These are especially stiff, stout, and downward directed around the mouth and inner surfaces of the lips. The pendulous lips are extremely flexible, almost prehensile, so the pads can grasp vegetation and tuck it to the rear of the mouth to the grinding teeth. The lips are turned outward into the food source then both lateral pads are closed inward with bristles effectively grasping the vegetation and pulling it into the cleft of the mouth.   The short tongue has little mobility.

Manatees have two, five-toed dextrous paddle-shaped flippers which are used to walk along the bottom of waterways, hold food to the mouth, clean the mouth, scratch the face and chest, and embrace other manatees.   The flippers are composed only of the forearm and horizontally flattened phalanges with nails, flexibly, bending at the wrist.   They may occasionally use their flippers to crawl onto banks to reach shoreline vegetation.

They have no hind limbs but have a horizontally flattened spatulate tail which is used as a propelling fluke undulating dorsoventrally.   It is also used as a rudder for steering , banking or rolling while the flippers are held loosely or against body.   Flippers can also assist in rudder action.   Manatees can also move on the bottom by alternate movements of the flippers along the substrate or by moving the limbs in unison in a clumsy "gallop".   Manatees are slow moving, cruising at 1-15 mph (2-25 kmph).   Although they have no major enemies except humans they can flee at speeds of 15 mph (25 kmph) in short bursts. They can't defend themselves having only rear teeth.

Manatees breath through their nostrils when resting, feeding or idling with only the tip of the snout exposed.   They often surface in groups in unison especially cows with their calves.   The average submergence time is approximately 4.5 minutes.   When not feeding they spend their time sleeping placidly on the bottom or dozing sideways and upside down as they float in slow river currents. They rest about 2-12 hours daily in 2-4 hour sessions with their eyes closed either suspended near the surface or lying prostrate on the substrate.   When active they surface every 2-5 minutes for air but they can submerge for as long as 20 minutes.

Social Behavior

Manatees are not especially social but they do occur in groups of 2-6 or as large as 20. These are ephemeral groups with only the cow-calf group lasting regularly.   The manatees communicate with squeaks, chirps, and squeals which convey

Manatee Resting Positions

moods such as fear, aggravation, protest, sexual arousal, and play. In flight, a cow and calf keep up a continual duet to maintain contact. They are extremely tactile animals, nuzzling snout to snout in a "kiss" greeting, embracing with their flippers and swimming in loosely synchronized formation. The muzzle-muzzle kiss begins beneath the surface and then muzzles are raised. Play occurs often in winter aggregates with 2-3 individuals involved in mutual kissing, mouthing, bumping, chasing, and sexual play. Aggression is rare in the species and they don't fight over food or territories. Males will show some placid aggressive behaviors in competition for estrus females.

Small breeding herds also form, centered around an estrus female, which may last for up to 1-4 weeks. Several to as many as 17 males follow and attempt to breed with the female. Initially she is in continual flight from the males who attempt to mouth and embrace her. She thwarts them by jack knifing, rolling away or turning her back. She may also head for shallower water where she is less vulnerable to the males.

Muzzle-Muzzle Kiss

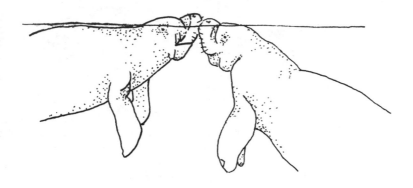

When ready to breed she may copulate with several bulls and sometimes the surrounding bulls mouth her as well. The bulls show little aggression with some pushing, shoving, and colliding with each other.

Females mature sexually at 7-8 years and breed sporadically throughout the year. Gestation is 385-400 days. Newborns weigh 60-80 lbs (25-35 kg) and are about 4 ft (1.3 m) long. At birth, the mother may aid the calf to surface on her flipper or back allowing it to breath before lowering it again. The calf can only use its tail after several days. Calves suckle underwater for 2 minutes each bout. Females nurse the calves for as long as 14 months to two years but the calf may begin to nibble vegetation at one month of age. Thus females breed probably every 2.5-3 years. They are long lived (to 33 years) but slow in reproducing.

The mother-calf bond is the strongest bond lasting beyond weaning when the calves still inhabit their mother's home range. Manatees mix and travel together during summer at which time these older offspring may tag along with their mothers. This may facilitate their learning how to get to refuges, feeding sites, and travel routes. Manatees may travel more than 900 miles (1550 km) along the entire length of Florida coast to reach warmer refuges. This learning period may be important since many first year juveniles die in cold weather.

Multi-Male Herd Courting Estrus Cow

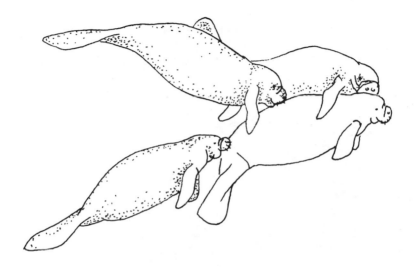

Copulating Manatee Pair

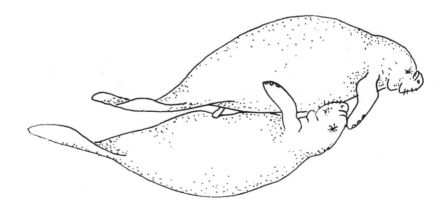

HUMMINGBIRDS

*A*lthough more than 300 species of hummingbirds range widely in the Americas from Alaska to Tiera del Fuego, most species are concentrated in the tropics. Hummingbird species are especially numerous in the northern mountains of South America. Twenty-one species occur in Belize.

Number of
Hummingbird Species
in the Americas

Besides their radiant irridescent colors, hummingbirds have a number of amazing adaptations for their specific lifestyle of gathering nectar from flowers. In a sense, they have taken over an insect's role. Hence, they are very small in size ranging from slightly larger than 2 in (5 cm) in the case of the Cuban bee hummingbird, to a length of 8 1/2 in (22 cm) in the giant hummingbird.

Flight

The extremely rapid wing beats which allow hummingbirds to hover while feeding and even to fly backwards, produce the "hum" which gives hummingbirds their name. They move their wings as fast as 50-80 beats per second and can fly as fast as 71 mph (115 kmph). When taking off, they don't use their feet to push off as other birds do, they instead arise directly from the power of their wing beats. Their typical flight movement is due to a modified wing structure and powerful breast muscles. These muscles may weigh 1/3 of the bird's weight. In hummingbirds, both the muscles which draw the wings up and down are very strong.

To hover, the body is held at a 45% angle and the wings are beat backwards and forwards describing a figure 8 in the air. The down stroking wings tilt to force air down and the bird up. Then the wing flips over so the back of the wing faces down. In rear flight, the wings are tilted so the air is forced forward and the bird is driven back. A helicopter is the

Hummingbird Wing   Hummingbird Hovering Flight

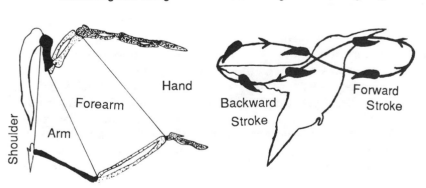

Pelican Wing

human's attempt to duplicate nature. To hover, helicopters achieve the same affect via the circular blades driving the air downward.

Nightly Hibernation

Any very small warm-blooded animal species has a very high surface area to volume ratio and can easily lose heat energy. In the hummingbird's case, its rapid flight also loses energy rapidly. Thus, hummingbirds must feed frequently throughout the day, with peaks at sunrise and sunset. Even at rest, a hummingbird's metabolic rate is 25 times that of a chicken. At night, however, it is unable to collect food and it conserves energy by going into a torpid state, a form of nightly hibernation. Some species reduce their metabolic rate 6 times, lowering their body temperature from 100 to 57° F (38 to 14° C) so as to match the surrounding air. Those species at the extreme northern and southern ranges must migrate to find food in winter. This is a stress to their metabolic system. They must store up to 1/2 their body weight in fat before setting off on the migration. Even then, it is thought that they may have an additional method for conserving their food reserves.

Plant Pollinators

Due to their nectar gathering lifestyle, hummingbirds have become important pollinators of the tropical rain forest. Many plant species depend on the birds for pollination and reproduction. Tropical hummingbirds and the flowers they frequent tend to fall into two groups which have loosely co-adapted to serve each other's needs. Hummingbirds with long decurved bills, form a group called "hermits" and the other group has short straight bills. Hermits forage from long curved flowers which secrete large amounts of nectar at the base of the flower tube. The nectar of these flowers is not accessible to the short billed hummingbirds. Hermit flowers are often widely scattered in the forest so the long billed hermits must follow a "trapline" from food source to food source. Hermits must also be strong fliers to cover long distances. Although they can get nectar from short flowers, they seem to prefer the long flowers owing to their large amounts of nectar.

In the Community Baboon Sanctuary, the long-tailed hermit (*Phaethornis superciliosus*) and the little hermit (*Phaethornis longuemareus*) are both very common. The long-tailed hermit is known to prefer the flowers of banana relatives of the genus *Heliconia*. These plants are found in early successional growth, 1-2 years after land is abandoned. Perhaps this is why hermits are common in the sanctuary. The other type of hummingbird has a short straight bill, and they forage from short straight flowers which may be more suited for insect visitors. These flowers secrete less nectar and may be clumped in large groups. These hummingbirds are thus more aggressive and maintain territories around these clumped food sources. They may chase hermits from their territories as well.

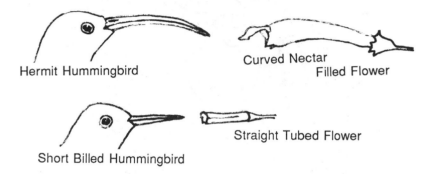

Hermit Hummingbird

Curved Nectar
Filled Flower

Short Billed Hummingbird

Straight Tubed Flower

The Hummingbird Tongue

Hummingbirds have evolved a long modified tongue for getting nectar from flowers. They don't suck it up as was once thought. Instead, they have long, forked extensible tongues whose sides roll up into grooves. The ends of these tubes are frayed or fringed. As they rapidly work the tongue in and out of the flowers, nectar and insects are entangled in the fringed tip and the nectar is drawn up into the grooves by capillary action and then swallowed.

Society in Miniature

The long-tailed hermit *Phaethornis superciliosus* is a hummingbird species which doesn't defend its food sources which are distributed in clumps along a 650 1,000 ft (200 500 m) foraging route. Instead, the males defend small 30-65 ft

(10-20 m) diameter breeding territories which are collectively composed of 5-25 males and are called a "lek". Lek breeding areas are located along streams or other long lived forests gaps because they contain good foraging areas, thickets along the forest edge, and open flight paths. Individual territories are arranged around a series of defended singing-perch sites on exposed slender branches about 6 ft (2 m) off the forest floor.

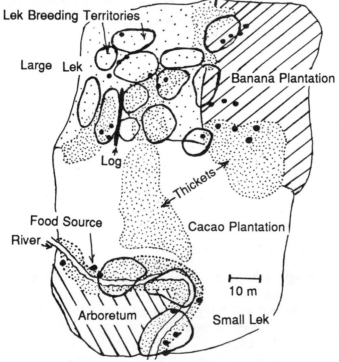

Hermit Lek Breeding Area Showing Individual Territories

During the breeding season from December to July, males wait for the females to arrive to mate with them. Females arrive on the lek infrequently, about one per day, so males must be very vigilant on their territories. The males arrive before dawn and sing simple repetitive songs from their perches. With the dawn light there is a peak of visual displays which resident males use to defend their territories from intruders. Young first year males need to establish a territory early during their first year or they may fail to breed. If they fail they may go to another lek up to 0.6 mi (1 km) away to try again.   They live only about 3 years so they have little time to breed and there is a high, 50% turnover in males during the year.   Many die in October-November when the food source of flower nectar is low.

By about 7-8 am, all males in the lek take a feeding break when the *Heliconia* and other food flowers produce the most energy rich nectar. They then quickly return to await the

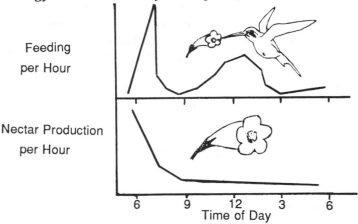

Feeding per Hour

Nectar Production per Hour

6   9   12   3   6
Time of Day

arrival of a well fed female to the lek area. Females are attracted by the singing males who sing both in early morning and late afternoon.   The dominant males hold central territories surrounded by others, giving them a breeding advantage.   The territory holders also chase intruding males at these times.   Young and more subordinant males maintain peripheral territories less likely to be visited by females.

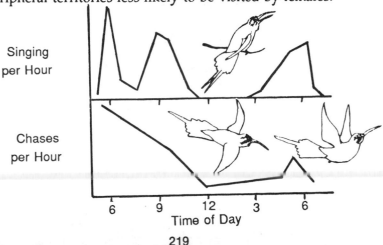

Singing per Hour

Chases per Hour

6   9   12   3   6
Time of Day

Except for size, both male and female hermit look alike so aggressive and courtship behaviors are similar. In mating, females choose their mates, staying to breed at the male's approach rather than fleeing. Males sing on their perch often wagging their tail, displaying the white tipped pattern when another approaches. Residents will often fly in front of an intruder displaying the facial pattern and an orange mouth lining which becomes visible as they open the mouth suddenly to make a popping sound. The resident may then hover over the intruder, approaching from the rear and attempt to land on his back. If the intruder is a male, the two may exchange perches in a similar manner until the resident chases the intruder from the territory. A female will remain on the perch to breed with the male. She eventually goes off away from the lek area to build a nest and care for the young herself.

Male Hermit Singing on Perch

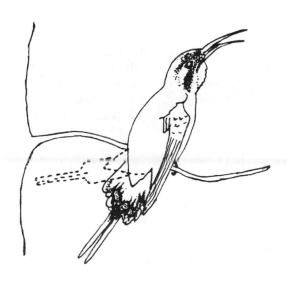

Courtship in Hermit Hummingbirds - Male approaches intruder from the rear. Intruding male is displaced (top) and visiting female remains to breed (bottom).

MIGRANT BIRDS

$\mathcal{B}$elizean forests form an important life-giving winter sanctuary for migrant birds from the United States and Canada. Although many North Americans think of the northern breeding birds as "their" birds, often these migrants spend only 3-4 months in the north. The remaining time they spend in other more southern areas and perhaps should be thought of as tropical species which breed in the north.

Due to the seasonally extreme cold which affects the insect and plant food sources in much of North America, many bird species have been forced to migrate to warmer tropical climates. Belize supports three groups of birds based on their migratory pattern: 1) permanent residents such as the toucan, parrots, and the groove-billed ani; 2) transients who are passing through Belize to other southern regions, such as the bank swallow, broad winged hawk, and the black poll warbler; and 3) winter residents which migrate and breed in the north, such as the black-and-white warbler and the blue winged teal.

Winter Residents and Transients

The black-and-white warbler and the northern water thrush are 2 examples of birds which breed in the U.S. and Canada but depend on areas like the Community Baboon Sanctuary for winter sustenance. The bank swallow and chimney swift breed in North America and winter in South America. However, they are species that may use Belizean forests as stopping areas to build up fat reserves while travelling between North and South America. The blue winged teal and pintail are two duck species that are winter residents in Belize. The blue winged teal is found in the Community Baboon Sanctuary. Some individuals spend the winter in Belize while others are transients, flying on to nearby areas in Central America. On the migration from North America, many species of ducks and other water fowl use the same migration routes forming "flyways". These routes are areas of species

congregations which probably insure that most individuals
will find their way to a secure winter feeding ground.

Migratory Range and Cycle of the Black-and-White Warbler

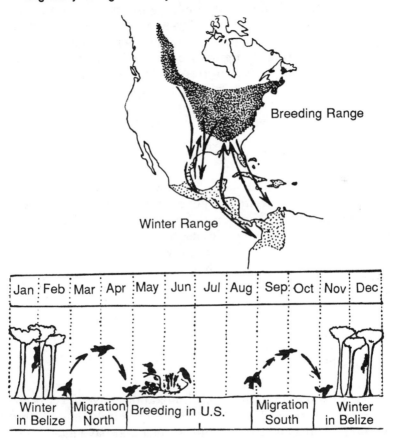

Breeding Range

Winter Range

| Jan | Feb | Mar | Apr | May | Jun | Jul | Aug | Sep | Oct | Nov | Dec |

| Winter in Belize | Migration North | Breeding in U.S. | Migration South | Winter in Belize |

Seasonal Migratory Cycles

Taking the black-and-white warbler as an example of
a common winter resident in the Community Baboon Sanctuary,
we see a yearly cycling of behavior. They arrive in the United
States in the third week in April and begin setting up breeding
territories. They arrive earlier than many insectivorous birds

because they are adapted to hunt insects who are still in hibernation under the bark of trees. They mate and lay 5 eggs which are incubated for about 2 weeks. The young fledge about 2 weeks after hatching. The full breeding cycle may extend into July. The adults then molt in July-August and develop fresh, strong feathers for the coming migration. At about the end of August they feed heavily to build up fat reserves prior to their migratory departure. Migrants begin arriving in Belize in October-November to feed on tropical insects until they ready themselves for the return trip in March-April.

The Mystery of Migration

What is Migration ?

Migration is the regular seasonal movement of a population of birds from one geographic location to another. Ancient peoples once thought that migratory birds hibernated or changed into another species as they saw one species arrive and another leave.   Now we know from many studies that birds migrate and we know their routes and destinations as well. Scientists study bird migration through direct observation, radio-tracking birds with transmitters on them, observing birds on radar screens, and by capturing , marking and recapturing birds.

Functions of Migration

Most questions about bird migrations have never been completely answered.   Birds most definitely benefit by migrating to areas which are both warmer and have more food available during the winter. In the spring, they get ample space for breeding.   But questions still emerge. Why do some bird species migrate so far?   Some theories propose that migrational behavior has evolved as a response to Pleistocene glaciations occurring in the Northern Hemisphere. Other theories propose that bird   species which evolved in the Southern Hemisphere have expanded their ranges and thus account for migrations.   While orioles, vireos, and tanagers originated in the tropics, many other species did not.

What Stimulates Migration ?

INTERNAL FACTORS

Birds prepare for migration by responding to internal changes which come about in response to environmental factors. Daylength triggers in birds the tendency to migrate both in spring and autumn. The lengthening and shortening of the day affects the pituitary and pineal glands which result in physiological changes in the bird. Birds build up a layer of fat, sometimes almost doubling their weight for the migration and their sexual organs enlarge or reduce in size. The counter current flow of blood and oxygen in their lungs also enables them to extract oxygen more efficiently and thus they can fly at high altitudes where oxygen content is low. They also become very restless. What the specific stimuli for migration are remains a mystery.

WEATHER FACTORS

Species vary radically as to time of their migration. Birds often leave before food becomes scarce. But it seems as though specific weather conditions influence the actual time of departure.

In the fall, the most intense passage of migrants occurs two days after a cold front low has passed and is being followed by a high. This is characterized by dropping temperatures, rising barometric pressure, and clearing skies. Beginning migration before the two days has elapsed is not always conducive to good passage because winds are too strong and turbulent in the trough between air masses. Birds possess an amazing understanding of winds. They look for moderate tail winds and cross-quartering breezes.

The spring migrations are just the opposite. Migrants move north on the warm sector of an incoming low. When a high pressure area has just passed, the influx of warm moist tropical air is extended and intensified cloudiness and rain in the low may curtail the migrations.

When Do Birds Migrate ?

Migrations occur both during the day and at night. Many of the smaller birds such as rails, flycatchers, orioles, sparrows, warblers, thrushes, and shorebirds migrate during the night, landing at daybreak to feed and rest throughout the daylight hours.

Species Examples

As a group, wood warblers probably travel more in mixed company than other North American bird families. Many other species keep strictly to themselves such as swifts, crows, and nighthawks. Sometimes young are more likely to move south together ahead of their parents. In a few species, the adults leave before the young; waterfowl and crane families travel together. In some species the sexes travel separately. In spring migrations, it is usually the males who travel first arriving first to establish their territories.

NAVIGATION

The main mystery of migration which has been studied by scientists is how migrants know how to navigate to where they are going. Getting from place to place and beginning and ending the migrations are actions based on complicated mechanisms within each bird species and we don't know all the answers about migration yet. Birds live in an expanded sensory world compared to humans. Birds and other animals, including humans, have "internal clocks" which have a cycle of about 24 hours. These clocks can be reset each day in response to the sunrise. In Belize, daylength doesn't vary much seasonally but in northern areas, daylength changes may stimulate breeding and migratory cycles.

Whereas humans use sextants, chronometers, compasses, charts, and mathematical tables in order to navigate, migrating birds depend on complex internal mechanisms. Initially birds show a tendency to orient in specific directions at certain times of the year. In order to do this, they use 3 internal "compasses" which allow orientation by the sun, the stars, and earth magnetism. They also have a remarkable awareness of time and atmospheric conditions including the ability to sense tail winds. They can also detect extremely small barometric pressure changes. Some species may even use smell and changes in the gravitational pull to home in on local areas. Many species originally learn routes or parts of them by following their parents or by flocking with other experienced birds.

Migrants have established routes. Once they have arrived on a familiar route or near a familiar area, they use vision to follow natural landmarks such as coastal outlines, rivers, lakes, shorelines or mountains. They seem to follow topography or "guiding lines" which are distinct features which seem to influence their travel. In many cases topography effects their route. Large water areas don't create good thermals and migrants are forced to travel around them. Thus shorelines may appear to be a guiding line but the birds may be forced to travel around them as updrafts are created by the land-water edge.

Routes

Different species follow different patterns for their migratory routes. Some form loops returning by a different route in the spring. Often seasonal loops are made to intersect more favorable feeding areas. Some show puzzling turns or twists which are often due to rigidly following traditional routes without regard to biological functions.

Banding has allowed ornithologists to plot migratory routes. Many warbler migrants migrate some 3,000 miles (4800 km) from Canada to Central and South America. Many individuals seek the same localities where they bred or wintered the year before, even utilizing the same trees. Birds generally can travel at two speeds of flight, normal flight and flight during escape. Migrations occur at speeds somewhere between those speeds. Larger birds generally fly faster than smaller birds, with ducks flying at 40-50 mph (65-80 kmph), flycatchers at 10-17 mph (16-27 kmph), and doves at 35 mph (56 kmph). Peregrines are the fastest birds and can fly at 60 mph (95 kmph) when chasing prey and as fast as 200 mph (320 kmph) during a dive. Thus during migration flights (about 10 hrs per day), small birds can cover 100-250 mi (160-400 km) per day. Ducks might cover 400-500 mi (640-800 km) per day. During migrations, radar has clocked shorebirds at 45 mph (47 kmph) and songbirds at 30 mph (48 kmph). In spring, the black poll warbler initially averages 30 mi (50 km) per day and later covers 200 mi (320 km) per day. In general, fall migrations are more leisurely with more feeding and resting occurring than in the spring.

Ninety-five percent of migrants travel under 10,000 ft (3100 m) high and most under 3,000 ft (940 m) but birds can and have been known to fly over 15,000 ft (4680 m) without problems. At 10,000 ft temperatures may be close to freezing. At 20,000 ft (6250 m) the oxygen is half what it is at sea level. Generally, the altitude flown depends on the species, weather, time of day, and geographical features. Nocturnal migrants fly at different altitudes at different times of night. Most small birds fly at 500-1,000 ft and nocturnal migrants fly a bit higher. Fall migrations are more leisurely but spring migrations are quicker and more scattered.

Migrations take a tremendous toll with over half the population dying every year. Most deaths occur in immatures and overland migrants which have strayed or been blown offshore to perish in the sea. Many also hit TV towers, powerlines, glass buildings or may be killed by spring storms. Many are starved out by cold temperatures which limit their food supplies.

Destruction of the Rain Forest

Individuals that maintain winter territories in the tropics and vigorously defend them are more successful than floaters. Species which maintain territories include summer tanagers, wood thrushes, redstarts, ovenbirds, white-eyed vireos, gray catbirds, northern and Louisiana waterthrushs, yellow-billed flycatchers, black-and-white warblers, worm-eating warblers, Kentucky warblers, hooded warblers, Wilson warblers, and black-throated green warblers. Both males and females defend the same forest area each year. Most forest breeding birds prefer forested wintering grounds. If their winter territories are destroyed, however, they will become floaters with less survival success. Floaters without territories have less chance for survival.

In the case of hooded warblers, clearing one acre of tropical forest might do as much damage as clearing five times that in North America. Swainson's thrush, black-and-white warblers and worm-eating warblers are particularly dependent on forests, both primary and secondary growth forests. However, tropical rain forests are disappearing at an annual rate of 1-2% due to timber and beef production.

U.S. censuses indicate a decline of many U.S. songbird species that winter in the shrinking tropical forests. Just over half of the 650 U.S. bird species winter in the south and 107 of those are dependent on tropical forests in Latin America. In Central America, if the present trends of timber harvesting, agricultural expansion, and human settlement continue, little forest will be left by the year 2000.

Studies since the 1960's reveal rapid population decreases in many bird species especially in hooded warblers, kentucky warblers, redstarts, and acadian flycatchers, all which require mature tropical rain forest habitat. Others dropping in numbers are black-and-white warblers, ovenbirds, Louisiana waterthrushs, parula warblers, yellow-throated warblers, red-eyed vireos, eastern wood peewees, great crested flycatchers, and wood thrushes. New Jersey studies conclude that worm-eating warblers, northern orioles, scarlet tanagers, and veerys are declining. Additionally, eastern phoebes, blue-winged warblers, solitary vireos, black-throated blue warblers, blackburnian warblers, pine warblers, black-throated green warblers, and chestnut-sided warblers are declining in number. Therefore eastern warblers, vireos, thrushes, and flycatchers are in serious trouble. In Wisconsin, redstarts, cerulean warblers, ovenbirds, least flycatchers, northern orioles, scarlet tanagers, blue-gray gnatcatchers, and yellow-throated vireos are showing population reductions. Thus, most of the warblers which migrate to the tropics are in danger.

BIRDER'S DELIGHT - AMERICAN WOOD WARBLERS

$\mathcal{A}$ favorite among North American bird watchers is the subfamily of American wood warblers. There are 53 warbler species which are a very beautifully colored and distinctly patterned group while in breeding plumage. They are, however, a challenge to identify when all sexes and ages are similarly colored in the confusing fall plumage. Wood warblers are small (half ounce - 14 gm) insectivorous birds with slender, sharp pointed bills. They are part of the passerine or perching bird order whose members have 3 toes projecting forward and one behind which are used to grip a perch. Their muscles grip tighter when the bird rests on its breast or sways backwards, an adaptation to keep them from falling off the perch at night when asleep

Originally confused with European warblers by early naturalists, wood warblers were later named American wood warblers because they are confined to American forest habitats. They do not warble but have non-musical songs which are an important part of their territorial defense and courtship. Another distinguishing characteristic of the group, which can only be seen when holding a bird, are the 9 primary feathers which are the largest flight feathers.

In spring, males arrive first on the breeding territory and the females accept a male with its territory and build a nest, laying 3-7 eggs (usually 4-5). The eggs are white or nearly white with brown, lilac or black spots or blotches concentrated at the larger end of the egg. Incubation lasts 11-14 days and young are reared by both parents in 8-11 days. As a family they are plagued by the brown cowbirds who lay parasitic eggs in their nests.

They migrate north after they spend 2/3rd's of their year in the neotropics, a home which has harbored them for thousand's of years. They depart for only a brief time to reproduce.   Many warblers average only 3 months in the U.S. breeding grounds with 2-3 months spent in migration and 6-7 months on the winter grounds.

They are nocturnal migrants flying 500-700 mi (800-1100 km) across the Gulf of Mexico in a single non-stop night of flight.   They migrate in mixed flocks.   When not migrating, their flight averages only 13 mph (21 kmph).

Resident tropical birds do not fill the niche left vacant by the migrants when they go.   They are instead territorial and show long-term site fidelity in order to compete with temporary residents for resources.   Half of the U.S. land migrants are funneled into Mexico, implying that migratory birds concentrate several-fold into the more lush and plentiful tropical rain forest.   Twenty-nine species of warblers winter in mature tropical rain forests and 24 of those species are found in Belize.

BLACKBIRDS, SOME ARE YELLOW

*I*n Belizean Creole, "blackbirds" include such varied black birds as grackles and anis but generally blackbird refers to a family of songbirds (Icteridae) which includes orioles, grackles, meadowlarks, cowbirds, caciques, and oropendulas. All blackbirds are not black; actually Icteridae comes from Greek meaning yellow or jaundice perhaps referring to the oriole's color.   As a group, blackbirds breed in almost every

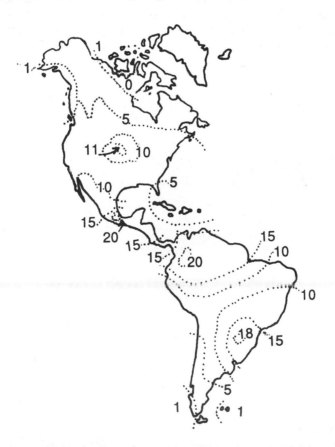

Number of Breeding Blackbird Species in the Americas

environment in the new world from Alaska to Tierra del Fuego. Belize, however, is close to the heart of blackbird country. The southern end of the Mexican plateau and its adjacent lowlands are where orioles evolved and where the highest number of blackbird species breed. Of the 94 blackbird species, 24 species breed there, 13 of which are orioles. Seventeen species are found in Belize of which 14 have been seen in the Community Baboon Sanctuary. Probably 9 species breed there.

Gaping

One particular behavior sets blackbirds apart from most other birds and enables them to exploit a wide variety of habitats and prey species in a way that other birds cannot. They all have an unusual way of feeding called gaping. It is subtle to observe but can be seen when a "bamboo cracker" (yellow-billed cacique) hammers at a bamboo stalk or when a boat-tailed grackle prods the earth in search of food. Gaping is when they insert their closed bill into an area such as the soil or bark of a tree and open the bill exposing the potential hiding place of a grub or resting insect. Whereas most birds forage on the surface of a branch or the ground, blackbirds probe inside, opening the twig or branch. Meadowlarks gape the soil

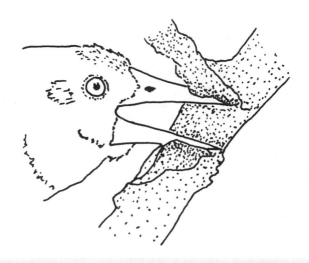

Gaping

or base of grass clumps for insects in their savanna home. Redwings similarly probe the base of aquatic weeds for small animals.   The yellow-billed cacique exploits bamboo and secondary growth thickets at all altitudes in Central America, seeking insects within.   The melodious blackbird may be seen in the pine ridge probing pine cones apart, prying bark or gaping through pine needles.   Both the forest dwelling caciques and oropendulas also probe bark in this same gaping manner. They also will probe curled leaves for any harbored insects.

The tropical riverine forests in the Community Baboon Sanctuary contain a relatively high number of epiphytic bromeliads. The bromeliads have broad, overlapping moist leaves which blackbirds gape apart in search of aquatic animals.   Orioles, oropendulas, and caciques, are the main exploiters of the bromeliads.   Orioles may also probe tubular flowers for the nectar and can destroy many of the orange and pink *Erythrina* (copna) blossoms, by pulling off the flowers and sucking the nectar from the flower's base.   Orioles compete with the howlers and other animals for these tasty flowers when they bloom early in the dry season.

Gaping may have been the main reason for the success of the blackbirds.   In the Community Baboon Sanctuary rain forest, they are able to obtain larger food supplies from the tree and shrub canopies by making foods accessible which are unavailable to other birds.

In addition to this unique use of the bill, many blackbirds are able to coordinate the use of their feet to hold the branch, leaf or flower while they gape into it with their bill.   This enables them to reach out for leaves or branches that are too slender to support them, pull them back, and hold them with their feet while resting on a larger branch.   They often hang upside down while foraging on slender branches.

While most birds have powerful muscles to close their bills to grasp or crush prey, blackbirds have strong muscles to open their bills against the resistance of wood, soil, rocks or other objects to explore for prey.   So, their muscles for lowering the lower bill are very large and strong.   Additionally, their eyes are situated in their head so as to focus directly into the space created by the open bill to see the prey they have just exposed. The eyes can sight along the bill which is shaped to preserve a direct line of sight from the eyes to the bill tip. The sight axis of both eyes runs parallel to the lower edge of the upper mandible giving them a characteristic "angry" appearance when viewed head on. Blackbirds have such a predeliction to gape that in captivity they seem unable to stop, gaping in situations which make no sense.

Blackbird Social Systems

Three main types of blackbird social systems are represented in the sanctuary. Blackbirds may form monogamous pairs or be polygynous whereby one male breeds with more than one female. In monogamous species such as the yellow billed cacique, meadowlarks, and the melodious blackbird, males and females have similar duties and thus look alike both in size and color. It should be noted however, that in all blackbirds, only the female incubates the eggs and almost always it is the female who builds the nest. In the melodious blackbird, however, the male does feed the female while she incubates the eggs. These males also help in nest building. Monogamous blackbirds jointly defend a territory to keep others of their species out of the area. This gives the pair a secure nesting and feeding area to rear young in. Melodious blackbirds again are extreme examples of both sexes doing similar jobs. They sing duets together to proclaim territory ownership. They sing while sitting within a foot of each other, directing the song at neighboring pairs or wandering individuals. Since males and females have different parts in the duet, birds who have lost their mates will remain on their territory singing their part of the duet. This helps them advertise for another mate.

A second type of sociality which is typified by redwings and boat-tailed grackles, is polygyny where one male establishes a large territory in which a number of females breed and nest. Size and colors are different in the sexes because in this case their duties differ. The redwing male is continually busy defending his territory against other males using song and the flashing of his epaulet (shoulder) patches, and attracting additional females. In contrast to the monogamous males, polygynous males rarely feed their young, leaving most of the rearing duties to the females.

Montezuma oropendulas have a polygynous social system but they are colonial. You may see groups of pendulous nests hanging from the branches of a tree, with a male singing and giving its active bowing display at the nesting site. Here again sexual dimorphism occurs and the females do most of the caring for the young.

Nestbuilding is very complex in many blackbirds such as orioles or oropendulas. Other members of the family, however, such as cowbirds are brood parasites who have lost the ability and the need to build nests or care for the young. Cowbirds lay their eggs in other bird's nests (called the host's nest) who never detect the strange eggs and raise the chicks as though they were their own brood.

The nest of blackbirds, although built in varied areas and in a variety of situations, use very similar materials and

Montezuma Oropendula Nests

always look similar in structure. Although first time breeders take more time to build a nest and need practice to build a good nest, eventually they build nests similar to those of their species. A Montezuma oropendula was observed extracting strips from a large banana leaf while standing on its midrib, pecking its underside to separate fibers. These were ripped off in 2 ft (0.7 m) strips. Orioles and oropendulas first construct a loop or ring of fibers from which the nest hangs. This is the most difficult part of the nest building. Most of the weaving is done while upside down and with the bill. Once a cup is formed then the combined movement of bill and feet are used to manipulate the materials. Oropendulas hold leaves down with their feet and shred them with their bill to produce fine materials to line the nest.

Nests serve for the protection of the eggs and young. Orioles' nests vary with latitude such that southern nests are more loosely woven to allow for air circulation. The meadowlark's nest, which is built on the ground, has a dome to protect it from the sight of predators. Most blackbird nests are hung in one way or another. Oriole and oropendula nests are often hung on outer branches away from predators and sometimes overhang water.

GOING - GOING - - GONE......
GAME BIRDS OF BELIZE

*T*wo families of birds which were once found throughout the rain forests of Belize are now becoming rapidly extinct from much of their former range. They are members of a group or order of chicken-like birds (Galliformes) which includes pheasants, chickens, grouse, and guinea fowl. They are the turkey family (Meleagridae) and the Cracidae, a family of chicken-like birds which includes the chachalacas (coc-re-co in Creole), guans, and curassows. Both families are specifically confined to the Americas. The ocellated turkey has the most limited range, similar to that of the black howler monkey. It once occurred around the Community Baboon Sanctuary areas and as far east as Burrell Boom.

While the curassow family has 38 species of chachalacas, guans, and curassows, most are found in South America and are in danger of extinction due to their dependence on the tropical rain forest. Of all the chicken-like birds, the cracids are most arboreal and thus doubly dependent on the forest. Only 3 species of cracids are found in Belize, the plain chachalaca (*Ortalis vetula*), the crested guan (*Penelope purpurascens*) and the great curassow (*Crax rubra*).

Despite the greater geographic ranges of the cracids, only the plain chachalaca or coc-re-co (named for its call) still reside in the Community Baboon Sanctuary. All these game bird populations have been pressured by over hunting and the destruction of the forest. Only the chachalacas have been able to withstand hunting pressure throughout Central America. Of all the magnificent and interesting game birds of Belize, only the ocellated turkey is protected by law. If more protection and better conservation is not practiced, all will soon be gone from Belize.

Geographic Range of the Crested Guan

Plain Chachalaca

Of all Belizean game bird species, the chachalacas are doing the best since they inhabit the vegetation of tangled thickets, secondary growth in abandoned fields, and forest edges. Although hunted in other areas, the plain chachalaca is common in the Community Baboon Sanctuary and is not hunted. Additionally, the many abandoned agricultural clearings in the sanctuary probably provide favorable habitat for the species. However, in other areas with more intense land use and increased mechanized agriculture, the chachalaca will soon disappear if nothing is done for it.

Plain chachalacas are small brown chicken-like birds which are social in all seasons. They live in flocks of 6 to 12 which fly in straggling fashion one after the other. As with most cracids, they are not strong fliers and usually glide from high areas with a few flaps. They move upward through the forest canopy by short flights from branch to branch. In general, all cracids are mainly vegetarians, feeding on seeds and fruits with a large amount of foliage in the diet. *Cecropia* fruits are a favorite food. Chachalacas forage on fruits directly in the treetops rather than scratching the forest floor like chickens.

Geographic Range of the Plain Chachalaca

The call of the chachalaca is where it gets its common name which sounds like "cha-cha-lac" which it repeats in loud raucus group calls mainly in early morning and sometimes at dusk.   The Creole name, "coc-re-co", is similarly based on its call.   As with other cracids, the loud call sound is amplified by an elongated trachea, which loops back between the skin and body before entering the thorax.   This same anatomical trait is even more exaggerated in the great curassow.

The chachalaca nests mainly in the dryer, first half of the year in low (3-8 ft, 1-2 m) bushes or small trees. It builds its nest as a shallow saucer of coarse dead branch materials. The female lays 3-6 eggs which are dull white and like other cracids have rough pitted shells.   The eggs hatch in 24-27 days.   As in other chicken-like birds, the chicks are precocial and are ready to move out of the nest within the first day. Although unable to fly they leave the nest and are led away on the ground by the female who raises them.   However, once they are able, she will take them to rejoin her flock.   The young chicks within a few days can hop and flit through low branches and vines.

The Great Curassow

The great curassow (*Crax rubra*) is the largest of all cracids. Its name comes from the Caribbean island of Curacao although the species resides only on the mainlands of Central and South America in low or medium elevation tropical rain forest. The male is black with a green glossy sheen to his feathers. He has white below which becomes visible during flight and displays. As with other curassows, he has a characteristic species bill structure called a "caruncle" which is a bright yellow knob on the forehead. He also displays a double-row crest of short, stiff, forward curling feathers. The female and juveniles are protectively colored in brown with black barring and a white and black crest.

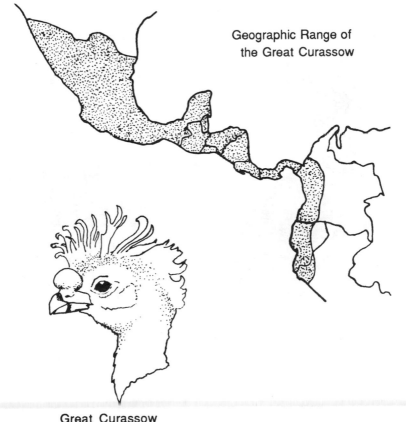

Geographic Range of
the Great Curassow

Great Curassow

Due to its large size which may reach 10 1/2 lbs (4.8 kg), great curassows are the most terrestrial of their group, feeding on fallen fruits, seeds, and insects, often scratching on the ground floor like a chicken.   They do however, nest in trees, sometimes as high as 30 ft (9 m) where they lay two pitted white eggs in a small coarse nest.   The chicks are quite precocial, climbing into branches within the first day and flying short distance at 4 or 5 days.

In contrast to the chachalaca, the species is monogamous with the male remaining with the family for its protection.   Males take up territories in the treetops emitting low pitched songs which carry long distances within the forest due to the long recurved trachea.   Once attracted, the male

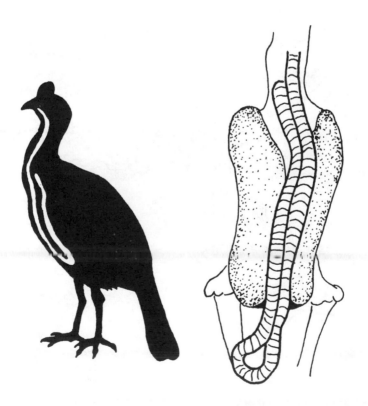

Position and Structure of the Extended Trachea Used in Calling

courts the female by strutting like other fowl with its tail raised and head high, its breast tilted low toward the ground, and wings drooped to display the white feathers underneath. The male may build a nest of twigs lined by green leaves which are replaced when they dry out. The female incubates the eggs in the nest for about a month.

Although they have predatory enemies like jaguars and other cats, humans are the most serious threat to their survival as a species. Once found in the Community Baboon Sanctuary, they have been hunted from the area and most parts of their range. They are sensitive to destruction of the rain forest as well. They still are found, however, in the Hill Bank and Gallon Jug areas. When Spaniards first came to the new world they saw Indians rearing curassows and thought they could be easily domesticated. However, many species of curassows do not breed well in captivity although the great curassow breeds regularly in zoos. Even so, they lay so few eggs per year that the captive population is still small.

Ocellated Turkey

There are only two species of wild turkey in the world. Both reside in the Americas. The American wild turkey ranges throughout the southeastern U.S. and northeastern Mexico. It is the ancestor of the domesticated turkey which was domesticated by the Aztecs long before white men came to the Americas. The second species, the ocellated turkey, does not do well in captivity and thus was never domesticated. It has a more restricted range and is endemic to the Yucatan Peninsula lowlands and is specifically found in tropical rain forest. Thus it is found only in the same limited region as the black howler and hickatee river turtle in the lowland forested areas of Belize, southern Mexico and northern Guatemala. Its numbers are rapidly declining due to cutting of the forest and hunting pressures. In Belize no hunting of turkeys is allowed. At one point in the late 1800's, ocellated turkeys were found in Burrell Boom and so must have thrived in the Community Baboon Sanctuary as well.

Geographic Range of the Two Turkey Species

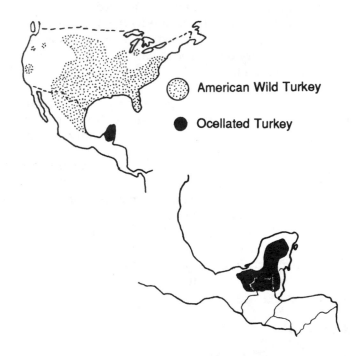

American Wild Turkey

Ocellated Turkey

The ocellated turkey, so named for the eye-like spots or ocelli on its tail similar to those of a peacock, is smaller than its northern relative. Males weigh about 11 lbs (5 kg) and females about 6 lbs (2.7 kg). Besides the colorful ocelli, the ocellated turkey differs from the wild turkey in having a blue head and neck with coral-red, warty caruncles on the head. It has bright copper bronze plumage, red legs, and a reddish green beak. Males have the typical galliform spurs which they use in fighting.

The species inhabits open forests as well as abandoned milpas and forest edges where it feeds on vegetation, including seeds, fruits, grasses and tender shoots as well as insects. The turkeys feed by stripping seeds off grass stalks and picking at flowers and exposed fruits. They show typical scratching for food in forested areas covered by dry leaves. Feeding occurs from 6 to10 in the morning in clearings. Flocks move to the shade of the forest during the heat of the day to preen and rest.

Later, they return to the clearing to feed again.   Their main habitat is tall or medium-height limestone forests of figs, gumbolimbo, mahogany, ramon, and chicle trees.

They flock in large groups of 10 or 11 individuals during the fall and winter with yearling males joining the flock at this time.   They roost in trees in the late afternoon on horizontal branches (often in *Cecropia* trees) about 15-35 ft (5-11 m) off the ground.   Roosts are often at clearing edges and may change nightly.   Gradually the flock size decreases to smaller breeding flocks as the males begin to display and gobble intensely, attracting small groups of females and yearling males.   At this time the males are only social in the early morning display periods.   Eventually the flocks become even smaller as females leave to begin egg laying.

Males breed at 2-3 years of age showing a courtship display similar to the domestic turkey.   He begins by lowering his head and tail feathers horizontal to the ground and wagging his partially spread tail.   He then raises his head and elevates and spreads his tail, displaying the blue-green ocellae to attract the hens.   With his head and neck held pressed back against his body feathers, the wings are drooped, touching the ground on which they are rattled similar to the domestic turkey.   The wing away from the female is vibrated while the male circles the females keeping them in a tight group.   He may reinforce the display by incorporating gobbling into it.   Sometimes the male may crouch like a soliciting female which seems to attract the hens.   He then gets up to strut and gobble.

Gobbling occurs during March and April when breeding occurs.   Cocks gobble on the ground or from tree roosts most often from 6 to 11 in the morning and again before dusk.   One to three males may gobble in a breeding flock but the dominant gobbles more and will be the main breeder.   The female solicits by squatting on the ground with her head and neck at a 45 degree angle to the ground.   The male then mounts and copulation occurs.

Nesting follows in April- May but may occur as late as July.   Nests are built as small depressions on the ground in

Courtship Strutting of the American and Ocellated Turkey

Gobbling of the American and Ocellated Turkey

which a female lays and incubates 8-15 buff colored eggs.   The precocial chicks hatch in 28 days and follow the female from the nest after hatching.   They can make short flights by two weeks at which time they may join the roosts.   Despite the large number of eggs, chick mortality is very high.

LIMPING BIRD

*A*n occasional visitor to the Community Baboon Sanctuary, the limpkin (*Aramus guarauna*), gets its name from its strange, long-legged limping gait. It walks by lifting its long toes high over matted swamp vegetation. Although they can swim they mainly walk and rarely fly except to roost in trees at night. The species is the sole member of an ancient family of birds (Aramidae) which has a fossil record going back to the Eocene period, 54 million years ago. They are relatives of and the link between rails and cranes. The colorful top-notch-chick or gray-necked wood rail is a common bird in the Community Baboon Sanctuary. Cranes however occur mostly in Asia and Africa. Two species, including the endangered whooping crane and sandhill crane, occur in North America but Cuba is the closest cranes come to Belize.

The two foot (0.6 m) tall limpkin occurs in freshwater marshes and swamps from the southern U.S. through Central and South America including some Caribbean islands. It was hunted almost to extinction in the U.S. and with widespread filling in of wetlands it is only found in a few wetland parks in Florida. Only small numbers are found in Central and South America.

It has also been called the crying bird, wailing bird or widow bird in reference to its loud, eerie wailing calls given mainly at night. They have a three syllabled call described as sad shrieks or wails and it is reminiscent of crane calls. In Belize it is called clucking hen.

Limpkins forage by wading in the shallow water of swamps and marshes feeding mainly on the large apple snail of the genus *Pomacea*, similar to the endangered snail kite. Both species are common in the Crooked Tree Wildlife Sanctuary. However, the limpkin can probe for prey in the mud with its long, sensitive decurved bill. Limpkins also supplement their diet with other molluscs such as freshwater mussels, worms, crayfish, and occasionally amphibians and reptiles.   Most limpkin feeding grounds, however, are littered with small piles of snail shells.

It captures the snails by probing for them in the mud and then carries them off to land or shallow water, holding the snail by its shell flange.   It eats the snail without breaking the shell. It lodges the snail in a crevice or branch fork with the shell opening pointed outwards.   It waits for the snail to relax and move out of its shell then it quickly grabs or spears the snail with its bill and with a quick head jerk pulls and detaches it from its shell.   It holds the denuded snail a minute or two before swallowing it.

The species form pair bonds during breeding and build a nest of reeds, sticks and other plant materials.   It is a bulky and flimsy nest platform lodged in either tangled vines, grass clumps, bushes or trees. Nests are usually 5-8 ft (1.5-2.5 m) high but may be as high as 17 ft (5.3 m) above the ground and usually located near or over the water.   The female lays a clutch of 4-8 pale green, brown-spotted eggs. Both sexes incubate the eggs.   The brownish-black chick resembles a rail chick and can swim and run almost immediately after hatching.   It leaves the nest on the first day after hatching but is guarded and fed by the parents for a long period.

TOUCANS

Of the 37 species of brightly colored toucans (Family: Ramphastidae) which are found exclusively in the neotropics, three species occur in Belize : 1) keel billed toucan (*Ramphastos sulfuratus*), 2) collared aracari (*Pteroglossus torquatus*), 3) emerald toucanet (*Aulacorhynchus prasinus*). The center of species abundance is in the Amazonian region of South America, and this is where toucans were thought to have evolved from some generalized woodpecker-like ancestor. Both the keel-billed toucan and collared aracari are common in lowland tropical forests such as in the Community Baboon Sanctuary. The toucanet is found in higher elevation forests.

Billbird: Keel-Billed Toucan

Related to woodpeckers, toucans share similar foot anatomy with both having two toes facing forward and two facing backward. Toucans are most notable for their extraordinary bill which is almost as long as the body.   It is very light, being filled largely with air and an inner network of delicate supporting bony fibers for strength. The thin outer shell adds to the bill's strength.

Although its functions are not fully known, the bill is important in feeding. Fruit eaters, toucans effectively use their bill tips to pluck fruits from small canopy branches. These are then raised in the tip of the bill, tossed back toward the throat and swallowed. Chunks of larger fruits are bitten off with the serrated bill and may even be held beneath the foot. The toucan's long tongue is fringed on both sides with bristles.

Toucan Feeding By Tossing Fruits Back Into The Throat

The bill is also used in social fencing and aggressive clashes. They may also toss or pass food from bill to bill . The males have been noted to feed fruit to females perhaps as part of a courtship ritual. The two sexes will also preen each other probably aiding in the formation of a pair bond. The bond is further strengthened by the males who defend fruit trees from other frugivores, allowing only his mate access to the fruits. These social uses of the bill along with the species specific coloration suggest a possible social function of the bill in courtship and/or species recognition.

Toucans have a curious ability to fold their tail up straight against their backs. This is thought to be an adaptation for sleeping in tree cavities. In sleeping, it turns back the bill and lays it along the back. It then brings the tail up until it covers the bill and fluffs its feathers until it resembles a round feathered ball. This peculiar action is found In other hole nesters like hornbills and kingfishers. They are

Collared Aracaris Bill Fencing

able to do this owing to the special articulation of the tail bone allowing rapid flipping of the tail against the back.

Toucans seldom fly for long distances. Their short rounded wings produce a characteristic flight pattern: a series of 8-10 wingbeats ending in an upthrust, followed by a short glide with stiffened wings. They fly in small flocks of less than a dozen birds which move in a loose flight pattern, one toucan following the next at intervals.

Toucans nest in cavities, laying 1-4 white eggs, but they are unable to do more than enlarge existing holes where the wood is rotten. They may line the nests with fresh leaves. Both sexes incubate these eggs and brood and feed the chicks.

Bill Bird - National Bird of Belize

This brightly colored bird with a brilliantly colored bill has been chosen as the national bird of Belize and is often seen as a symbol of the new world tropics. It is a large,

17-22 in (43-56 cm) long bird. Even without its multicolored bill and pale green bare skin surrounding its dark eye, its mixtures of white, yellow, red, and black give it a spectacular appearance. Males are a bit larger than females including the bill. The rainbow-billed or keel-billed toucan inhabits lowland humid forests, ranging from southern Mexico through Central America to northern South America. In Central America, it occurs mainly on the wetter Caribbean side and is mainly confined to lower altitudes below 2,000 ft (625 m) above sea level but has been recorded up to 4,000 ft (1250 m) in Costa Rica and to 5,000 ft (1560 m) in Columbia. Although primarily a resident of the forests, they may venture from the forests into milpas, pastures, and second growth forests. They are not a common bird in the Community Baboon Sanctuary.

They travel in small flocks of up to 12 members. They move in a straggling single file, one behind the other, in an alternation of wing beats and gliding undulating flight. They are among the most frugivorous of birds in the Central American forests eating trumpet tree spikes and figs among other fruits in the Community Baboon Sanctuary. They supplement this diet with insects, small lizards, snakes, other bird species eggs and nestlings.

They are non-melodius vocalists and have a limited vocabulary. They give low harsh croaks and may also make castanet like rattles using their vocal chords, not their bills as is often thought. When calling, they throw their heads and bills up and down and side to side, bowing and turning.

Bill birds nest during the dry season; one was noted to hatch in early April. The birds take possession of the nesting site 4-6 weeks before laying. They nest in tree cavities resulting from decayed wood. Usually the opening is quite small, just large enough for the toucan to squeeze into. The cavity must have sufficient depth so that the young will be inaccessible to the probing heads or forearms of predators such as small cats, tayras, coatis, and raccoons. Since toucans cannot peck their own hole, they are dependent on ready made holes in large trees, a scarcity which may limit the population of this large species of toucan. Nests range in height from 9 to 90 ft (3-28 m) above ground. The cavity may be lined with regurgitated seeds rather than any soft lining, on which rest 1-4 dull white eggs pitted with length-wise grooves.

Both parents incubate the eggs, spending collectively 70% of the time in attendance for sessions of 20 minutes to almost two hours. The incoming parent, alights high above the nest, calls, then moves down near the nest entrance. From that point it looks around alternately, putting its beak through the nest hole. In nest changeovers, the incubating parent leaves before the other enters and the two parents don't share the cavity together with the eggs.

The newly hatched young resemble newly hatched woodpeckers, pink and naked with eyes closed. The lower bill is slightly longer than the upper. The heel joint has projections which fits over the nest substrate seemingly to grip it. The young are slow in developing, showing a feathered appearance by 5 weeks and fledging at 7-8 weeks. Both parents alternately brood the young nestlings but only one stays in the nest at night with them.

Collared Aracari

This small, slender, very social species is commonly found in the Community Baboon Samctuary. Although showing similar colors to the bill bird it is not as brilliant. Its bill is more slender showing a hooked tip and coarse serrations along its edge.

The collared aracari inhabits both rainforests and less dense, drier seasonal woodlands having the same range as the bill bird, from southern Mexico, through Central America to northern South America. It is more confined to the lowlands. It is a gregarious species, living in flocks of up to six which move through the treetops in the typical toucan straggling social flight. During the non-breeding season, it roosts communally in tree holes sometimes in groups of as many as six.

The same roosting cavity may become a nesting cavity when the female takes over possession of it for egg laying. Females lay 2-3 eggs during the dry season in late March.

With hatching, communal use of the cavity is resumed and all bring food to the nestlings and may brood them as well. They also remove waste from the nest. These nest helpers are probably offspring from previous years. They are wary in approaching the nest, usually carrying insects for the young which are replaced with small fruits when the young are a month old. Some of the food is regurgitated for the chicks. When older, feeding occurs through the nest hole instead of inside the nest. Fledging occurs at about 6-7 weeks of age.

Aracaris appear to play by striking their bills against tree trunks. Playing pairs will also strike their bills together while facing each other as though fencing. Then they grasp mandibles and push until one falls below the limb. Others then may challenge the victor. The aracari's voice differs from the keel-billed toucan, being thin and high-pitched. It gives short, high-pitched barks, swinging the head side to side.

Adults feed mainly on small fruits which they pluck with their slender bill tips, transferring the food to the throat with an upward jerk of the head. They will also feed on insects and small invertebrates, especially when they are feeding nestlings. They also may occasionally feed the nestlings with other bird species nestlings.

MANAKINS - SNAP CRACKLE POP
by Jevra Brown

If you walk far into the forest during the right season (April-August) you may hear loud snaps (similar to popcorn popping), grunts, rolled snaps, and whistles. If you follow these sounds you will discover that they are made by small birds only 5 1/2 in (14 cm) long. These sounds are actually an important portion of the mating display of the male white-collared manakin. Adult male manakins are easily seen because of the conspicuous feathers around their neck. Females and immature males look alike, being olive- green with yellow abdomens, and are much quieter than the males. Both sexes have strong, brightly colored orange legs that are a distinguishing characteristic of the species.

Manakins belong to the bird family Pipridae. This family is only found in the new world tropics. Almost every member of this family participates in an unusual mating system called a "lek". People from North America will be most familiar with the leks of the Prairie Chicken and Sage Grouse. When mating season approaches, the males begin to defend a very small territory called a "court" that will be used to attract a female to the male so that he may mate with her. The male usually performs a display on his court to advertise his presence and encourage a female to approach. Often males of lekking species will clump their courts close together. A clump of courts is also called a "lek" or an "arena". This clumped distribution is thought to send a stronger signal to females who may be in the area.

Although lekking is an unusual mating ritual among animal species in general, it is used by a few species of all the vertebrate groups, and even by some insects. Lek systems are probably unusual for two reasons. First, the males spend all of their energy during the mating season in defending their territories and displaying for females, leaving the females to raise the young all by themselves. This is far too big a job in most environments for one parent to accomplish alone. Second, it is known that in lek systems, a few males will get a disproportionate number of the matings. In a single breeding season, one male may sire up to 95% of all the offspring of that season, while other males will not have any offspring. Researchers working with lekking species often question how such a mating system can be maintained and how it evolved.

Near the end of the winter wet season, male white-collared manakins begin to prepare their courts for the upcoming breeding season, though some maintenance may have been done throughout the months since the last breeding season. The male makes a court by clearing a circle, about 3 ft (1 m) in diameter on the forest floor. All the leaf litter is removed from this circle and it is typically surrounded by small saplings whose lower leaves are either absent or are removed by the male. The male defends an area about 16 ft (5 m) in diameter around his court. Throughout the day, most males only rarely leave the area around their court. They spend a great deal of time resting and advertising their location with rolled snaps and whistles.

White-collared manakins are known locally as the "machine bird" because of the many machine-like sounds they make in association with their mating display. The popcorn-like snapping, rolled snaps, grunts and the whirring during flight, are not produced with the vocal apparatus, but by movements of the wing feathers. Sounds produced in these and similar ways are referred to as "mechanical sounds". Snaps and rolled snaps are made using the secondary flight feathers, the long feathers that run the length of the wing. The whirring sound heard when the birds fly is called "wing noise" and is made by wind passing between the primary feathers at the tip of the wing. Both the primary and the secondary feathers are specialized to make these sounds. Human observers usually realize a female is present at the lek before they see her because of the increase in the number of these sounds and of the display behavior exhibited by the males.

When a female flys into the area or when other males can be heard displaying, the male will fly onto his court and begin his display. He will make acrobatic jumps from sapling to sapling around his court using his strong legs. In mid-jump the male will usually make a loud, abrupt "snap" with his wings. Sometimes the male will jump to the ground and remove a leaf which has fallen into the court, leaving his court or he may jump back onto a sapling making a low "grunt" sound with his wings. If the male is lucky, a female may join in this dance around the court. She will also jump between the saplings, sometimes leading and sometimes following the male. After a short time she will either mate with the male or leave his court.

Sometimes males can be seen interacting with other males. Usually these interactions are between two neighbors at the lek and take place at the boundary between their territories. These male interactions are often initiated by one male flying toward or into the territory of another male. The second male will then approach the first and the two will stay close together, often on the same branch within a foot (0.3 m) of each other. The males will make very small jumps sideways, toward or away from each other. They extend their chin feathers so they resemble a beard and move their heads from side to side as if shaking their heads "no". They may fly to other branches or "leapfrog" over each other. When the argument is particularly intense, the males will chase each other all around the lek or even grab one another with their feet in mid-air and fall to the ground, but this is rare.

Sometimes these interactions may revolve around an unoccupied court and may include many males, all competing for ownership of the court. Court ownership is not a random process. Males spend much energy maintaining and defending their courts. How courts are acquired and held varies with the species, but in general, young males need to acquire courts before they can attract females. Males can certainly make their own courts but it appears that not all courts are created equal, and the display takes much practice to perfect. The location of the court within the lek and the precision of the display performance may have a great influence on the male's ability to successfully attract a mate. It may be five or more years before they get their first mate.

Male-Male Interaction

Male Displaying on Court

THE HICKATEE (*Dermatemys mawii*)

by Robert Horwich and John Polisar

*T*he hickatee, tortuga blanca, or Central American river turtle (*Dermatemys mawii*) is the lone survivor of an ancient family of turtles which originated in Asia and was once widespread throughout the world. The hickatee is most closely related to mud turtles of the family Kinosternidae.

The hickatee is recognized by a primitive characteristic, a row of 3 to 6 (usually 4) shell plates between the upper (carapace) and lower (plastron) shells. The shell is smooth, large and flattened without keels in adults and may become flared at its rear in adults. The carapace is black, brown or dark olive with a cream colored undershell. The young have a keeled shell with serrated edges. The shell scales are thin and tender and easily subject to abrasion. This is further evidence of the animal's aquatic lifestyle.

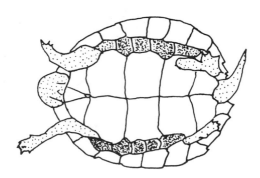

Underside of Hickatee Showing Primitive Shell Plates
(dark stippling)

Tortuga blanca, the name used in Veracruz, Mexico may refer to the meat color or the color of the lower shell. The Creole name, hickatee, comes from the Spanish "jicotea" which is a common name for many different turtle species within Latin America.

Range

Today, this remnant species has a limited range similar to the black howler monkey, in the Atlantic coastal lowlands of Belize, northern Guatemala, and southern Mexico. It is absent from most of the Yucatan Peninsula proper. It may also occur in northwestern Honduras. It lives primarily in larger, deeper, lowland rivers, their larger tributaries, and

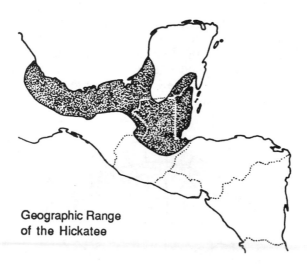

Geographic Range
of the Hickatee

the large freshwater lagoons which are found mostly in northern and central Belize. It also occurs in at least two river systems of extreme southeastern Belize but they are not found in the high gradient streams which drain the Maya Mountains. Hickatee are found in the Belize River from its mouth to San Ignacio. They are also found in the deeper sections of Mussel

Creek (Botlass Creek, Cooks Lagoon, Cox Lagoon, and Mucklehany), Spanish Creek, and Southern Lagoon. All major tributaries to the Belize River (Black Creek, Labouring Creek, and Freshwater Creek) harbor some hickatee. Because the turtle rarely rises to the surface, it is rare that a visitor will glimpse one.

**Geographic Range
of the Hickatee
in Belize**

Natural History

With its webbed feet, the hickatee is well equipped for its almost completely aquatic lifestyle. Hickatee do not even bask on logs but rather rest on the bottom, only rising to the surface of the river for air. They can spend long periods underwater by taking in dissolved oxygen from the water through their nasopharyngeal lining, a portion of the pharynx directly behind the nasal cavity. Submerged turtles continually suck in water through the mouth and expel it from the nostrils. Feeding occurs mainly at night in inland waters and may be correlated with incoming tides in areas with tidal influence. Hickatee are totally herbivorous, feeding on leaves and fruit which drop into the water, as well as aquatic plants. The young may take small amounts of animal matter in their diet. The aquatic grass *Paspalum peniculatum*, which forms beds in shallows, is an important food. Hickatee may move into these beds soon after dark and graze throughout the night. Turtles from the Rio Grande estuary population in southern Belize fed on three species of mangrove leaves.

Foods of the river animals appear to be broadleaved riparian tree leaves, seed pods, fruits, and bankside grasses. Figs are eaten as they fall into the water. In some lagoons, hickatee rely heavily on submergent and emergent aquatic vegetation. The turtles are usually nocturnal in activity, spending the day hiding on the bottom. Rising water levels seem to stimulate foraging activity regardless of the hour.

Reproductive Biology

Mature males have long tails which extend beyond the carapacial rim (edge of the shell). Females have smaller tails that barely reach the rim. In males the dorsal head surface is yellow-ochre through bright orange to reddish-brown depending on the water body in which they live. The coloration extends to spotting of the same color on the sides of the head. Females and juveniles have an olive gray head, although females may show obscure spotting.

Old accounts report a maximum size of 24 in (60 cm) carapace shell length and 48 lbs (22 kg) in body weight. Animals caught locally in recent times are generally smaller (maximum of 19 in [48cm] carapace length and 35 lbs [16kg]). Evidence suggests that this discrepancy is due to harvesting the older, larger animals. Size at maturity varies somewhat among populations. Belize River turtles mature at somewhat smaller sizes, 1.4-1.5 in (350-375 mm) for males, 1.6 in (400-405 mm) for females. In lagoons, mature sizes are 1.4-1.5 in (365-390 mm) for males and 1.65 in (420-425 mm) for females. Maximum female size always exceeds male size.

The breeding season seems to be in April through June. The females then visit land only for the purpose of laying eggs during the rainy season from September through mid-December, with a peak in October-November. Females may have double clutches within this period, nesting in September and again in November, with the ovarian follicles regressing after December. During flooding, the females are carried to flooded areas where they then lay 6-17 eggs on the river edge and cover them over with about 4 in (10 cm) of soil or vegetable matter. The Belize River is subject to dramatic oscillations in water level during the rainy season due to a vast watershed and rapid runoff. Smaller river systems have dampened and less extreme and less recurrent oscillations. Egg laying roughly coincides with peak water levels. For the last 7-8 years the greatest water flow has occurred in October. Thus many nests in the Belize River experience repeated floodings. This flooding could even happen as late as January.

Female hickatee lay in a variety of places, ranging from densely covered to exposed riverbanks. The laying season is still unclear. Most probably laying is between October and December, tapering off in January. However, a few females have been found with eggs during the dry season. Besides being hunted by humans and crocodiles, the eggs and juvenile turtles are eaten by racoons, coati mundis, otters, and some birds including the clapper rail, gray-necked wood rail, limpkin, and both black-crowned and yellow-crowned night herons.

An Exploited Endangered Species

The hickatee is an endangered species because it is widely hunted for its meat throughout most of its range. It has been listed by CITES as Appendix II (CITES 1984) and as endangered under the provisions of the Endangered Species Code (Code of U.S. Federal Regulations 1987). Although the species is still thriving in the unpopulated regions of Belize, in habitable regions where it is hunted, it is disappearing fast. Although once plentiful in western Belize, it is now only rarely found in the Macal River or the upper Belize River. There are indications that the number of hickatee are declining in the Community Baboon Sanctuary waters as well. Captures in the severely exploited Belize River are more skewed toward immature animals than captures in less intensely exploited areas. In Mexico, there is a grave possibility of it being hunted to extinction. Because of its economic importance, its limited range, and its unique biological significance, the Community Baboon Sanctuary has targeted it, as well as the baboon, as an important species for study and management. Its limited range makes it another important wildlife heritage of Belize.

Most of the hunters in the Community Baboon Sanctuary, on the Belize River, strike the turtles with a long harpoon (peg) as they float on the river surface. The peg is a 12- 14 ft (3-4 m) long, narrow cylindrical wood staff with a detachable barbed tip 3-4 in (8-10 cm) long which is attached to the staff by a strong thin cord. Hunters strike animals two different times, during the heat of the day in large eddies when turtles come to breath or blow, and at night along the shore as the turtles feed. At night, hunters have a shotgun, fish harpoon, peg for hickatee, and a head lamp to hunt along the riverbanks. They go out "progging" which is a term for the lifestyle of one who hunts and fishes.

Some hunters capture large numbers of hickatee in a short period by diving and capturing them in the dry season. The Belize River fluctuates from about 3-25 ft (1-8 m) in depth but some eddies get to as much as 65 ft (20 m) during the high water. During the dry season the turtles congregate in deeper river pools. The shallower, clear water makes it easier to capture the hickatee.

For river diving, hunters use mask and fins and grab at the front and rear of the shell and turn the turtle upside down, bringing it up to the surface. Hunters may also put nets across the river and drive the animals into the nets. This is very efficient, but it has alarmed some locals that it might eradicate the resource. Short inshore nets can also be placed in short calm stretches of rivers and baited with fig leaves and thus function like a trap. Nets are successful in moderate and low water levels. In the past, dynamiting has been used but resulted in overkill and major habitat destruction.

Hickatee are marketed locally for special occasions, or in Belize City. Consumption peaks during the dry season around Easter. Some hickatee caught in the Rio Grande River are marketed in Punta Gorda. Recent Belize City market surveys in 1989-90 when compared to similar surveys in 1983-4 show a major decrease in the availability of the species for sale. In 1990, hickatee were priced at about $10Bz per 10 lbs.

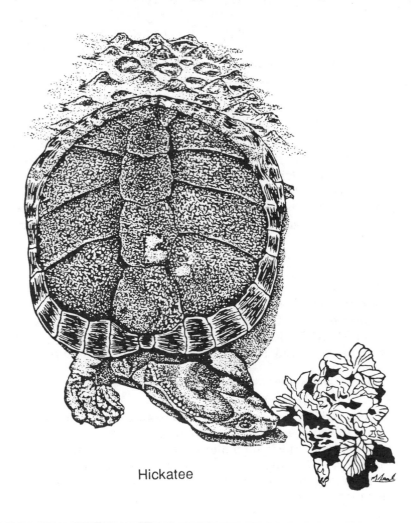

Hickatee

CROCODILES OF BELIZE

*T*here are 2 crocodile species in Belize, the American crocodile (*Crocodylus acutus*) which occurs mainly in coastal areas and Morelet's crocodile (*Crocodylus moreleti*) which is found within inland water bodies. The latter is found in areas in the Community Baboon Sanctuary and is especially abundant in nearby Mussel Creek. Although the two species of crocodilians in Belize are technically in the crocodile family, the Creole name for both is "alligator". It is interesting to note the derivation of the common names as they have been derived from two diverse cultures. The name crocodile was first used 2,000 years ago by Greek travelers in Egypt. The huge crocodiles reminded them of a tiny Greek lizard called "krokodeilos". Similarly when Spaniards saw alligators in Florida they called them "el lagarto" meaning lizard. English sailors who followed, adopted the Spanish name but ran it together and corrupted it into its present form.

Despite their armor which protects them from most predators, all crocodilians are threatened with extinction. Hunting of their skins for luxury leathers and development of their habitat have made humans responsible for their precarious state. CITES (Convention on International Trade in Endangered Species of Wild Flora and Fauna) now bans the trade in skins of most crocodilians including the two Belizean species.

The Order Crocodylia includes 3 families of the largest reptiles living today. They are a living vestige of a group of reptiles , called archosaurs or the "ruling reptiles" of the Mesozoic era 225-65 million years ago, which included the dinosaurs and flying reptiles. They were the most advanced and intelligent reptiles but they died out. Crocodilians survived but their ancestors, including a 50 ft (15m) long crocodile, became extinct.

The three living families include crocodiles

(Crocodilidae- 14 species), alligators (Alligatoridae- 7 species), and Gavials (Gharialidae- 1 species). They all have the characteristic lizard-like shape with a thick leathery skin covered with large rectangular partially ossified horny plates on the back, called osteoderms, which protect them like shields. They live in the subtropical and tropical warm areas throughout the world. Most species live in freshwater areas although a few species do make use of saltwater. They show their relation to two-legged ancestors by having longer hind legs which they slant forward when they stand.

Their most characteristic crocodilian features, however, are internal. Despite their ancient history they are the most advanced living reptiles having an enlarged brain and cerebral cortex indicating their increased ability to learn. Additionally, they have a 4 chambered heart whose ventricles are completely divided so there is no mixture of the arterial and venal blood within the heart. Therefore more oxygenated blood gets to their enlarged brain.

Views of Alligator and Crocodile Heads Showing Differences: Crocodile (top), Alligator (bottom)

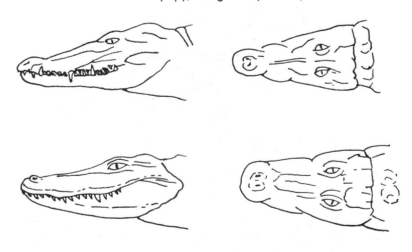

Crocodiles can be distinguished from alligators by the shape of the head and the dentition (arrangement, type and number of teeth). Crocodiles have longer and narrower heads than alligators. Alligator upper teeth are arranged to close over the lower teeth so that when the mouth is closed only the upper teeth show in the "crocodile smile". All teeth show in crocodiles since the upper and lower teeth are arranged in a line. Additionally, the fourth tooth of the lower jaw of both groups is larger than other teeth. In alligators it fits into a laterally closed pit in the upper jaw. In crocodiles it lays in a notch of the upper jaw and is visible when the mouth is closed. There is only one species of gavial from India, which has a long narrow skull with small, even teeth used for eating fish.

Geographic Range

Although the American crocodile has an extensive range from southern Florida, throughout Central America into

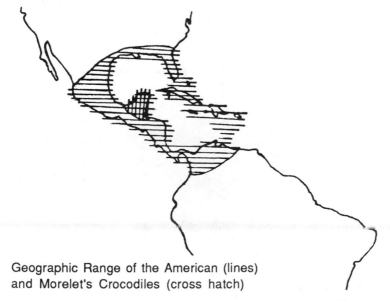

Geographic Range of the American (lines) and Morelet's Crocodiles (cross hatch)

northern South America, it exists only in small remnant populations and is rare in Belize. Because it is an estuarine species, able to tolerate saltwater, it also occupies many of the Caribbean islands and is found on both the Atlantic and Pacific coasts. Although it freely enters salt water it prefers large rivers and inland swamps. Ten years ago the U.S. population was censused at only 200 individuals with only 12 breeding females. Recent population counts include about 560 crocodiles. The American crocodile is much less aggressive than the American alligator which has been overrunning Florida in recent years. American crocodiles actively shun human activity and are more limited by cold temperatures.

The Morelet's crocodile was first described in 1851 as a new species from Peten in Guatemala and was named after P.M.A. Morelet, its discoverer. The species was described in Belize in 1870 and specimens found in the Sibun swamp west of Belize City in 1923, secured it as a different species from the American crocodile. The Morelet's crocodile has a limited range endemic to the Yucatan peninsular area in Mexico, Guatemala, and Belize. It may also extend into Honduras. The American crocodile is a much larger animal capable of reaching to 22.6 ft (7 m) long. Morelet's crocodiles generally are only about 7-8 ft (2.5 m) in length but may get as large as 15 ft (3 m).

Geographic Range of
Morelet's Crocodile
in Belize

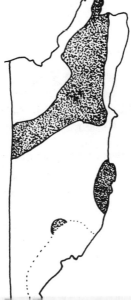

In Belize, the American crocodile is mostly found by river mouths and in mangrove swamps along the coast. It has also been found in lagoons of the mangrove cays. The northernmost two cays in Lighthouse Reef once had a thriving population and thus the species has been locally referred to as the "salt water crocodile". In contrast, Morelet's crocodile is mostly found in inland lagoons and slow flowing rivers. Crocodiles were said to be seen sunning themselves in areas of Lake Independence in Belize City near the St. Martin DePorres School. The two species may overlap but can be told apart by the snout. The Morelet's crocodile has a broad massive snout while the American crocodile snout is more slender.

Snout Profiles
of Salt Water (left)
and Morelet's (right)

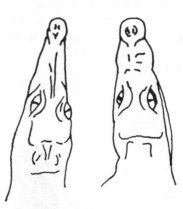

Aquatic Lifestyle

Crocodiles are adapted to an aquatic predator lifestyle. They are cryptically colored in dark green, brown or black. While they do not spend much time moving on land they have 3 gaits of locomotion: 1) they can use a serpentine movement sliding on their belly, especially when moving from the shore into the water; 2) they can walk on extended legs with the belly off the ground; and 3) they are capable of short bursts of galloping if needed. They are, however, unable to move well from side to side due to the rigidity of their belly ribs. Thus prey animals can escape on land by quickly changing direction since the crocodile has to turn in a large curve.

Their main aquatic characteristic is the long, muscular, laterally flattened tail which is used to propel crocodilians through the water by skulling in a sepentine swimming motion.

The tail's height is extended by a crest of tall scales. While the 4 fingers are long and unwebbed, the 5 toes are completely webbed and perform some swimming functions. However, the limbs generally are folded to the sides while swimming. When threatened the webbed rear feet allow a swimming crocodile to sink quickly by a sudden upward movement of the feet with spread toes. They are also adept at floating and moving slowly to stealthily stalk prey on the shore. Their adaptations of raised nostrils and eyes permit them to see and smell the prey while remaining almost totally submerged.

Crocodilians have at least 60 large conical teeth, variable in form and size, that are situated in deep hollows (alveoli) in the jaws . They serve only for seizing and holding prey and not for chewing. Teeth may be lost in prey encounters but they are quickly replaced. Each tooth contains a small replacement tooth within its pulp cavity and sometimes a third tiny tooth is ready to erupt within the replacement tooth as well. Crocodilians may go through as many as 3,000 teeth in a lifetime.

The tongue is barely moveable and firmly fused to the mouth floor. A Belizean folk story even notes that crocodiles have no tongue . This situation, according to the tale, came about when the crocodile lent his tongue to his friend the dog who had no tongue. Being so useful, the dog refused to return it, which is why to this day crocodiles have no tongue and are enemies with dogs. The stable tongue and its second palate go along with its lacking a well developed Jacobson's organ for smell and a poorly developed sense of taste. A long esophagus connects to the round, muscular, two-chambered stomach.

The eyes, ears, and mouth are all adapted for an aquatic life. The eyes have 3 lids, an upper and lower lid and a semi-transparent nictitating membrane which crosses the eye from its inside corner. The membrane protects the eye while underwater yet still allows the crocodile to see. Vision is sharp and the vertical pupil permits greater dilation at night. It additionally has rhodopsin which glows rosy-pink at night and makes night vision possible.

The American crocodile like other animals living in

saltwater must be able to dispose of absorbed extra salt which it does by lacrimal glands (tear glands) and glands associated with the nictitating membrane which are similar to salt glands in sea birds. Crocodile tears, which symbolize false grief, probably come from either tear glands used to keep their eyes moist or water which is trapped in their lids which may run from the corner of their eyes.

Both the ears and nostrils can close when diving. The nostrils are secondarily protected by a second palate. Above this palate is an air passage connecting the nostrils far back in the mouth which leads directly to the throat. Air from the outside never enters the mouth at all. A skin flap at the back of the mouth closes the glottis preventing water from entering. This flap allows the crocodile to both feed while submerged in the water and breathe with its mouth open underwater. The external ears are a fold of skin which can be closed over the eardrum.

Because crocodiles are coldblooded, they spend the day basking in the sun to raise their body temperature. When too hot, they open their mouth exposing the mucous membranes where blood is closest to the surface of the mouth. Since they have no sweat glands this mouth opening acts to cool them. During the main heat of the day they will retreat to the shade or may enter the water for short periods.

They spend the night in the water usually hunting. Adults use surprise and their camouflage coloration of drab green, brown or black. They stalk prey from the water, moving slowly, grabbing and pulling prey into the water when it comes to drink. They may drown the animal in the process and then tear it into pieces by holding the prey firmly and suddenly rolling over and over in the water, turning on the long axis, and throwing the tail out of the water. They swallow the large pieces and digestion proceeds rapidly. Although they have huge powerful muscles to snap their jaws shut, the muscles to open the mouth are weak. Large numbers of stones have been found in the stomachs of crocodiles which were thought to function in grinding food. These stones are now thought to act as ballast in stabilizing the body while swimming.

Breeding Behavior

Male crocodiles establish territories along river or shore banks and the females choose the male based on the best sunbathing areas. The dominant male swims up and down the shore taking only short rests while others remain basking on the shore. He will pause at his territory boundary at the same place for 5-10 minutes. If approached by another male he will chase it, half out of the water, bellowing and snapping at the challenger and then return again to his swimming patrol. During fights, males may blow up little bubbles of water next to their snouts. One may then suddenly, while growling with mouth open wide, leap at the other, emerging half out of water. The two combatants may bite at each other grasping their opponent by the jaws.

Crocodiles have one of the few well developed voices in reptiles and males are known to give an extended bellow during the breeding season with the head lifted and mouth open wide. During this season they also give off a strong musk smell from 2 pairs of glands under the jaw and from the cloaca. Both the calling and musk attract females to them. Breeding season of caimans in Venezuela occurs in the latter part of the dry season or early wet season which may be similar to the Morelet's crocodile in Belize since their nesting is dependent on rains. Nests must be located away from flooding yet close to water for the hatchlings. Hatching in the American crocodile in south Florida coincides with the rainy season. The nesting occurs in mid-August through late October and hatching occurs from October to December.

Courtship takes place in the water. When a smaller female approaches, the male lifts his tail from the water, sometimes holding it at the water surface, straight up or arched over with the tip touching the water. This tail display may give both males and females an indication of the male's size and also function as a territorial display. The male may also swell his neck up, filling his lungs with air, and expel hissing air from his mouth and nostrils. The pressure of air shoots a column several feet into the air. The fountain plays 5-6 seconds and may be repeated several times. As his excitement grows he lifts his head and bellows, vibrating his flanks so vigorously that water sprays up on both sides of his body.   He also agitates the water by clapping his jaws open and shut and beating the water with his tail.

The female may approach and nibble the male's mandibles.   Juveniles have been seen to nibble adult jaws in captivity so in courtship it may function to reduce the males aggression.   She is mostly passive but performs a nuptial dance making rearing movements in which she also angles the head out of the water and utters gutteral sounds.   She also snaps her jaws and rears up again, displaying for some minutes.   The male then follows the female, overtaking her, forcing her to swim in a circle.   She may lift her mouth from the water uttering throaty sounds.   She then flees or allows the male to lay a forefoot on her shoulder and mount her.   They intertwine tails as copulation ensues and they may swim together while mounted.   In deep water, the female may be totally submerged during copulation which lasts from a half-minute to 2 minutes.   Fertilization is internal by the single grooved penis of the male which protrudes from the cloaca through a longitudinal slit.

Motherhood

There are 2 kinds of nests dug by crocodilians for the purpose of keeping their eggs warm.   Often, however, the problem is not in gaining heat but in preventing excessive heat exposure during the hot mid afternoons. Most female crocodiles will dig a hole in the ground for their nest in the same area each year.   They dig with the forepaws, pushing the sand away with the rear legs, to dig a pit 8-20 in (20-50 cm) deep. They may lay over 40 hard, heavily calcified shelled eggs which they cover again with grass or soil.   They carefully arrange them in 2 or 3 layers covering them with sand to keep them warm.

Some crocodilians like the American alligator and Morelet's crocodile build a mound nest of leaves and other vegetation gathered in the mouth and piled between and over the eggs.   The female scoops out a hole in the middle for the eggs and recovers them.   Occasionally turning over the leaves

Morelet's Crocodile Mound Nest

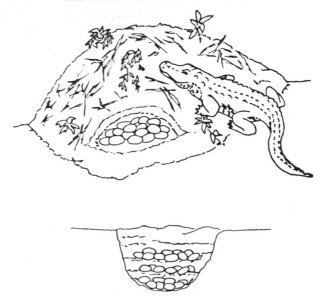

Crocodillian Underground Nest

ensures that the eggs will remain moist and allows some of the heat generated by fermentation of the pile to be vented. Both types of nests ensure both a uniform temperature around the eggs which doesn't vary more than 5.5° F (3° C) as well as a uniform humidity. Development takes about 3 months during which the female guards the nest continuously. She may occasionally move into the water and drip water over the nest when she returns.

Maternal care in many crocodilians rivals some of the best mammalian mothers yet shares some of the characteristics of birds with precocial young (capable of movement when hatched). Prior to hatching, the young begin to squeak with loud high-pitched grunts. Squeaking increases in response to noises or vibrations made above the nest when the female walks on it or in response to other young making sounds. Their calls can be heard over considerable distances. As they pip the egg using an egg tooth (a caruncle on the snout tip) they call louder and more frequently. This is a communication which stimulates other young to hatch synchronously and is also found

in ducks and chickens.   It also stimulates the mother to push
the earth away with her belly and dig the eggs out with her
forelegs.   The young initially stay together in the area of the
nest.

Young Crocodile Emerging

The young emerge with an egg sac which can provide
food for several months. The young are especially vulnerable
at 3 stages: when eggs; as hatchlings before they reach the
water; and during the early months when they fall prey to
large wading birds and fish.   Only about 2-5% of the brood
reaches sexual maturity at 8-12 years. Thus maternal care is
very important at hatching.   The Nile crocodile leads its new
hatchlings to the water. They follow her in the water, climb
onto her head and snout, and swim after her when she dives.
She and the young will call to each other when approached by
humans.

Mothers of other species of crocodilians may actually
help the young to hatch by gently crushing the egg shell of
pipped eggs in their jaws.   The mother will also scoop up a
number of the newly hatched young and carry them in her
gular or throat pouch to secluded areas in back waters. If
threatened, mothers may even gather young in the mouth
before diving . Sometimes females dig small secluded nursery
areas.   Maternal care occurs for 3-4 months and yearlings have
been seen in these nurseries indicating that perhaps maternal

care may last as long as 1-2 years.

Female Crocodile Carrying Young Hatchlings

Very young crocodiles are most susceptible to predation and remain hidden in weedy inlets. They stay away from areas frequented by strange adults who may cannibalize them. Initially they eat snails, dragonfly larvae, crickets, beetles and other insects. Young crocodiles have been seen cornering mosquito larvae by curving their bodies and tails around them. The American crocodile, born into a saltwater environment that could quickly kill them, avoid dehydration for the first few months by drinking lenses of rainwater that float on top of the saltwater or by snapping up raindrops as they fall. Later in life they eat crustaceans, toads, fish, small birds and rodents. Crocodilians grow rapidly and continuously throughout their life, sometimes growing 1-3 ft (0.3-1 m) in a single year. They are also long-lived, achieving ages of 70-100 years in captivity.

SNAKES: GOOD, NOT EVIL

Snakes or serpents get their name from the Latin "serpere" which means to crawl or creep. While having both good and evil symbolic associations in various cultures, most people have a general fear and distrust of snakes and often kill them on sight. A study in the United States showed that drivers go out of their way to drive over snakes. This occurs in Belize as well. The distrust of and desire to kill snakes is often not related to their poisonous abilities and indeed most people do not know which snakes are dangerous and which are not. It has been stated that perhaps people and other primates have an innate fear of snakes but research does not back this assertion up. Although not appreciated anywhere, snakes hunt many animals, especially rodent pests, which need to be kept in check. In India for example, which has many poisonous snakes, attempts to eradicate these snakes resulted in huge crop losses by rodents after crops were stored; Without the snakes there was nothing to control the rodent populations.

Evil Symbols

Probably the Christian symbolism of the serpent or snake has left the most damaging and ill-deserved reputation for snakes. Symbolically in Christian mythology, snakes represent the powers of evil of that which has been reduced to the level of the earth. In some parts of the Bible they are referred to as Satan incarnate. Pre-Christian symbolism associated the snake with sex due to the snake's form. A snake ready to strike resembles the erect phallus or male sex organ. The Judeo-Christian images, building upon this, let the snake represent the tempter of Adam and Eve in the Garden of Eden which represented the fall into sin. The relationship of the serpent, sin, and sex was obvious, as the first thing Adam and Eve did after the fall, was to cover their genitals equating sin with sex.

Yet snakes no more deserve this misidentification with Satan and evil than any other animal does. There are 2,500 species of snakes in the world of which only   20%   are poisonous.   They are animals which have evolved to lead a specific lifestyle with the adaptations they have.   Despite their general similarity in legless, elongated form, they show a variety of habits, many of which are beneficial to humans.

In Belize, one often comes across lifeless snake bodies which have been needlessly killed and casually tossed to the side of the road: bluetails, wowlas, and bocaturas all harmless, beautiful, and wasted.   In the Community Baboon Sanctuary, only the yellow-jawed tommygoff or fer-de-lance is poisonous and aggressive enough to pose harm to humans.   Even the beautiful coral snakes which are poisonous are harmless if left alone, having   neither the disposition nor large mouth with fangs to attack a person.

What is a Snake ?

A lthough developed from a lizard with well developed limbs, almost all snakes have subsequently evolved without limbs, ears and eardrums or moveable eyelids, although they have evolved other specializations.   They have also lost the pectoral girdle and urinary bladder.   Their skull bones are only loosely joined as are the jaws so that they can become widely separated during feeding and can swallow large food items.   Their elongated body is due to a large number of vertebrae and attached ribs.   Most species have over 200 vertebrae and some have as many as 400.   Humans have 29.

Many of the paired internal organs have been reduced to fit the elongated body.   They have only one main lung with an air sac near the tail. The air sac is used when the lung is blocked during the swallowing of large prey.   Constrictors have special muscles to pull the wind pipe opening in the floor of the mouth forward, past the prey as it is being swallowed, to prevent their own suffocation.   Swallowing is also assisted by muscles that rotate the jaw forward then pull it backward to "walk" the head over the victim. The more primitive boas and pythons retain two lungs. Many other organs like the esophagus, stomach, liver, urinary organs and genitals are also elongated. While the flexible stomach has a huge capacity, the intestine can only handle smaller digested materials.

Although hearing has degenerated in snakes restricting them to perceive only low-frequency sounds, vision is highly developed responding mainly to movement. The snake's forked

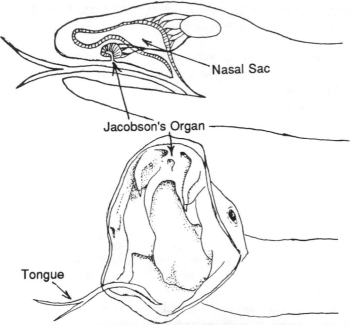

Snake Heads Showing the Tongue, Jacobson's Organ and Nasal Sac

tongue is also very complex having 3 sensory capabilities, perceiving smells, touch, and some auditory vibrations. Sometimes the snake will flick out the tongue touching the tips to the ground and at other times will wave it in the air.   By putting the tongue in the air it is picking up smell molecules which it brings back in to pass over organs in the roof of the mouth. By touching the ground it is perceiving vibrations from the ground.

Snakes move in a variety of ways, not having the use of limbs.   Some snakes like boas move in a slow caterpillar motion using the scutes on the lower surface of their body to push along the ground.   Internal muscles attached to the ribs then pull the rest of the body forward.   Some snakes use a faster undulatory movement forming S-shaped curves pushing the rear curve against the ground to move forward.

Snakes are stripped down predators. They have invaded a variety of habitats and niches. Prey is limited by its diameter and the capacity of the snake to swallow it. By having evolved flexible jaw bones and specialized mouths they can swallow prey even larger than themselves. They can open the mouth at a 150 degree angle. The blunt headed tree snake found in Belize specializes in eating sleeping anoles. The lizards sleep far out on ends of fern fronds, leaves or vine tips. Since the perch begins to vibrate whenever an animal starts to crawl onto the leaf, the vibrations warn the anole who drops off and runs away. The snake, however, can extend its reach by extending its backbone and vertebrae scales without support thus enabling long extensions and capture of the fleeing anoles. Its large eyes probably also aid in seeing anoles in the dark.

Shedding the Skin

Ecdysis or shedding of the epidermis is one of the snake's most remarkable habits, giving ancients the impression of a snake's immortality and its symbolism of rebirth, as though it is reborn each time it casts its skin. It sheds its skin to renew it as it becomes worn, especially as it travels against the ground. The new skin, once it keratinizes, becomes tougher and more resistant. Keratin is a tough, fibrous, modified protein which is found in skin, horns, nails and hair. Keratinization also prevents extra moisture loss and protects the snake from ultraviolet rays.

Shedding the skin depends mainly on the snake's food intake. It may cast its skin 3-4 times per year. More rapid metabolism, which depends on food intake and external temperature, leads to more shedding. Feeding may be seasonal and thus shedding may occur so as well.

Shedding is accompanied by a sudden loss of appetite, and the colors dull and markings become less distinct. The eyes also become opaque caused by the thickening of the outer skin. During this phase the snake is hidden and does not hunt. Casting occurs 2-5 days after the eyes clear and the snake becomes restless. Peeling begins at the head and is aided by a secretion exuded by the underlayers of the skin. It rubs its nose and sides of its jaws against rough edges causing the skin to break free of the mouth's edges.   As the skin breaks from the head, the snake then begins to push through dense vegetation so the skin catches on branches or bark as the snake moves forward.   It uses a muscular action involving alternative contraction and expansion of a small section of the body at a time.   This loosens the skin and pushes it backward toward the tail.   It eventually pulls off inside-out, usually in one piece and is left dangling in the environment.

Boa Constrictor

The boa constrictor (*Boa constrictor*) is a member of mainly neotropical constrictor type snakes such as the African pythons and the anaconda from South America.   Their method of feeding gives them their name-- constrictors.   They lie in wait for prey, responding to smell, movement, and heat sensing organs in their lips.   These very sensitive heat receptors can distinguish direction and distance of prey objects by

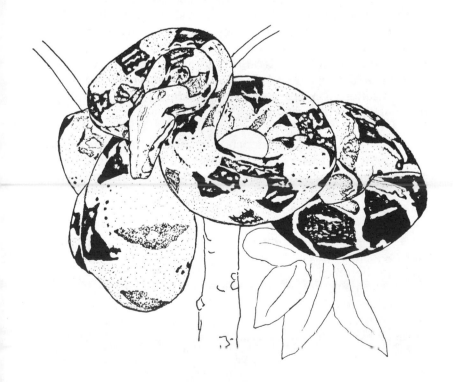

detecting changes of less than 0.002° F. They strike quickly, darting forward at the prey, which are usually small mammals, birds, and reptiles. They have been known to eat prey as large as young deer, coatis, and ocelots. They have a great number of sharp, rear-pointing teeth which hold the prey fast while they throw two or more thick, powerful coils of their body over the struggling animal constricting its body. The prey is not crushed but held fast as the coils are tightened around the prey's chest and ribs preventing inhalation until it suffocates or the blood vessels rupture. Once dead, the boa sniffs the prey and begins to swallow it head first, consuming it slowly. It loosens its upper and lower jaws from their linkage, enabling it to swallow large animals. The lower jaw with teeth is pushed forward with the larynx, thus permitting breathing as it swallows.

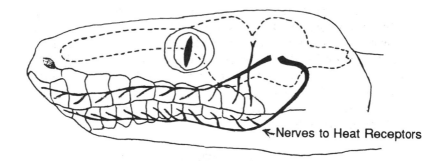

←Nerves to Heat Receptors

Boa Head Showing Nerves to Heat Receptors in the Lips

The other interesting characteristic of boas is the presence of a pelvis and the remnants of hind legs indicating that they are primitive snakes. The legs are not used for locomotion. Instead, males having larger, claw-like remnant hind legs (called "anal spurs") on either side of the anal vent, use them during courtship to stroke the female around her cloaca stimulating her to breed. Eventually she raises her tail allowing the male to wrap his around her and he inserts one of his pair of hemipenis in copulation. Breeding occurs from August to March. Births of 20 to 60 young from 14 20 in (35-50 cm) long occur from May to August. Boas breed when

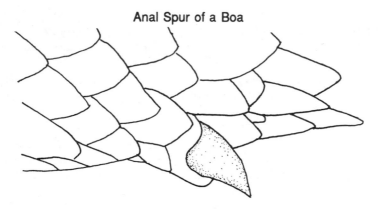

Anal Spur of a Boa

they are 4-6 feet (1.5-2 m) in length. Boas may grow as long as 20 feet (6 m). One boa has lived in captivity for 38 years but boas may live to 40-50 years in the wild.

Boa constrictors are large snakes colored in camouflage with dark dorsal blotches on a brownish background. The head is arrowhead-shaped and the tail tends to be more reddish in color They inhabit a variety of environments usually near water from southern Mexico throughout much of South America. They are mainly active at dawn and dusk frequenting both the ground and trees where they actively seek good areas to wait for prey.

Pit Vipers

There are two main poisonous snakes of the pit viper family (Crotalidae) in the sanctuary, the fer-de-lance or yellow-jaw tommygoff and the Central American rattlesnake, or cascaval. The family includes 6 genera and 130 species worldwide. The two most distinguishing characteristics of the venom apparatus are the fangs capacity to fold and the tubular injection mechanism. The two upper jaws which bear the fangs are shortened, each having a special joint which permits the jaw and fang to rotate 90 degrees. With the mouth closed, the fangs lie back, tips inward, covered by a mucous membrane fold. When opened, a lifting mechanism activates, with certain bones pushing the fangs vertically. Being able to fold the fangs backward allows them to be longer.

Pit vipers also have highly evolved long tubular poison fangs with a highly developed mechanism for activating them. Instead of grooves, their fangs have enclosed

Pit Viper Head With Venom Glands and Tubular Fang

canals from which poison is injected like a hypodermic needle. Contractions of the muscles surrounding the venom glands control the amount of venom which is then directed by a mucous membrane covering to the hollow teeth. After biting prey, often the fangs remain in the prey and may be excreted. Fangs may be replaced 2-4 times annually by reserve teeth.

Poisonous snakes are said to have one of two types of toxins, neurotoxins which paralyze parts of the nervous systems and hemotoxins which destroy blood and tissue. Venoms are actually a rich complex of numerous proteins and other compounds. Other toxic elements which might be found in venom include blood clotting agents, those which reduce blood clotting , some which reduce red blood cells, bacteriological

285

agents, and some which stimulate digestion. Research on venoms has resulted in the synthesis of compounds to treat blood clotting disorders in humans.

Pit viper venom contains primarily hemotoxins, poisons which are injurious to the blood and its vessels. A bite results in local irritation and symptoms of severe blood poisoning. This includes pain, inflammation, discoloration, sudden drop in blood pressure, internal bleeding, and tissue degeneration. Death may occur because of heart stoppage.

The main function of the venom is to quickly immobilize prey especially fast moving aquatic or arboreal prey. The bushmaster, a South American relative of the tommygoff, injects large volumes of venom into the agouti which predigests the prey. Production of venom in some species follows a seasonal pattern, peaking in summer when most food is available, and then declining in winter, paralleling the natural cycle of feeding and fasting.

Most venomous snakes avoid wasting venom on non-food items. It takes a milked rattlesnake over a month to fully replenish its venom supply although it can produce enough venom to be dangerous in 3 days. Studies have shown that dried rattlesnake venom still can retain its toxicity after 50 years.

Some prey are resistant to venom. Opossums which evolved in the Americas with rattlesnakes and pit vipers are highly resistant to their bites. The common Virginia opossum can withstand the bite of large snakes such as the eastern diamondback rattlesnake with no ill effects. Opossums have withstood up to 60x a lethal dose of pit viper venom for other animals with only a slight change in blood pressure which disappeared in a half hour. This resistance enables them to hunt venomous snakes such as cottonmouths. This sort of natural immunity is what allows snakes such as the mussurana, which occurs in Belize, to specialize in eating other snakes including the highly toxic fer-de-lance. It is said the black tail can kill and eat the tommygoff as well. If so, perhaps it has a similar immunity.

When bothered, pit vipers show a threat posture by slightly flattening the body and forming a spiral, lifting the forebody and bending it into an S-shape. The end of the tail is also raised and shaken even though it may have no rattles. This is a warning behavior.

Pit vipers have a unique pit organ for detecting prey, chiefly small mammals and birds, some reptiles, amphibians and fish. The pit organ is a deep pit between the nostril and eye in an indentation of the upper jaw bone, the opening being larger than the nostril but smaller than the eye and can be opened by a sphincter muscle. The function of this strange organ became apparent when experiments were carried out on snakes by presenting them with normal or covered light bulbs when their eyes were normal or covered. It became obvious that the snakes were excited by the heat. The pits are heat

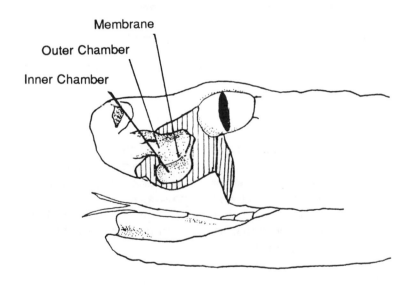

Membrane
Outer Chamber
Inner Chamber

Anatomy of a Pit Organ

sensing organs which respond to ultra-red radiation. The organ has an outer and inner chamber separated by a membrane. When radiant heat impinges on the membrane, the nerve endings in it respond to the temperature difference between inside and outside of the snake. The pit organs are so sensitive they can detect a 0.003° C difference and can perceive warm blooded prey at a distance of 20 in (50cm). It has been suggested that this complex organ evolved from the joining of two simple lip pits similar to those of the boa constrictor.

The fer-de-lance related snakes have a triangular or heart shaped head which is distinct from its body. It gets its common name from a Creole-French word originating in Martinique where the species is now rare. It is however, common in the Community Baboon Sanctuary and throughout the forests of Belize and Central America. It has a high fertility and can have as many as 71 young at a time. It is rightly feared in Belize because its bite is very dangerous and can be fatal, especially if it strikes a blood vessel.

While originating in tropical Asia, today, two thirds of all pit vipers occur in the Americas. Most rattler species occur in North America but only the species in Belize is found in Central and South America. The most distinctive characteristic of rattlers of the genus *Crotalus*, are the segmented rattles on their tail tip.

Rattlesnakes

The 30 species of rattlesnakes of the genus *Crotalus* occupy many habitats. They prefer dry, rocky, shrubby terrain where they can conceal themselves in rock crevices. Mexico has the most species. Despite their poison, very few people die from rattlesnake bites. They are slower and more sluggish than the fer-de-lance and don't bite as readily. Additionally, they have the warning rattles. These are a hard, dry, chain of loosely joined rattle elements at the tail tip. They are actually remnant shed skin from the previous moltings. They are related to age but you cannot tell the age of a rattler from the number of rattles. A newborn rattler's tail ends in a single spherical scale. While other snakes cast off this scale at every molt, rattlers do this only at the first molt at 7-10 days. The last scale then hardens into a hollow structure with a ring like construction before the second molt. During each succeeding molt the last scale then loosens without falling off.

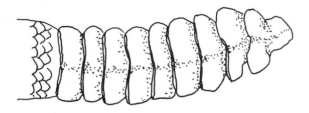

Instead the new and wider terminal scale develops inside the first one , holding it.   This continues but after 6-8 rattles some begin to break off.   The snake may molt three times a year.

The rattling cannot be heard by the snake itself who is deaf.   It can perceive only ground vibrations. When ready to strike, like the tommygoff, the rattler holds its body in an ascending spiral with head and neck in an S-shaped posture. They can very rapidly strike up to a half their body length.

Female rattlers reach sexual maturity at 3 years and bear clutches of 8-15 live young after a gestation of 140-200 days.   Males perform ritualized battles which were once thought to be mating.   The two males lift their forebodies in the air and wrap around each other usually orienting head to head and move in a swaying motion back and forth, pushing with their forebodies until eventually one moves off.

Mating differs in that the female is passive.   The male will give tongue flicks to her and crawls onto her, vigorously jerking the hind portions of his body.   He presses his tail beneath the female who lifts her tail and their cloacas contact each other.   The male's hemipenis then penetrates the female. Copulation periods can take as long as 22 hours.

The Central American or tropical rattlesnake *Crotalus durissus* is the most dangerous of rattlers, its venom containing a substantial amount of neurotoxin as well as hemotoxins.

Seventy-five percent of untreated bites cause death. However, it is a sluggish, non-aggressive species and it is rare to see one in a threat posture. Thus few actual deaths are attributed to the species. However the symptoms of a bite include initial paralysis of the neck muscles causing the head to drop to the side. Later there is auditory and visual impediments which can lead to unconsciousness and death. Despite the danger, even rattlesnakes have uses for humans, many of which we don't yet know. It was accidentally discovered that the venom can be used in treating epilepsy.

Rattler Striking Posture

IGUANAS

*A*lthough the family of Iguanidae is large, the subfamily of iguanas (Iguaninae) includes only 30 species most of which reside in the tropical and subtropical regions of the Americas. Their distribution is centered in Mexico where 4 of the 8 genera occur. Most of the species occur in dry environments where they take refuge in holes in trees, the ground, rocks or in arboreal termite nests. The iguana family includes the anoles and basilisks which are commonly found in the Community Baboon Sanctuary.

Usually only 1 to 3 species are found together sympatrically. This is the case in the Community Baboon Sanctuary which has the two large Central American rain forest iguanas, the green iguana (*Iguana iguana*) and the spiny-tailed iguana or wish-willy (*Ctenosauria similis*). Both species range from southern Mexico to northern South America. The green iguana is colored grayish to brownish green with patterns of stripes on the shoulder, belly, and tail.

Herbivorous Lifestyle

Their large size and specialized herbivorous diet are what are most notable about iguanas. Although many lizards will take some plant material in their diet, iguanas as a group are almost totally herbivorous, feeding on plants the day they hatch. Only the wish-willy is omnivorous when young. The smallest spiny-tails feed primarily on insects. Older, larger wish-willys feed progressively more on plant material although leaves are not the primary food source of any size or age class. Wish-willys are opportunistic feeders, grazing on lawns, feeding on trumpet trees, and even taking birds from mist nests of scientists. Green iguanas in contrast, are not insectivorous at any stage, even hatchlings feeding on plants. The smallest greens feed heavily on flowers, although flowers are not major food items for adults. Green Iguanas of all sizes feed primarily on leaves.

As herbivores, similar to the howlers, iguanas spend the majority of their time resting, since it takes little time to fill their gut. The common or green iguana, called bamboo chicken in Creole, spends 90-96% of its time resting or inactive, feeding only 1% of its time. They face some of the same problems as other herbivores. Despite the abundance of plant material, plant food may still be limiting. Many of the plant leaves have secondary toxic compounds as protection against herbivores. Like the howlers, the common iguana prefers new leaves, flowers and fruits. During certain seasons however, the iguana depends on mature leaves which are fibrous, difficult to digest and not very nutritious. Their efficiency to digest plants is low, ranging from 30-70%.

Despite the problems facing them as herbivores, iguanas have evolved specific characteristics which help them in their herbivorous lifestyle. They have a colon partitioned with valves which are formed by infoldings of the inner colon. The numbers of these partitions increases in larger animals. These partitions seem to slow the passage of plant materials through the digestive tract allowing prolonged digestion. The partitions also increase the absorptive surface area thereby promoting enhanced digestion. Most importantly they provide microhabitats for symbionts in their colon such as nematode worms, protozoans and bacteria, which help them digest plant materials.

Nematodes are ingested by young iguanas soon after hatching by licking the soil or eating feces of other iguanas. The large numbers of these worms in all healthy iguanas suggests that they are not parasitic but aid the iguana. It is thought that they break the vegetation down in the gut thereby increasing the surface area of food particles. Nematodes also produce usable waste products and regulate the abundance of the gut microbes which they feed on.

Green iguanas are primarily arboreal and spend much of their time in arboreal basking sites in direct sunlight. They prefer riverine forest habitats. Except for an occasional descent for feeding, tree to tree moves, escape from predators, and nesting iguanas remain in the treetops both day and night. The well camouflaged young, however, bask during the day in grass thickets or in semi-aquatic plants. In the evening, the young climb up into vegetation 6-10 ft (2-3 m) high.

Long range movements are prompted by food availability. An iguana may shift its center of activity for several days or weeks to follow seasonal fruiting and flowering as, for example, when green iguanas congregate to feed on hog plum fruits during August-September. Sometimes longer term shifts occur. Adult males have the smallest home ranges, around 0.20 acres (0.08 ha), and maintain exclusive breeding territories. Females and young males have larger ranges from 0.5-0.6 acres (0 .22-0.25 ha).

Spiny-tailed young choose different sites as they grow. Bright green juveniles spend time in the riverine forest understory, most commonly on the ground in direct sunlight. At night, like the common iguanas, they move into low vegetation. For the young, the most important priority is to find a place to retreat for protection, such as a burrow or tree hollow. Predators of both species include humans, small carnivores and snakes. The basilisk lizard is also a major predator of very young common iguanas, taking hatchlings up to 2-3 months old.

Territoriality and Aggressive Displays

All members of the family Iguanidae exhibit aggressive displays which involve temporal movements of the head. The two main displays are head bobs or nods and pushups of the head and front trunk area or even the whole body. Larger species, like the iguanas show only head bobs while smaller species perform pushups. These displays are performed primarily by males, usually as a declaration of territory ownership or as an aggressive threat.

The pattern and form the display takes is species-specific and can vary in time, temporal patterning of the display, and amplitude of the movement. The displays are also enhanced by posture and modification of particular body parts to emphasize the communication. Thus the lizards usually present themselves laterally to their opponent and often compress their body laterally with crests and throat pouches (dewlaps) extended to give a larger more formidable appearance. The tiny anoles common throughout Belize show the most exaggerated dewlap expansion, exhibiting the hidden bright red or orange patch to their adversaries.

Aggressive Head Nodding In the Green Iguana

The green iguana has a large pendant gular flap or dewlap while the spiny-tailed iguana exhibits a pendant but smaller gular enlargement. Both may slightly compress their body laterally and will raise a section of skin on the head, neck and trunk topped by an erect crest of serrated scales. When highly aroused, the common iguana can change to a lighter body color with darker belly stripes within 3-5 minutes.   The tail is not used in the display but may be used in fighting or defense by lashing it with wide swings as it hisses and snaps at its adversary.

The spiny-tailed iguana displays on a raised or level site, expands its dewlap, gapes, and bobs its head in 2-5 single fast and low bobs in its territorial display.   The common iguana displays on a raised site, usually an exposed tree top, laterally compresses its body , expands its crest and dewlap, gapes and bobs and vibrates its head.   It shows an initial high bob followed by a series of smaller bobs.

The green iguana lives in the light/shade mosaic of trees along rivers, lakes, and mangrove swamps and may be found in more open areas if food is available. Adult males hold territories which they defend against other adult males. They will, however, allow several smaller males, juveniles as well as females to live within their territories.

Nesting and Breeding

Other than nest construction, egg laying, and in a few cases nest guarding, parental care is lacking in iguanas. Polygyny is the rule and competition of males for females leads to greater male activity.

During the breeding season, the male changes color to a bright gold or red orange. His coloration is partly related to social factors since males who are deposed from their territory may change within a few hours to dull brown. The breeding male establishes a territory on a large tree on a high open conspicuous perch. He maintains this area throughout the breeding season, rarely feeding and losing a lot of weight. He mainly displays at other adult males. He may allow small males into the territory but medium-sized males avoid him.

These perches are also preferred basking areas and may be used by females as well. Thus large males are more frequently in the company of adult females, especially at this time. Increases in territorial display rates by the large dominant males are correlated with growth of the testes. Overt aggression indicates the marked onset of breeding. The male territories are well spaced and conspicuous. The territorial males alternate periods of rest with display bouts, courtship bouts, and territorial patrols. Patrolling consists of a series of short perch changes within the tree, followed by a signature bob at each perch. Studies of Panamanian iguanas showed that after late November, males were rarely observed to feed and by late December were very emaciated. The highest display rates were in December and January. These dates would probably be delayed by around a month in Belize.

The Panamanian studies also found that large conspicuous trees were preferred as mating territories but no specific tree species was preferred. Food availability was not an essential part of the mating territory. Females within the territories without food moved singly or in groups to nearby areas to feed. Males follow receptive females to the feeding areas and stay within a few yards (meters) of them, displaying frequently but rarely feeding.

Pair bonds are formed in three ways: by males moving to trees where females are found and establishing territories there; by males leaving their territories to court females in other areas; or by females visiting several male territories and eventually residing in one. Females are courted for at least four weeks before becoming receptive. They may remain receptive for at least 15 days and perhaps longer.

Courtship in the green iguana begins with the male approaching the female from the rear and performing rapid, low-amplitude, vibratory head nodding accompanied by ritualized tongue flicking. The female then moves her tail to one side. Receptive females are more likely to reciprocate with head bobbing in response to the males bobbing. The male may then bob again and attempt to mount and grab the female's neck skin. The pair may walk slowly together in this exchange. He then straddles the female and tucks his tail under hers, and copulates by extruding his hemipenis into her cloaca. Copulation may last 2-12 minutes and the male only mates once per day. Females will mate 1-5 times during the receptive period, usually with the same male.

The entire course of iguana breeding, however, does not occur as quickly and simply as described above. Rather, it takes place over a long time span in which the male courts the female for four weeks before she is ready to breed. At least the last two of these four weeks the female spends with the male who she will mate. After the pair has copulated 2-3 times, the amount of courtship is dramatically reduced.

A dominant territorial male may have 1-4 females in his territory. He will engage in more courtship bouts with the non-receptive females and receptivity periods in the females will overlap. Thus, a male with more than one female, courts each female daily but copulates with them on alternate days.

The younger, smaller males try to participate in the breeding by employing different strategies but are usually not very successful. The medium-sized males remain on the periphery of a dominant male's territory for anywhere from one week to the whole breeding season. They rarely display, patrol, or feed and are chased by the dominant male if they come too close. They court the females as they come in and out of the territory but are rarely successful in copulating with them. On occasion, a territory becomes vacated and the peripheral males can come in and assume a full breeding social position.

The small males are tolerated by dominant males and they move in and out of the territory unchallenged. The small males quickly drop from the tree if the dominant comes within 6 ft (2 m) of them. Otherwise they will be lunged at and head-butted from the tree by the dominant male. The small males will attempt to copulate with the females when the dominant male is elsewhere. In such instances, they run at the female, leap on her back and try to secure a neck bite. The female thrashes violently, threatens with her mouth open and attempts to bite him. The dominant, if he sees what is happening, comes to her defense. Neither this rape strategy nor the medium-sized males waiting methods bears much success since 90% of all copulations are by the dominant male. Probably an even lesser number of small and medium-sized males produce any offspring by these methods.

Iguanas reach sexual maturity later than other lizards, at 2-3 years. Both the common and spiny-tailed iguana females can breed at about 22 months. Males are capable of breeding at a year of age but due to the dominance and territoriality of their social system, they don't breed with any success until they are 2-3 years of age.

Gravid females select ground nest sites in sunlit areas and excavate burrows, 3-6 ft (1-2 m) in length, large enough to accomodate the females entire body. The burrow terminates in an egg chamber, 10-20 in (25-50 cm) deep, and wide enough to allow the female to turn around in it. She lays only one clutch per season in this burrow, filling it in and packing the entrance with dirt. Most species leave a packet of air over the eggs, although the common iguana does not.   These nest sites are defended against other females during and prior to nest preparation.   These sites may be reused during the 5-8 reproductive seasons a female survives.   Clutch size is larger in larger females and averages about 43 in both iguana species but may vary from 12 to 88.

In some cases, the wish-willy utilize a network of subterranean passages where several females lay eggs within the same burrowing system but with individual clutches laid in separate chambers.   The common iguana has maintained group areas for nesting in some instances as well.   Although the females generally leave the nest after laying the eggs, some populations of common iguanas return to the nest for 4-15 days piling on sand or debris and making repairs to the nest. These nest   visits are unusual because following nesting, the females have lost a lot of weight and must again begin feeding in other areas.

Green iguana eggs have a narrow temperature range around   86°F (30° C) which cannot vary more than a few degrees or the eggs will die.   Incubation takes 10-14 weeks. The eggs hatch in synchrony and the young dig their way to the surface on their own. Predation is a key factor determining iguana survival patterns.   The young are very vulnerable at this stage and have developed cryptic coloration.   Hatchlings quickly disperse from the nest, sometimes in groups, shortly after hatching.   Studies on hatchlings have shown that they have incredible abilities to orient to areas suitable for their growth.   Both the common and spiny-tailed iguana show extremely rapid growth.

Iguanas concentrate nesting activity into a 1-3 month period, females laying a single clutch each season.   Both the common and spiny-tailed iguanas lay their eggs during the dry season which provides insulation and high nest temperatures, minimizing the probability of nest flooding.   Then hatching occurs near the onset of the rainy season when food becomes more plentiful.

Green iguanas studied in Panama show a seasonality in

breeding similar to the green iguanas in Belize although Belizean iguanas probably breed somewhat later. Females breed when 2-3 years old with courtship and mating occurring in December-January, coinciding with the beginning of the dry season. The females migrate to a nesting area at this time. A clutch of 24-72 eggs are laid in February to early March and they hatch in late April through May at the beginning of the rainy season. In Belize, the dry season normally starts in January and the rains start in June. Females may migrate as much as 1.8 mi (3 km) to a suitable nesting site.

The green iguanas breed seasonally to take advantage of specific seasonal characteristics. Males can stay for longer periods on their exposed territory display areas during the windy periods of the dry season. The dry season is also favorable for incubation; wetter soils would lead to flooding and fungal infections and ultimately egg mortality. Hatching occurs when the flush of new foliage is available to the young. Young leaves are higher in protein and general food quality for rapid growth of the hatchlings. Rains at hatching also make it easier for the young to climb out of the nest.

Panamanian spiny-tailed iguanas have one short reproductive season in the mid dry season from December to February. The reproductive season is probably somewhat later in Belize. Egg laying and hatching take place in burrows prepared by the females, usually away from the riverine forest. Hatchlings emerge in April-June at the onset of the rains. Young are attracted by the forests and the insects in them but don't show a strong site attachment. With the rains, they move more into the non-riverine areas. In the first year they change to a more herbivorous diet and also change from green to brown in color. By the end of the first year , they leave the riverine forest to find safe refuges in burrows or hollow trees in other areas.

Green iguanas use the riverine forests throughout their life. Their reproduction also is concentrated in mid dry season with egg laying probably occurring in the riverine forest. However, in the sanctuary, females have been seen in the drier broken ridge forests during egg laying season. Hatchlings emerge between April-June and begin to feed on leaves, flowers

and fruit.   Green iguanas have greater site fidelity than spiny-
tails and may remain in the same site for over a year.   Females
reach minimum reproductive potential by 20 months but may
not breed until the third year.   For the first two years, both
species grow at constant, rapid growth rates.

In the Panama studies, hatchings of both species
occured in April although small spiny-tailed iguanas were
found into June and green iguanas until August. The hatching
phase is probably a bit later in Belize.   Different species of
iguana hatchlings differed in behavior, however.   Young
wish-willys which were mostly bright green in color, chose
night perches on low branches and were rarely clumped
together.   Green iguana youngsters, on the other hand, used
low branches, they were often found in groups, with commonly
10-20 in a space of only several square meters.   They were also
often in direct physical contact with each other.   Such
aggregations were most common in grass thickets at hatching.

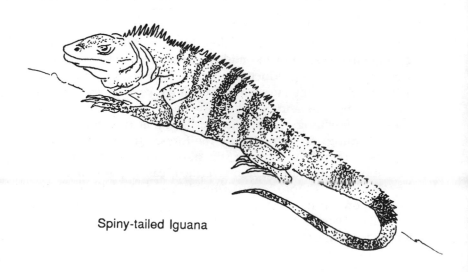

Spiny-tailed Iguana

FROGS AND TOADS

*O*f the 40,000 living vertebrates, only 4,000 are amphibians. These 4,000 species are what remain of a once flourishing group which moved onto land and eventually gave rise to the reptiles. The amphibians were the first vertebrates to give up the aquatic lifestyle of their fish ancestors some 350 million years ago. Amphibians probably moved onto land as an adaptation to a climatic drying trend. This gave them an increased ability to cross land and to find water to live in.

Frogs and toads, of the order Anura, share the class Amphibia with salamanders (order Caudata) and the legless caecilians (order Gymnophiona). Although amphibians don't have a specific characteristic, such as feathers in birds, which separates them from all other vertebrates, they all still have some link to the aquatic lifestyle from which they evolved. In most cases, in order to avoid dessication, they return to water to produce young. The Greek word amphibia means both lives, a reference to their existence first as an aquatic larvae, followed by metamorphosis into an adult which leads a terrestrial lifestyle.

Amphibians developed ribs to protect their inner organs, and a skin to aid them in water balance within the two environments. Besides having color producing cells (chromatophores) the skin also includes groups of cells which produce mucous. These mucous cells keep the skin moist and enhance gas exchange on the skin surface. Other mucous cells produce poison glands which manufacture toxins for protection against predators. Frogs shed their skins as often as every 3 days, pulling it off with the mouth and swallowing it.

In addition to lungs for breathing, adult frogs take in oxygen and give off carbon dioxide through the skin when it is moist. Water can also pass through the skin to maintain a water balance in the body. Frogs don't have the muscular lungs of other vetebrates but pump air in and out by raising and lowering the floor of the mouth which is noticeable from throat movements of the frog. Although of no real biological consequence, the common division of frogs and toads is characterized by frogs being smooth skinned, long limbed and living in water whereas toads are wart skinned, more stout-bodied, and live in dark, damp places away from water.

Being a Frog

There are 3,500 species of frogs and toads. All are distinguished by the absence of a tail in the adults. The richest variety of species is found in the tropics. Both frogs and toads evolved a specialized jumping lifestyle, developing long and powerful hind legs and feet where a tail would be a hinderance. They have thus evolved a fused bone of the last tail vertebrae into a long , flexible rod . A short, rigid backbone (with only 9 vertebrae compared with 30-100 in salamanders) has also proven essential to withstand forces involved in leaping and landing.

Most frogs are nocturnal with pupils which close down in bright light to protect their sensitive retinal cells. The slit may be vertical or horizontal. The eyes have special glands to keep them moist and have moveable lids. Some frogs have a third eyelid known as the nictitating membrane which can be drawn up over the eye to protect it while still allowing some underwater vision. The ear is marked by the presence of an external ear drum or tympanum. Frogs' large eyes and nostrils are set on top of the head, an adaptation to concealing themselves in the water while resting.

The coloration of frogs is important and is produced either by pigment granules in the outer epidermal skin layer or by specialized pigment containing cells of the lower dermal layer called chromatophores. In the latter method of color production, the frog, like some other amphibians and reptiles, can change its body color. Since amphibians are cold-blooded, color changing can help regulate body temperature.

The chromatophores can be evenly distributed throughout the cell or contracted into its center. Since these cells are irregularly branched and overlay each other in a complex lattice, the frog can change its color from dark to light by dispersing or contracting the pigment granules within each cell. Movement of the pigment within the chromatophores is temperature and humidity linked since dark bodies absorb radiant energy. Warmth and dryness results in a contraction of the pigments and a pale color while cold and dampness causes dispersal which is displayed as a darker color. This process is controlled by the pituitary gland which produces a chromatophore stimulating hormone.

In general, frog colors are for concealment from predators or prey. Some bright colored frogs, however, are so colored to warn potential predators of their poisonous nature. Other frogs show colorful patterns which are hidden at rest and flash when hopping to confuse pursuing predators.

Feeding

Three quarters of all frog species are found in tropical rain forests and hence they are affected by the rapid rate of deforestation. Additionally, the use of pesticides and herbicides are contributing to their demise. Adult frogs eat the contaminated arthropods while agricultural run-off makes ponds, lakes and streams unsuitable for the developing tadpoles.

Adult frogs lead a carnivorous life although the spring chicken, *Bufo marinus*, will eat some vegetable matter and even carrion. All frogs seek living prey and are stimulated by movement. They feed on ants, termites, beetles, slugs, snails, earthworms and other small animals and even small vertebrates in the case of larger frogs which can swallow food whole.

In prey capture, a frog first studies the prey, then raises the front part of its body and when the prey moves, the frog flicks its tongue out from the front of the mouth. When the sticky, mucous coated tip hits the prey it is brought back in and swallowed. In many species such as the tree frogs, the tongue is small and can't be distended. These species simply lunge forward and grab the prey in their mouth, sometimes using the forearms or hands to cram the prey in or prevent its escape.

Most frog species have teeth for grasping the prey. Swallowing occurs in 2-3 gulps often looking painful. Swallowing is followed by the retraction of the eyeballs into the skull. As they are pressed down into the buccal (mouth) cavity they help to force the food down the frog's throat. This is made possible by the flexibility of the roof of the mouth and the tough protective casing around the eyeballs.

Reproduction

The main defense of frogs is fecundity so most frogs produce large numbers of young, most of which fall prey to predators. Clutch sizes can vary from 1 to as many as 30,000 as in *Bufo marinus*. The numbers of eggs are greater in larger species. Medium-sized frogs have clutches of 500-5,000. Lesser numbers of eggs are produced by species which show parental care or specialized methods of egg deposition, such as laying eggs out of water or in small arboreal pools. Eggs may be laid in a variety of places including large permanent bodies of water, small temporary pools, streams, arboreal pools such as in bromeliads or other plants, and even in pools especially constructed by males for the eggs.

Frogs were the first vertebrates to develop a true voice produced by moving air across a series of vocal cords. The male inhales, closing the mouth and nostrils and passes the air forward inflating a balloon-like vocal pouch which is either single or double, formed from the floor of the mouth. The sound is produced by moving air back and forth from body to pouch over the vocal cords. Generally, smaller frogs produce higher-pitched calls and larger species have lower calls. In the Community Baboon Sanctuary, the difference in calls is illustrated by the only two species of toads which occur in Belize. The huge spring chicken, *Bufo marinus*, produces a low pitched, slow trill while the much smaller *Bufo valliceps* calls with a typical toad, high-pitched rapid trill. Additionally, note repetitions are affected by the temperature. As the temperature rises, the rate increases, the note duration decreases and the pitch rises.

These calls are primarily breeding location calls

which tell females where the breeding males are located. The breeding or position call is different in each species, helping to isolate species which live in the same area from interbreeding and in some cases hybridizing, since each only responds to its own species call. Some species in the same area which look alike to humans have been found to be different species based on their having different calls and thus not interbreeding, a phenomenon known as behavioral isolation.

There is also some indication that these calls function along with similar calls to advertise to and repel other males. If an intruder male approaches, the calling male will move toward the newcomer and give a similar call and often another encounter call which will usually chase the intruder away. If not, some grappling between males may occur.

Once the female is attracted, the male grabs her from the rear and amplexus (copulatory embrace) occurs. In species which have huge generalized breeding congregations there is no social organization of the calls and the females are attracted en masse to the breeding pond. Once they enter the water they are grasped by any available male who uses a nuptial pad on the thumb to help restrain the female. If another male is grabbed accidentally he gives a short release call and the male lets him go. In amplexus, the female then extrudes the eggs which the male fertilizes.

In non-aggregate species in which the male calls from an isolated perch or in which a few may call, two or more male callings are organized into duet or trio sequences such as the hylid, *Smilisca baudinii*, commonly heard in the Community Baboon Sanctuary. Females approach or touch the calling male before it clasps her in amplexus. Then the eggs are laid in a gelatinous coating, fertilized by the male as they are laid. Different species of frogs lay eggs in different ways sometimes singly, in small clumps, in large masses, in strings or as surface sheets floating adhered to the water surface.

Metamorphosis

Metamorphosis in frogs and toads is a very radical

change which may last for a few days to three years depending on the species. The process is controlled by thyroxine, a hormone produced by the thyroid gland in the throat which also stimulates skin shedding. The thyroid can be inhibited by cold temperatures. Following hatching from the eggs, frogs begin life as tadpoles which are essentially feeding machines with a head and enormous intestine, adapted to an herbivorous lifestyle for rapid growth. The change or metamorphosis is dramatic both physically and in terms of lifestyle.

The tadpoles resorb their propulsive tails, lose their larval teeth, and grow limbs. The forelimbs develop inside the chamber housing the gills. Internally, the tadpoles have a long tightly coiled intestine with a large absorbing surface for processing vegetation. In adults the intestine becomes radically reduced in length. As they change to adults, space becomes available in the body for the reproductive organs.

Tadpoles are adapted to either a suspension-feeding way of life in which they filter particles of food from water or to a grazing-browsing life in which they tear and rasp off plant material from algae and other water plants. In filter feeding, water is taken in through the mouth and passed over the gills to filter out plankton and expelled through the tube-like spiracle. Oxygen is extracted similarly. In some species, especially those species which use small water bodies, tadpoles do not eat but survive on food from the yolk sac until they metamorphose.

Tadpole mouth parts used for feeding consist of a pair of fleshy lips and sometimes beaks with serrations. These horny "teeth" are arranged in transverse ridges or "tooth rows". The numbers of rows can be as high as 7 with the greatest proliferation of teeth in stream tadpoles. Some species have no teeth.

The generalized type of pond tadpole approximates the hylid type, with ovoid body, moderate caudal (posterior) muscles, and a small to medium-sized anteroventral mouth. From this general type evolved stream, pond, and arboreal tadpole types. The pond adapted tadpole has short, high fins with slender caudal musculature, extension of the dorsal fin onto the plump body. It develops a ventral spiracle and a terminal mouth. The stream dweller has a shallower more streamlined body, longer tail with heavier caudal musculature and shallower fins. They also have a large, more ventrally placed mouth which is often enlarged and modified with sucker-like discs for adhering to rocks in strong currents. Pond forms use their mouths only for food ingestion.

Tadpoles Showing Environmental Adaptations. Pond (top), Stream (middle), and Red-Eyed Tree Frog Tadpole (bottom)

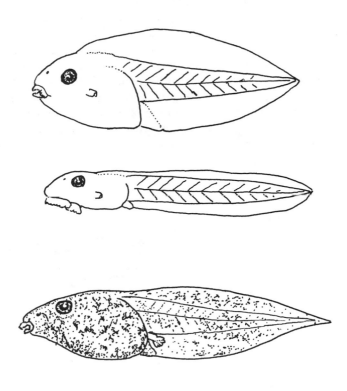

Arboreal types have a long tail with reduced fins, a ventral mouth or a mouth modified for eating frog eggs. Arboreals show striking physiological adaptations since they develop under limited water conditions with much decaying vegetable matter, low oxygen supply and low food supply. Food limitations may be compensated for by ingesting eggs of frogs probably of the same species.

Tree Frogs

Tree frogs (family Hylidae) or hylids are one of the most diverse and widespread of frog families. There are 630 species worldwide with 115 species occuring in Central America. Hylids are rather slender frogs and are much flatter than land-living frogs. This gives hylids an even weight distribution and enables them to balance and move with great agility on branches and leaves. The snout is rounded and the pupil of the eye is horizontally elliptical except for four genera in Central America including that of the red-eyed tree frog which is vertically elliptical. A frog tympanic ring is evident in most hylids. The tongue is not distensible and it is barely free for less than half its length. The vocal sacs can be single, double or include forms in between. In *Smilisea*, the

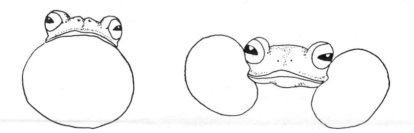

Tree Frogs Calling with Single (left) & Double (right) Vocal Sac

vocal sacs form paired bulbous protrusions. In *Hyla microcephala*, a common breeder in the roadside ditches of the Community Baboon Sanctuary, the vocal sac is a single bright yellow, greatly distensible sac.

Most of the Central American hylids are brown or green in color with a small minority being yellow. Most are patterned plainly or blotched with a few species striped. The most common coloration is brown with splotched patterning. The ability to change color in hylids is well documented. They typically turn dark in cool dark environments and lighter in light warm areas. However, pond breeders such as *Hyla microcephala* and *Hyla staufferi* are lighter at night and darker with conspicuous markings by day, in contrast with other species such as the red-eyed tree frog whose colors are darker and more intense at night. These two opposing trends in color change do not seem correlated with habits or habitat and are unexplained at this time.

Tree frogs have large areas of sticky webbing between their fingers and toes. The ends of the toes are expanded into circular adhesive discs enabling them to climb up smooth vertical surfaces. The loose belly skin acts similarly.

Hylid Life History

There is a close correlation in the time of breeding of most pond breeders with the onset of the rainy season whereas

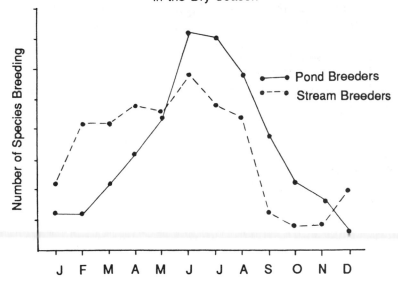

Seasonal Hylid Species Breeding Showing Pond Species Peak During the Rainy Season and Stream Species Breeding in the Dry Season

there is a less noticeable negative correlation with stream breeders and the dry season. Bromeliad breeders seem to have an extensive breeding season.

Dry season breeding activity in many stream breeding hylid species is understandable since many of these species inhabit humid montane forests which are moist throughout the year. Moreover, the streams are usually clear and calmer during the dry season. At the height of the rainy season such streams are rushing torrents and poor habitat for fragile tadpoles. The positive correlation between breeding season and the rains in pond breeders is even more predictable since many of these species utilize temporary ponds formed by heavy rains which are only wet during certain seasons. Indeed, research has shown that frogs emerge and breed on the night following a heavy rain.

Red - Eyed Tree Frog (*Agalychnis callidryas*)

This large most colorful of Central American frogs which gets its name from its vertical pupiled iris, occurs in the Community Baboon Sanctuary forests. It is distinguished from closely related frogs by having dark flanks (usually blue) with pale vertical bars. Their striking coloration is thought by scientists to confuse predators. A number of tree frogs show flash colors on the flanks, thighs, and surfaces that are concealed when the frog is at rest. They become visible, however, when it leaps, contrasting strikingly with the body colors. These flash colors are visible only momentarily to a predator while the frog leaps. When the frog then assumes a resting position, its green body blends with its leafy environment.

The gaudy leaf frog, as it is sometimes called, ranges throughout most of Central America. Like most amphibians and frogs in particular, it is dependent on water for part of its life. In the forest, it can minimize water loss by resting in a shady area and tucking its limbs in close to its body keeping its toes and fingers between its body and the tree or leaf. By thus reducing the surface area exposed to the air they reduce their evaporation water loss. By being quiescent (inactive) in the heat of the day they also slow down their metabolic processes,

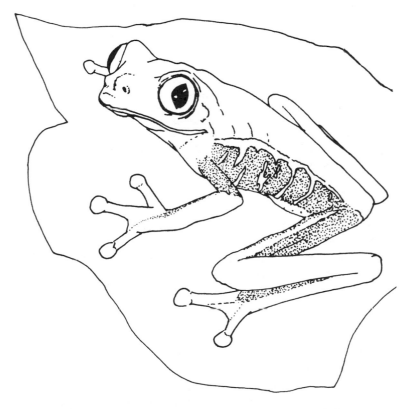

Red-Eyed Tree Frog Showing Flank Flash Colors

slowing breathing, and thus reducing moisture loss through respiration.

Breeding calling occurs from October-November through March during the rainy season near temporary or permanent ponds. Expanding the single subgular vocal sac, males call from trees and bushes or at the edge of ponds. They sit perpendicular to the branch or vine grasping it with large discs on the toes of their half webbed foot. Shortly after sunset males call from trees, usually about 10 feet (3 m) but as high as

25-30 feet (8-10 m) above the water. Usually the males are well spaced around the pond. The male then descends to the pond and produces a mating call which consists of a single or double-clucking note repeated at widely   spaced intervals of

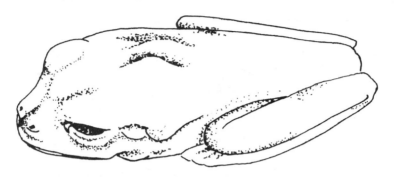

Red-Eyed Tree Frog Resting to Conserve Body Water

ten seconds to one minute. The round of clucking from high trees by the red-eyed tree frog at dusk may be territorial.   In areas away from the breeding sites, some hylids give certain calls just before and during a diurnal shower in a series of short notes "cluck-cluck-cluck" repeated at 0.1 second intervals which may be territorial or an awakening call.

The gravid female (laden with eggs) approaches a chosen male face to face. Once the male sees the female, she turns around and the male mounts and clasps her with his nuptial thumb pads which are enlarged during the breeding season. The tight clasping process in frogs is called amplexus. Following amplexus, the male then becomes very placid, closing his eyes.   Carrying the male on her back, the female climbs down to the water to fill her bladder by absorbing water through her skin.   She must do this or her eggs will die of dehydration.   The clasping pair then moves back into the tree and the female lays her eggs on an overhanging leaf while releasing water from her bladder over the eggs as they are laid.   The male fertilizes the eggs as they are laid.   She lays about 30-50 pale green eggs in a mass of clear jelly at one time but may repeat the whole process, laying 3-5 clutches in the night. Sometimes the female lays eggs on tree leaves which curl, further protecting the moist eggs.

In 5 days the pale blue tadpoles hatch by vigorously wriggling and rupturing the egg membrane and then fall into the water below. They orient head up near the surface of the water and congregate in sunny areas. In the warm waters they metamorphose into a frog in 74-79 days. The young frog doesn't attain its striking coloration until several weeks later when the tail is totally resorbed. As adults, the frogs spend most of the time in the forest canopy often using the bromeliads. Only about 30% of the young will reach maturity with most succumbing to predation and dehydration. The adults also have many enemies the most spectacular being some species of bat which are attracted to the frogs' vocalizations.

Frog-Eating Bat Attacking Red-Eyed Tree Frog

Hyla microcephala

This species is found in the Community Baboon Sanctuary because it occurs in disturbed areas such as cut over forest, secondary growth, and pasture land and is not an inhabitant of primary forest. It is distinguised from other *Hyla* by a lateral brown stripe extending to the groin region and bordered above by a narrow white line. It is a small

313

slender frog, yellowish-tan with two brown longitudinal stripes on its back and brown longitudinal stripe on the flank bordered by a narrow white line.

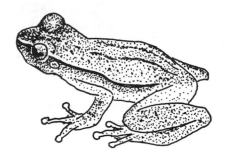

Hyla microcephala breeds throughout the rainy season from May through January. Breeding sites usually are shallow ditches, marshes or temporary ponds. Calling males perch on grasses or reeds in or at the edge of the water. Males have singular median vocal sacs and their mating call consists of a primary note followed by a series of secondary insect-like notes-- "creek-eek-eek-ekk". The primary note is unpaired and the secondary notes are paired. Eggs are deposited in small masses that float near the surface of the water and usually are attached to emergent vegetation. The caudal (tail) fins of the tadpoles are transparent except for an orange periphery.

Hyla staufferi

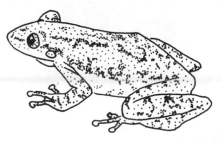

The species *Hyla staufferi* is common in the Community Baboon Sanctuary even frequenting around buildings and breeding in roadside ditches. It ranges from lowland, tropical subhumid forests and savannas to moderate elevations where rainfall is highly seasonal. Because of the seasonal rainfall, they are active only part of the year. During the dry season, they have been found in axils of leaves of elephant ear plants (*Colocasia*) and in bromeliads.

This species is distinguished by its very small size of 1.12 - 1.25 in (29-32 mm), the presence of dark longitudinal markings on its body and the absence of such markings on its thighs, a pointed protruding snout, and vestigial webbing between the fingers. Its long and slender toes bear discs that are noticeably smaller than those on fingers. Its color is tan or dull brown with irregular darker markings on the dorsum and limbs and an inter-orbital spot.

Breeding activity begins with the onset of rain in May and June and continues at least into September. Breeding takes place in shallow temporary ponds. Males call perched on grasses, herbs or low bushes with a series of short nasal "ah-ah-ah-ah" of 2-30 notes. After a heavy rain, large numbers may congregate at breeding ponds and at these times males compete for calling sites. Eggs are deposited in small clumps in shallow water. Tadpoles develop in these ponds where they prefer areas of dense grass or aquatic vegetation.

Smilisca baudinii

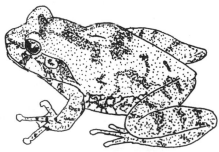

Smilisca baudinii is a large member of its genus being 3-3.5 in (76-90 mm) long and is identified by a large, high, elliptical inner metatarsal tubercle (large, wart-like bump on the hind feet). It is one of the most abundant species in Belize and is conspicuous owing to its loud and distinctive call.

Their dorsum is marked with large spots or blotches and is generally pale green or brown with dark brown markings. Juveniles are uniformly dull green above and lack marks on the thighs and flanks. They also have a broad white spot below the eye. The species inhabits dry and subhumid regions having a prolonged dry season. During unfavorable seasons they take refuge in bromeliads, elephant ear plants, tree holes, under tree bark, and under the outer sheaths of banana plants.

It breeds from June through October but has a longer season in the more humid Caribbean lowlands. Males call from nearly any body of water including cisterns and buckets, thus their common occurrence around human habitations. Usually their breeding sites are shallow temporary pools. · They call from the ground or at the edge of the water but may sit in shallow water or perch in bushes and trees while calling.

Males have paired gray vocal sacs which are subgular and greatly distendible. The males call in duets with each chorus made up of several pairs of calling males and successive choruses apparently are initiated by the same duet. The mating call is a series of short explosive notes "wonk-wonk-wonk" of 2-15 notes. Whereas most hylids don't give a territorial call, both *Smilisca baudinii* and *Agalychnis callidyas* produce widely spaced notes like the first notes of the mating call which may be territorial in nature. Several hundred eggs are spread by the gravid female in a surface filament on the water.

Inland Sharks ?

*W*e know that the area along the Belize River in the Community Baboon Sanctuary was once under ocean waters. Portions of what is now riverine and cohune forest was once under ocean and the lip of pine ridge where villagers now reside was a beach with waves lapping at its shores. We know that the sea came up this far by the fossil record left by the numerous species of sharks and rays who shed their teeth here millions or perhaps only thousands of years ago [an estimated guess is from the Miocene, 26 million years, to upper Cretaceous, 65 million years ago].

Sharks and rays are related in a group named Chondrichthyes which means having a cartilage skeleton. They differ from the typical bony fish found in the Belize River such as bay snook, tuba, and prana or from the many varied bony reef fish in a number of important ways:

1. They have cartilaginous skeletons.
2. They have no swim bladder for floating and must swim or they will sink to the bottom. This is not important for rays which are bottom dwellers, feeding on fish, molluscs, crustaceans, and sea urchins which live on the ocean bottom. Thus rays have little need of an air bladder.
3. Their teeth are not imbedded in a jaw bone but come from denticles (placoid scales) which are generalized skin teeth or scales.
4. They have a method of salt regulation.
5. They lack gill covers and thus have a number of gills slits at the surface. One specialized slit is a spiracle behind the eye in sharks or on top of rays, which acts as a water intake valve.
6. Males have claspers which are used for internal fertilization much like a penis in mammals functions. Although eggs are fertilized inside the female, sometimes they are retained and the female gives birth to live young with yolk sacs still attached. This occurs in sand or mako

sharks. In other species, such as most rays, the egg may be enveloped by a horny shell and extruded into the ocean. These egg cases may be found on the seashore and are sometimes called "mermaid's purses".

7. They have a small brain with a large smell organ (olfactory bulb). Smell is how sharks detect prey from a distance.

8. They have a short but efficient intestine with a spiral structure inside, called a spiral valve, for increasing absorptive surface. As an example, a 10 ft (3 m) shark has a 9 ft (2.8 m) intestine, while a 6 ft (2 m) man has a 25 ft (8 m) intestine.

Modern sharks are a primitive group of vertebrates which are related and very similar to many species which occur as fossils from the Cretaceous period (70-140 million years ago) or even the Jurassic Period (140-170 million years ago). The earliest shark lived some 350 million years ago yet they haven't changed much since then.

There are about 250-350 species of sharks and rays in existence of which only 12 are harmful to humans. These include the most formidable great white shark and to a lesser extent the tiger and mako shark. Living sharks range in size from 3 in (8 cm) to 45 ft (15 m). Rays are closely related and might be thought of as flattened sharks. Whereas sharks have gill slits on the side of their head, rays have them underneath.

Since sharks and rays have a cartilaginous skeleton, which disintegrates more rapidly than bone, they do not fossilize easily but their teeth and spines do. In fact, since sharks are continually growing rows of teeth and losing them, they shed a tremendous number of teeth. Teeth in the front drop out or are lost while teeth in the second row move into place. In most sharks, 5 or 6 replacement rows lie behind the functional teeth, one on top of the other, covered by tissue. As the tooth or denticle ages the root deteriorates and eventually the tooth falls out. The degradation can be seen from the teeth displayed. The spare teeth are always larger than those in use to keep up with the shark's growth. During a period of 10 years a tiger shark may produce, use, and shed some 24,000 teeth, hence the high numbers of fossils found in the area.

Shark Teeth

Shark teeth are usually one of two main types or shapes serving two main predatory functions: 1) seizing and grasping prey; and 2) cutting the prey into smaller pieces for swallowing.   Shark teeth alone can often be used to identify a species and give an idea of the shark's lifestyle and ecology. A 6 in (15 cm) tooth suggests the great white shark (*Carcharodon carcharias*) had a Miocene ancestor whose average length was 80 ft (25 m). The plate-like, triangular tooth is the most common in sharks and similar teeth of all sizes are found in the area.   Species such as the tiger shark

Triangular Teeth For Cutting

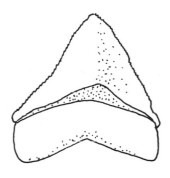

White Shark Relative
Carcharodon megalodon

Tiger Shark

feed on large prey which must be cut into smaller pieces before being eaten.   The triangular shaped tooth is used for this purpose.   However, the teeth also have serrations and cut more like a bread knife does, using the serrations in a sawing action.   Sharks like the sand and mako sharks also have long, round, spike-like teeth which are easily used to hook and seize small fishes, squid or octopi which they can swallow whole.

The placoid scales of shark skin, of which a shark has millions, are actually preformed undifferentiated teeth. The scales have the same structure as a tooth, composed of dentine with a pulp cavity at its center, covered by a layer of enamel. A base plate secures the scale to the skin.   The similarity of

Spike Teeth For Seizing

Sand Shark

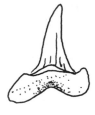

Mako Shark

the scale and shark teeth is so exact that scales are called denticles or dermal teeth to distinguish them from jaw teeth. Unlike mammals, the teeth are not implanted in sockets but are simply attached at their bases to a sheath of connective tissue called a tooth bed. The teeth are anchored by a root which is the equivalent of a base plate of a denticle. The cartilaginous jaws of sharks are loosely attached to the cranium allowing them to be removed easily.

Denticles come in a wide variety of shapes and sizes and may be arranged tightly or sparsely in ranks, giving the shark skin a rough sandpapery feel. In some areas shark skin has been used as sandpaper. Denticles are the main unit from which more specialized structures have arisen. Teeth are the most obvious. An embryo shark shows no difference between denticles around the mouth and those lining the jaws. But as they grow, the teeth differentiate. In rays, spines such as those in sting rays, are also modified denticles. The poison spines of sting rays, which have also been found in the sanctuary, are notched with rows of tiny barbs. They release a venom that affects blood and causes swelling and cramps.

Although formidable, the spines do not protect them from sharks and often one finds ray spines imbedded in the

Rows of Replaceable Shark Teeth

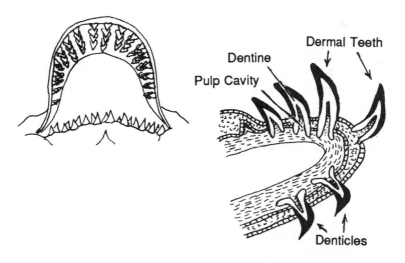

mouth or skin of sharks. The sawfish has a long snout armed with rows of teeth on either side. These teeth are also modified skin denticles which the sawfish uses to slash its prey in shoal water where it lives. The function of the general skin denticles affords some protection but it may also be that their rough surface helps to maintain a layer of water close to the shark's streamlined body to aid in movement while swimming.

When feeding, because their mouths are situated underneath the head, sharks lunge at prey from below, opening the mouth wide, closing it and shaking the entire forward part of the body violently from side to side to tear off large chunks of tissue. Bull sharks (*Carcharhinus leucas*) eat rays, shads, crabs, mackeral, and porpoises; tiger sharks eat porpoises, hammerhead sharks, turtles, crabs, mackeral, sharks; mako sharks eat bluefish.

GLOSSARY

Adaptation- adjustments to new or altered environmental conditions based on genetic changes due to natural selection acting on a species or population

Adventitious- in plants referring to any structure arising from an unusual location on the plant

Altruism- the act of one individual(A) enhancing the survival and reproduction of an unrelated individual(B) that is detrimental to individual(A)

Amplexus- the copulatory embrace of frogs and toads

Anterior- located near or towards the front or head of an animal

Arboreal- refers to species which live primarily in trees

Canopy- the uppermost portion of a tree where the leaves spread out

Carbohydrate- a group of organic compounds consisting of carbon, hydrogen, and oxygen, including cellulose, starches, and sugars

Carnivore- species which exclusively eat flesh or nutrients obtained from animal matter

Carrion- dead and/or decaying flesh of animals

Carrying capacity- the number of individuals that the resources of a given habitat can support

Caudal- at or near the tail or hind end of an animal; posterior

Cecum- a blind sac at the beginning of the large intestine

Chromatophore- pigment cell in the skin giving color

Climax community- the end point of a successional sequence; a plant community that has reached a steady-state under the particular climate of a given geographical region

Cline- changes in population characteristics along some environmental or geographical gradient or transition

Cloaca- posterior chamber of the digestive tract receiving waste discharge; in some animals it also functions as a reproductive canal

Cold-blooded- animals that cannot internally regulate their body temperature thus having body temperatures nearly the same as the changing temperatures of their environment

Copulation- the sexual union of two individuals

Crepuscular- animals active during both twilight and near the dawn

Cross-pollination- the transfer of pollen from the flower of one individual to another

Decomposition- the breakdown of organic matter

Dewclaw- claw terminating the vestigal digit on the feet of mammals

Dewlap- a fleshy fold of skin hanging from the neck of reptiles

Diversity- the number of species in a given community or region

Dorsal- located near or at the back of an animal or one of its parts

Ecdysis- molting or shedding of the outer skin

Ecosystem- a complex system including all interacting organisms together with their environment

Edentate- an order of mammals having few or no teeth, includes anteaters, armadillos,and sloths

Edge effect- the resulting vegetation at an interface between two different community types or at the edges of a clearing; edge species prefer these types of habitats

Epiphyte- plant which lives on other plants, usually above ground, but is not parasitic on its host

Evapotranspiration- evaporation or discharge of water from plants (mostly occuring through the leaves) and the soil

Extinction- either the worldwide or regional population death of a species or group of species

Fecundity- rate at which an individual produces offspring

Gene- the basic unit of inheritance, part of the DNA molecule that encodes a single enzyme or structural trait

Generalist- a species with a broad range of food and/or habitat preferences

Gland- a structure which produces substances vital to the survival of the organism

Gravid- a female carrying eggs or young

Gular- located in the upper throat; in turtles it is a horny shield on the plastron

Habitat- physical place where a plant or animal normally lives, eg. stream, forest, mountain

Herbivore- an animal that eats only living plants or plant parts

Heredity- genetic transmission of traits from parents to their offspring

Home range- an area in which an individual restricts most of its normal activity; intruders may or may not be excluded from the home range (see also territory)

Hybridization- the crossing of individuals from different populations, subspecies or even species

Hyoid- a bone or bones at the base of the tongue, much enalrged in the howler monkey

Inbreeding- mating among related individuals

Inheritance- the genetic transmission of characteristics from parent to offspring

Invertebrate- an animal lacking a backbone or an internal skeleton

Kingdom- the classification of species falls into an established hierarchy as follows: Kingdom
Division
Class
Order
Family
Genus and species

Leaching - the dissolving and removal of nutrients and minerals from soil by the action of downward moving, percolating water

Lek- a communal courtship area on which several males hold territories and court females

Loam- a soil consisting of sand, silt, and clay

Mammae- milk-secreting organs found in all mammals

Mangrove- a plant community occuring in coastal areas and commonly containing species of mangrove trees

Melanism- the occurence of a black pigment

Metabolism- the sum total of processes whereby an organism gets energy by processing foodstuffs, either synthesizing or breaking down compounds

Metamorphosis- a dramatic or gradual change in development from one form to another

Mimicry- one species assuming the color, form or behavior of another species; Mullerian mimicry is the mutual resemblance of two equally distasteful or poisonous species to avoid predators; Batesian mimicry is the resemblance of a "mimic" edible species to a "model" unedible species

Monogamous- having only one mate for life

Monogynous- having only one female in a colony or mating with only one female

Mutualism- interactions between two species which are beneficial to both species

Mycorrhiza- a mutual relationship whereby a fungus invades the roots of a host plant; the fungus provides needed nutrients for the plant and vice versa

Niche- the functional relationship of an organism to its environment

Nictitating membrane- a membrane found in vertebrates located in the inner angle of the eye or below the eyelid that covers the eye

Nocturnal- animals only active at night or plants with flowers that open only at night

Omnivore- an organism with a wide-ranging diet including both plants and animals

Opportunisitc- an individual or species that takes advantage of temporary changes in habitat and/or environmental conditions

Pappillae- a small, nipple-like projection

Parasite- an organism that lives in or on another species, called a host, usually not killing the host

Perennial- an organism that lives for more than one year

Phenology- the study of periodic biological events such as flowering, fruiting or breeding

Pheromones- chemical substances used for communication between individuals or to influence behavior

Photoperiod- length of daylight each day

Pigment- any coloring material or substance in plant or animal cells

Polymorphic- the occurence of two or more distinct forms of individuals in a given population or species

Posterior- the back end or hind of an organism

Precocial- birds that hatch covered with down, with eyes open, and able to move about immediately

Predator- an animal adapted to kill and eat other animals

Respiration- the use of oxygen to break down organic matter for energy

Riparian or *Riverine-* refers to the environment along rivers, lakes or other waterways

Savanna- vegetation type with trees scattered in a grassland matrix

Scute- a bony, horny or chitnous plate

Sibling- individuals having the same parents; a brother or sister

Soil horizon- a distinct zonation of different soil layers which make up the soil profile

Species- a group of interbreeding or potentially interbreeding populations which cannot breed with any other type of organism

Subspecies- subpopulations within a species that have distinct morphological, behavioral or physiological characteristics

Succession- the directional and continuous pattern of change in species composition, abundance, and importance over time

Symbiosis- interrelationship between two species which have co-evolved

Sympatric- occuring in the same place; refers specifically to regions of overlap in species distributions

Territory- any area defended by one or more individuals against intrusions by the same or other species

Thigmonasty- movement of an organism in response to touch

Trophic- refers to food or nutrition; trophic levels are positions in the food chain determined by the number of energy transfers required to reach a given level

Ungulate- any hoofed mammal

Ventral- situated close to or on the belly or lower surface

Vertebrate- a group of animals which all have backbones; ranges from fish to humans

Warm-blooded- any animal that can maintain a relatively constant body temperature

REFERENCES

Development of the Sanctuary, Community Baboon Sanctuary, and Future of Community Sanctuaries

Horwich, R.H. 1990. How to develop a community sanctuary: an experimental approach to the conservation of private lands. *Oryx* 24: 95-102.

Horwich, R.H. 1988. The Community Baboon Sanctuary: an approach to the conservation of private lands, Belize. In: *Saving the Tropical Forests*, J. Gradwohl & R. Greenberg (eds.), Earthscan Publications, Ltd., London.

Horwich, R.H. & J. Lyon. 1987. Development of the "Community Baboon Sanctuary" in Belize: An experiment in grass roots conservation. *Primate Conservation* 8: 32-34.

Horwich, R.H. & J. Lyon. 1988. An experimental technique for the conservation of private lands. *Journal of Medical Primatology* 17: 169-176.

The Baboon or Black Howler Monkey

Bolin, I. 1981. Male parental behavior in black howler monkeys (*Alouatta palliata pigra*) in Belize and Guatemala. *Primates* 22: 349-360.

Coelho, A.M., C.A. Bramblett, L.B. Quick, and S.S. Bramblett. 1976. Resource availability and population density in primates: A socio-bioenergetic analysis of howler and spider monkeys. *Primates* 17: 63-80.

Horwich, R.H. 1983. Breeding behaviors in the black howler monkey (*Alouatta pigra*) of Belize. *Primates* 24: 222-230.

Horwich, R.H.1983. Species status of the black howler monkey, *Alouatta pigra*, of Belize. *Primates* 24: 288-289.

Horwich, R.H. & K. Gebhard. 1985. Relation of allomothering to infant age in howlers, *Alouatta pigra*, with reference to old world monkeys. *Current Perspectives in Primate Social Dynamics*, vol.1, D.M. Taub & F.A. King, p.66-88.

Horwich, R.H. & K. Gebhard. 1983. Roaring rhythms in black howler monkeys (*Alouatta pigra*) of Belize. *Primates* 24: 290-296.

Horwich,R.H. & E. Johnson. 1986. Geographic distribution of the black howler, *Alouatta pigra*, in Central America. *Primates* 27: 53-62.

Smith, J.D. 1970. The systematic status of the black howler monkey, *Alouatta pigra*, Lawrence. *Journal of Mammalogy* 51: 358-369.

Conservation of Howler Monkeys

Baker, B. 1986, 1987, 1988. *Regional Studbook Black Howler Monkey Alouatta caraya.*

Estrada,A. & R. Coates-Estrada. 1988. Tropical rain forest conversion and perspectives in the conservation of wild primates (*Alouatta* and *Ateles*) in Mexico. *American Journal of Primatology* 14: 315-327.

Happel, R.E., et al. 1987. Distribution, abundance, and endangerment. In: *Primate Conservation in the Tropical Rain Forest*. C.W. Marsh & R.A. Mittermeier (eds.), pp. 63-82. Alan R. Liss, N.Y.

Johns, A.D. 1983. Tropical forest primates and logging - can they co-exist? *Oryx* 17: 114-118.

Konstant, W.R. & R.A. Mittermeier. 1982. Introduction, reintroduction, and translocation of Neotropical primates: past experiences and future possibilities.
Int.Zoo Yrbk. 22: 69-77.

Marsh, C.W., Johns, A.D., & J.M.Ayres. 1987. Effects of habitat disturbance on rain forest primates. In: *Primate Conservation in the Tropical Rain Forest*. C.W. Marsh & R.A. Mittermeier (eds.), pp. 83-107. Alan R. Liss, N.Y.

Mittermeier, R.A. 1987. Framework for primate conservation in the Neotropical region. In: *Primate Conservation in the Tropical Rain Forest*. C.W. Marsh & R.A. Mittermeier (eds.), pp.305-320. Alan R. Liss, N.Y.

History of the Area

Dobson, N. 1973. *A History of Belize*. Longman Caribbean, Jamaica.

Education Task Force. 1984. *A History of Belize*. Sunshine Press, Belize City.

Foster, B. 1987. *The Bayman's Legacy*. Cubola Productions, Benque Viejo, Belize.

Krohn,L.H. et al. 1987. *Readings in Belizean History*. St. John's College, Belize City.

Belizean Trees and History

Anonymous. 1984. *Belize Today: A society in transformation*. Sunshine Books, Belize CIty, Belize.

Bolland, O.N. 1986. *Belize, a new nation in Central America*. Westview Press, Inc., Boulder, Colorado.

Bolt, A. 1961. Chicle chewing gum from British Honduras. *World Crops* 13(2): 58-59.

Gregg, A.R. 1968. *British Honduras*. H.M.S.O., London.

Naylor, P.A. 1989. *Penny Ante Imperialism*. Associated University Presses, Inc.

Standley. P.C. and S.J. Record. *Forests and Flora of British Honduras*. Field Museum of Natural History, Bot. Ser. 12, 432 p.

Waddell, D.A.G. 1961. *British Honduras: a historical and contemporary survey*. Oxford University Press, London.

Belizean Forests, Forest Types Within the Sanctuary

Anderson, R.C. and J.S. Fralish. 1975. An investigation of palmetto, *Paurotis wrightii* (Griseb. & Wendl.) Britt., communities in Belize, Central America. *Turrialba* 25(1): 37-44.

Beard, J.S. 1955. The classification of tropical American vegetation types. *Ecology* 36(1): 89-100.

Chapman, V.J. 1976. *Mangrove vegetation.* Weinheim: Cramer Verlag.

Dwyer J.D. and D.L. Spellman. 1981. A list of the Dicotyledoneae of Belize. *Rhodora* 83: 161-236.

Field Museum of Natural History, Botany: Flora of Guatemala. Fieldiana, Botany, volume 24 part I-XIII. Chicago, USA.

Furley, P.A. and W.W. Newey. 1979. Variations in plant communities with topography over tropical limestone soils. *Journal of Biogeography* 6: 1-15.

Lambert, J.D.H. and J.T. Arnason. 1978. Distribution of vegetation on Maya ruins and its relationship to ancient land- use, Lamanai, Belize. *Turrialba* 28: 33-41.

Spellman, D.L., J.D. Dwyer, and G. Davidse. 1975. A list of the Monocotyledoneae of Belize. *Rhodora* 77: 105-140.

Standley, P.C. and S.J. Record. 1936. *Forests and Flora of British Honduras.* Field Museum of Natural History, Bot. Ser.12, 432 p.

Stevenson, D. 1928. Types of forest growth in British Honduras. *Trop. Woods* 14: 20-25.

Wright, A.C.S., D.H. Romney, R.H. Arbuckle, and V.E. Vial. 1959. Land in British Honduras. *Col. Res.* Publ. No.24.

Forest Phenology

Boinski, S. and N.L. Fowler. 1989. Seasonal patterns in a tropical lowland forest. *Biotropica* 21(3): 223-233.

Borchert, R. 1983. Phenology and control of flowering in tropical trees. *Biotropica* 15: 81-89.

Bullock, S.H., and J.A. Slois-Magallanes. Phenology of canopy trees of a tropical deciduous forest in Mexico. *Biotropica* 22(1): 22-35.

Frankie, G.W., H.G. Baker, and P.A. Opler. 1974. Comparative phenological studies of trees in tropical wet and dry forests in the lowlands of Costa Rica. *Journal of Ecology* 62:881-913.

Janzen, D.H. 1967. Synchronization of sexual reproduction of trees within the dry season in Central America. *Evolution* 20: 249-275.

Lieberman, D. and M. Lieberman.1984. The causes and consequences of synchronous flowering in a dry tropical forest. *Biotropica* 16(3): 193-201.

Rathcke, B. and E.P. Lacey. 1985. Phenological patterns of terrestrial plants. *Annual Review of Ecology and Systematics* 16: 179-214.

Reich, P.B. and R. Borchert. 1984. Water stress and tree phenology in tropical dry forest in the lowlands of Costa Rica. *Journal of Ecology* 72: 61-74.

Forest Succession

Brokaw, N.V.L. 1985. Gap-phase regeneration in a tropical forest. *Ecology* 66: 682-687.

Denslow, J.S. 1980. Gap partitioning among tropical rainforest trees. *Biotropica* 12 (Suppl): 47-55.

Ewel, J. 1983. Succession. In, *Tropical rain forest ecosystems: structure and function* , ed., F.B. Golley,Amsterdam, Elsevier Scientific.

Hubbell, S.P. and R.B. Foster. 1986b. Biology, chance, and history and the structure of tropical forest tree communities. In J. Diamond and P.J. Case eds., *Community Ecology* , pp. 314- 329. Harper & Row, New York.

Pickett, S.T.A., S.L. Collins, and J.J. Armesto. 1987. Models, mechanisms and pathways of succession. *The Botanical Review* 53: 3365-371.

Pickett, S.T.A. and P.S. White. *The ecology of natural disturbance and patch dynamics* . New York, Academic Press.

Land Use in the Sanctuary

Arnason, J.T., J.D. Lambert, and J. Gale. 1984. Mineral cycling in a tropical palm forest. *Plant and Soil* 79: 211-225.

Birchall, J.S. and R.N. Birchall. 1979. *The agricultural potential of the Belize Valley.* Land Res. Div. Suppl., ODA, London.

Jenkin, R.N., J.S. Birchall. 1976. The agricultural potential of the Belize Valley. *Land Res. Div.*, ODA, London, Land Resources Study No. 24, 348 p.

Kellman, M.C. and C.D. Adams. 1970. Milpa weeds of the Cayo District, Belize (British Honduras). *Canadian Geographer* 14(4): 323-343.

Lambert, J.D.H., and J.T. Arnason. 1978. Distribution of vegetation of Maya ruins and its relationship to ancient land use at Lamanai, Belize. *Turrialba* 28(1): 33-41.

Lambert, J.D.H., and J.T. Arnason. 1980. Nutrient levels in corn and competing weed species in a first year milpa, Indian Church, Belize, C.A. *Plant and Soil* 55: 415-427.

The Importance of Tropical Rain Forests

Almeda, F and C.M. Pringh. 1988. *Tropical rainforests, diversity and conservation.* San Francisco, California Academy of Sciences.

Longman, K.A. and J. Jenik. 1974. *Tropical forest and its environment.* London, Longman Group.

Richards, P.W. 1952. *The tropical rain forest.* Cambridge University

Press.

Tomlinson, P.B. and M.H. Zimmerman. 1978. *Tropical trees as living systems*. Cambridge University Press.

Leigh, E.G. Jr. 1982. *The ecology of a tropical forest*. Washington, D.C., Smithsonian Institution Press.

Pomeroy, D. and M.W Service. 1986. *Tropical Ecology*. London, Longman Group.

Ridpath, M.G. and L.K. Corgett. 1985. *Ecology of the wet-dry tropics*. Melbourne, Darwin Institute of Technology.

Whitmore, T.C. and A.C. Chadwick. 1983. *Tropical rainforest: ecology and management*. Oxford, UK, Blackwell.

Rivers and Water Resources

Gonzalez, V.J. 1980. *A limnological investigation of a tropical freshwater ecosystem: The Belize River, Belize, Central America* Western Michigan Univ., Kalamazoo, Ph.D. dissertation.

Lee, R. 1980. *Forest Hydrology*. Columbia University Press, New York.

Lowrance, R.R. et al. 1984. Riparian forest as nutrient filters in agricultural watersheds. *Bioscience* 34: 374-377.

McColl, J.G. 1970. Properties of some natural waters in a tropical wet forest in Costa Rica. *Bioscience* 20: 1096-1100.

Payne, A.I. 1986. *The ecology of tropical lakes and rivers* . John Wiley & Sons, New York.

Riparian ecosystems and their management: reconciling conflicting uses. 1985. *Proceedings of the First North American Riparain Conference*, Tuscon, AZ, USA.

Whittan, B.A. 1975. *River Ecology*. Blackwell Scientific, New York.

Epiphytes

Benzing, D.H. 1970. Foliar permeability and the absorption of minerals and organic nitrogen by certain tank bromeliads. *Botanical Gazette* 131: 23-31.

Benzing, D.H. 1980. *The Biology of the Bromeliads*. Mad River Press, Eureka, Calif.

Nadkarni, N.M. 1981. Canopy roots: convergent evolution in rainforest nutrient cycles. *Science* 214: 1023-1024.

Perry, D.R. 1978. Factors influencing arboreal epiphytic phytosociology in Central America. *Biotropica* 10: 235-237.

Perry, D.R. 1984. The Canopy of the tropical rain forest. *Scientific American* 251(5): 138-147.

Spellman, D.L., J.D. Dwyer and G. Davidsee. 1975. A list of the Monocotyledoneae of Belize. *Rhodora* 77: 105-140.

Strong, D.R. 1977. Epiphyte loads, treefalls, and perennial forest disruption: a mechanism for maintaining higher species richness in the tropics without animals. *Journal of Biogeography* 4: 215-218.

Vines and Lianas - Tie-Ties

Janzen, D.H. 1979. How to be a fig. *Annual Review of Ecology and Systematics* 10: 13-51.

Putz, F.E. 1980. "Lianas vs. Trees". *Biotropica* 12 (Suppl): 224-225.

Putz, F.E. 1984. The natural history of lianas on Barro Colorado Island, Panama. *Ecology* 65: 1713-1724.

Strong, D.R. Jr., and T.S. Ray, Jr. 1975. Host tree location behavior of a tropical vine *Monstera gigantea* by skototropism. *Science* 190: 804-806.

Rain Forest Adaptations

Black, H.L. and K.T. Harper. 1979. The adaptive value of buttresses to tropical trees: additional hypotheses. *Biotropica* 11: 240.

Dean, J.M. and A.P. Smith. 1978. Behavioral and morphological adaptations of a tropical plant to high rainfall. *Biotropica* 10: 152-154.

Henwood, K. 1973. A structural model of forces in buttresses in tropical rain forest trees. *Biotropica* 5(2): 83-93.

Lee, D.W., J.B. Lowry, and B.C. Stone. 1979. Abaxial anthocyanin layer in leaves of tropical rain forest plants: enhancer of light capture in deep shade.*Biotropica* 11: 70-77.

Smith, A.P. 1972. Buttressing of tropical trees: a new descriptive model and new hypotheses. *American Naturalist* 106: 32-46.

Smith, A.P. 1979. Buttressing of tropical trees in relation to bark thickness in Dominica, B.W.I. *Biotropica* 11: 159-160.

Plant Defenses

Coley, P.D. 1983. Herbivory and defensive characteristics of tree species in a lowland tropical forest. *Ecological Monographs* 53: 209-233.

Coley, P.D., J.D. Bryant, and F.S. Chapin. 1985. Resource availability and plant antiherbivore defense. *Science* 230: 895-899.

Futuyma, D.J., and M. Slatkin. 1983. *Coevolution.* Sinauer Associates, Sunderland, MA.

Hedin, P. 1983. *Mechanisms of plant resistance to insects.* American Chemical Society Symposium.

Myers, N. 1984. *The primary source: tropical forests and our future.* W.W. Norton, New York.

Rosenthal, G.A. and D.H. Janzen. 1979. *Herbivores: their interactions with secondary plant metabolites.*`New York, Academic Press.

Wallace, J.W. and R.L. Mansell. *Biochemical interaction between plants and insects.* New York, Plenum Press.

Fruits

Estrada, A. and T.H. Fleming. 1986. *Frugivory and seed dispersal*. The Hague, Dr W Junk.

Foster, R.B. 1982. The seasonal rhythm of fruitfall on Barro Colorado Island. In, *The ecology of a tropical forest*, eds., E.G. Leigh, Jr., A.S. Rand and D.M. Windsor. Washington, D.C., Smithsonian Institution Press.

Foster, S.A. and C.H. Janson. 1985. The relationship between seed size and establishment conditions in tropical woody plants. *Ecology* 66(3): 773-780.

Herrera, C.M. 1982. Defense of ripe fruits from pests: its significance in relation to plant-disperser interactions. *American Naturalist* 120: 218-241.

Howe, H.F. 1977. Bird activity and seed dispersal of a tropical wet forest tree. *Ecology* 58: 539-550.

Janson, C.H. 1983. Adaptation of fruit morphology to dispersal agents in a neotropical forest. *Science* 219: 187-189.

Smythe, N. 1970 Relationships between fruiting seasons and seed dispersal in a neotropical forest.*American Naturalist* 104: 25-35.

Wheelwright, N.T. 1985. Fruit size, gape width, and the diets of fruit-eating birds. *Ecology* 66: 808-818.

Orchids

Ames, O. and D.S. Correll. 1985. *Orchids of Guatemala and Belize* . Dover, New York, 779 p.

Passionflowers

Bisacre,M., R. Carlisle, D. Robertson &J. Ruck (eds.). 1984. *The Illustrated Encyclopedia of Plants*. Exeter Books, N.Y.

Edlin,H. 1973. *Atlas of Plant Life*. The John Day Co., N.Y.

Fogden, P. 1987. War and Passion. *International Wildlife* Jan- Feb pp12-17.

Heyward, V.H. 1978. *Flowering Plants of the World*. Mayflower Books, N.Y.

Lehner, E. & J. Lehner. 1960. *Folklore and Symbolism of Flowers, Plants, and Trees*. Tudor Publishing Co., N.Y.

Mitchell, A.W. 1986.*The Enchanted Canopy*. Macmillan Publishing Co., N.Y.

Pesman, M.W. 1962. *Meet Flora Mexicana*. Dale S. King Publ., Globe, Ariz.

Rest, F. 1973. *Our Christian Symbols*. The Christian Education Press, Philadelphia.

Figs and Wasps

Janzen, D.H. 1979. How to be a fig. *Annual Review of Ecology and Systematics* 10: 13-51.

Sisson, R.F. 1970. The wasp that plays cupid to a fig. *National Geographic* 138: 690-697.

Wiebes, J.J. 1979. Co-evolution of figs and their insect pollinators. *Annual Review of Ecology and Systematics* 10: 1-12.

Amazing Ants

Bentley, B.L. 1977. Extrafloral nectaries and protection by pugnacious bodyguards. *Annual Review of Ecology and Systematics* 8: 407-427.

Janzen, D.H. 1966. Coevolution of mutualism between ants and accacias in Central America. *Evolution* 20: 249-275.

Newman, L.H. 1967. *Ants from Close Up*. Thomas Y Crowall, Co., N.Y.

Wilson, E.O. 1974. *The Insect Societies*. Harvard University Press, Cambridge, Mass.

Wilson, E.O. 1975. *Sociobiology*. Harvard University Press, Cambridge, Mass.

Endangered Species of Belize

Anon. 1987. *Endangered & threatened wildlife and plants*. U.S. Government Printing Office.

Ehrenfeld, D.W. 1970. *Biological Conservation*. Holt, Rinehart and Winston,Inc. N.Y

Edentates - Toothless, Not Quite

Schueler, D.G. 1988. Armadillo make me smile alot. *Audubon Magazine* July: 72-77.

Shaw, J.H. & T.S. Carter. 1980. Giant Anteaters. *Natural History* 189(10) : 62-67.

Smith, L.L. & R.W. Doughty. 1984.*The Amazing Armadillo*. Univ of Texas Press, Austin.

Storrs, E.E. 1982.The Astonishing Armadillo. *National Geographic* 161(6): 820-830.

Cats

Cohen, I.E. 1978. *The Predators*. New Burlington Books, London, WI.

Ewer, R.F. 1973. *The Carnivores*. Weidenfeld and Nicolson London.

Guggisberg, C.A. 1975. *Wild Cats of the World*. Taplinger Publishing Co., N.Y.

Tinsley, J.B. 1987. T*he Puma, Legendary Lion of the Americas*. Texas Western Press, Univ.Texas, El Paso.

Trowbridge Bohlen, J. 1987. Jaguars - Why protect a killer? *InternationalWildlife* Mar-Apr. 4-11.

Wexo, J.B. 1981. *Big Cats*. Zoo Books Wildlife Education, San Diego.

Gray Fox
Fox, M.W. 1975. *The Wild Canids*. Van Nostrand Reinhold Co., N.Y.

Hoofed Mammals - Ungulates
Sowls, L.K. 1984. *The Peccaries*. Univ. Arizona Press Tucson.

The Manatee
Bateman, G. (ed.). 1984. *Sea Mammals*. Torstar Books, N.Y.
Bruemmer, F. 1986. How the mermaid perished. *International Wildlife* Jan-Feb : 24-27.
Hartman, D.S. 1979. *Ecology and Behavior of the Manatee* (Trichechus manatus) *in Florida*. Special Publication No. 5, The American Society of Mammalogists.
Husar,S.L.1977. *The West Indian Manatee* (Trichechus manatus), U.S. Dept. Interor, Fish & Wildlife Service Wildlife Research Report 7.
O'Shea, T.J. & C.A. Salisbury. 1989. *Status of Manatees*, Trichechus manatus (Mammalia: Sirenia), *in Belize, with results of a May 1989 aerial survey*. Report.
Sleeper, B. 1986. A far cry from a sea nymph. *Audubon Magazine* Mar: 86-99.

Hummingbirds
Biel, T.L. 1987. *Hummingbirds*. Zoobooks. Wildlife Education, Ltd., San Diego.
Feinsinger, P. 1978. Ecological interactions between plants and hummingbirds in a successional tropical community. *Ecological Monographs* 48: 269-287.
Grant, K.A. and V. Grant. 1968. *Hummingbirds and their flowers*. Columbia University Press, N.Y.
Russell, S.M. 1964. A distributional study of the birds of British Honduras [Belize]. *Ornithological Monographs* No. 1.
Stiles, F.G. 1980. The annual cycle in a tropical wet forest hummingbird community. *Ibis* 122: 322-343.
Stiles, F.G. & L.L. Wolf. 1979 Ecology and evolution of lek mating behavior in the long-tailed hermit hummingbird. *Ornitholopgical Monographs* No. 27. A.O.U., Wash, D.C.

Migrant Birds
Fisher, A.C. 1979. Mysteries of bird migration. *National Geographic* 156: 154-193.
Fitzpatrick, J.W. 1982. Northern birds at home in the tropics. *Natural History* 91: 40-47.
Howe, J.R. 1983. The vanishing birds of Vera Cruz. *Defenders of Wildlife* Nov-Dec. 18-28.

Keast, A. and E.S. Morton. 1980. *Migrant birds in the neotropics: ecology, behavior, distribution, and conservation.* Washington, D.C., Smithsonian Institution Press.

Lincoln, F.C. and S.R. Stevenson. 1979. *Migration of Birds.* Circular 16. U.S. Fish and Wildlife Service, U.S. Dept. Interior.

Birder's Delight - American Wood Warblers

Harrison, H.H. 1984. *Wood Warblers World.* Simon and Schuster, N.Y.

Wood, D.S., R.C. Leberman, and D. Weyer. 1986. *Checklist of the birds of Belize.* Pittsburgh, PA, Carnegie Museum of Natural History, Special Publication No. 12.

Blackbirds

Orians, G.1985. *Blackbirds of the Americas.* Univ. of Washington Press, Seattle.

Going, Going, Gone... Game Birds of Belize

Delacour, J. & D. Amadon. 1973. Curassows and related birds. American Museum of Natural History.

Lint, K.C. 1977-8. Ocellated turkeys. *Journal of the World Pheasant Association* :14-21.

Steadman, D.W., J. Stull, and S.W. Eaton. 1978-9. Natural history of the ocellated turkey. *Journal of the World Pheasant Association* :15-37.

Limping Bird

Pellowski, M.J.1987. *Birdwatcher's Digest* July-Aug: 30-32.

Manakins

Bradbury, J.W. and R.M. Gibson. 1983. Leks and mate choice. In: *Mate Choice*, ed. P. Bateson, pp. 109-138.

Sick, H. 1967. Courtship behavior in the manakins (Pipridae): ar review. *Living Bird* 6: 5-22.

Snow, D.W. 1962. A field study of the black and white manakin, *Manacus manacus*, in Trinidad.
Zoologica 47: 65-105.

The Hickatee

Alvarez del Toro, M. Mittermeier, R.A., and Iverson, J.B. 1979. River turtle in danger. *Oryx* 15: 170-173.

Campbell, J.A. 1972. Observations on Central American river turtles. *International Zoo Yearbook* 12: 202-204.

Lee, R.C. 1969. Observing the Tortuga Blanca. *International Turtle and Tortoise Society Journal* 3(3): 32-34; 20-26.

Mittermeier, R.A. 1970. Turtles in Central American markets. *International Turtle and Tortoise Society Journal* 4(5): 20-26.

Moll, D. 1986. The distribution, status, and level of exploitation of the freshwater turtle *Dermatemys mawei* in Belize, Central America. *Biological Conservvation* 35: 87-96.

Moll, D. In press. Food and feeding behavior of the turtl, *Dermatemys mawei* in Belize *Journal of Herpetology*

Pritchard, P.C.H. 1979. Taxonomy, evolution, and zoogeography. PP1-42. In: Harless, M. and Morelock, H. eds. *Turtles : Perspectives and Research*. John Wiley and Sons, N.Y.

Crocodiles of Belize

Abercrombie, C.L. et al. 1980. Status of morelet's Crocodile *Crocodylus moreleti* in Belize. *Biological Conservation* 17: 103-113.

Echternacht, A.C. 1977. *How Reptiles and Amphibians Live*. Gallery Press, N.Y.

Halliday, T. & K. Adler. 1986. *Encyclopedia of Reptiles and Amphibians*. Facts on File, Inc., N.Y.

Kondo, H. 1972. *Illustrated Encyclopedia of the Animal Kingdom, Reptiles*. The Danbury Press, CT.

Norales, V. Crocodiles. Printed for Belize schools by RARE, USAID, CCA.

Toner, M. 1985. The Croc holds its own. *National Wildlife* June-July: 12-15.

Wexo, J.B. 1986. *Alligators and crocodiles*. Zoobooks Wildlife Education, Ltd., San Diego.

Snakes : Good, Not Evil

Appleby, L.G. 1987. Snakes shedding skin. *Natural History* 64-71.

Forsyth,A. 1988. Snakes maximize their success with minimal equipment.*Smithsonian* Feb: 158-165.

Gamow,R.I. and J.F. Harris. 1978. The infrared receptors of snakes. *Scientific American* 228: 94-100.

Ubertazzi Tanara, M. 1975. *The World of Amphibians and Reptiles*. Gallery Books, N.Y.

Iguanas

Burghardt, G.M. & A.S.Rand. 1982. *Iguanas of the World*. Noyes Publ., Park Ridge, NJ.

Frogs and Toads

Duellman, W.E. 1970. *The Hylid frogs of middle Americ* Monographs of the Museum of Natural History, Univ. Kansas, vol 1&2. pp. 1-753.

Duellman, W.E and L.Trueb. 1985. *Biology of Amphibians*. McGraw-Hill, N.Y.

Halliday, T.R. & K. Adler. 1986. *The Encyclopedia of Reptiles and Amphibians*. Facts on File Publications, N.Y.

Mattison, C. 1987. *Frogs and Toads of the World*. Facts on File Publ., N.Y.

Inland Sharks?
Budker, P. 1971. *The life of sharks*. New York, Columbia University Press, N.Y.
Case, G.R. 1982. *A pictoral guide to fossils*. Van Nostrand Reinhold Co., N.Y.
Lineaweaver, T.H. and R.H. Backus. 1969. *Natural History of Sharks*. T.H. Doubleday, Garden City, N.Y.
Schnyder, E.K. and H. Rieber. 1986. *Handbook of Paleozoology*. Johns Hopkins University Press, Baltimore.

General References For Species
Ayensu, E.S. 1980. *Jungles*. Crown Publishers, N.Y.
Burton, M & R. Burton (eds.). 1969. *International Wildlife Encyclopedia*. Marshall Cavendish Corp., N.Y.
Carr,A. 1963. *The Reptiles*. Time Inc., N.Y.
Grzimek, B. 1971. *Grzimek's Animal Life Encyclopedia*. Van Nostrand Reinhold Co., N.Y.
Janzen, D.H. (ed.). 1983. *Costa Rican Natural History*. Univ. Chicago Press, Chicago.
Macdonald, D. 1984. *The Encyclopedia of Mammals*. Facts on File Publications, N.Y.
Matthews, L.H. 1971. *The Life of Mammals, vol 2*. Universe Books, N.Y
National Geographic *Book of Mammals* (2 vols). 1981. National Geographic Society, Washington, D.C.
Nowak,R.M. and J.L.Paradiso. 1983. *Walker's Mammals of the World*. John Hopkins University Press, Baltimore.
Skutch, A.F. 1983. *Birds of Tropical America*. Univ.of Texas Press, Austin.
Vaughan, T.A. 1972. *Mammalogy*. W.B. Saunders Co., Phila.
Whitfield, P. 1979. *The Animal Family*. WW Norton & Co. Inc., N.Y.

COMMON TREES and SHRUBS FOUND in NORTHERN BELIZE

CM = coastal mangrove   PR = pine ridge   BR = broken ridge
HR = high ridge   CR = cohune ridge   HR* = wet areas in high ridge

Common name	Botanical Name	Family	Habitat Type			
Annatta	*Bixa orellana*	Bixaceae	PR	BR		
Bay cedar	*Guazuma ulmifolia*	Sterculiaceae		BR	HR	
Billy Webb	*Sweetia panamense*	Fabaceae		BR		
Black mangrove	*Avicennia germinans*	Avicenniaceae	CM			
Black poisonwood	*Metopium Brownei*	Anacardiaceae		BR	HR	
Botan palm	*Sabal morrisiana*	Palmae	CM	BR		
Bribri	*Inga edulis*	Mimosaceae			HR*	CR
Bucut	*Cassia grandis*	Caesalpinaceae		BR	HR	CR
Bullet tree	*Bucida buceras*	Combretaceae		BR	HR*	CR
Buttonwood	*Conocarpus erecta*	Combretaceae	CM			
Cabbage bark	*Andira inermis*	Fabaceae		BR		
Cabbage palm	*Euterpe macrospadix*	Palmae	CM		HR*	CR
Calabash	*Crescentia cujete*	Bignoniaceae	PR			
Cedar	*Cedrela mexicana*	Meliaceae			HR	CR
Chicle	*Manilkara zapota*	Sapotaceae		BR	HR	
Cockspur	*Accacia* spp.	Mimosaceae		BR	HR	CR

Common name	Botanical Name	Family	CM	PR	BR	HR	CR
Cohune	*Orbigyna cohune*	Palmae			BR	HR	CR
Cojotone	*Stemmadenia donnell-smithii*	Apocynaceae				HR	CR
Copna	*Erythrina fusca*	Fabaceae				HR*	CR
Cotton tree	*Ceiba pentandra*	Bombacaceae				HR	CR
Cowfoot	*Piper auritum*	Piperaceae			BR		
Craboo	*Byrsonima crassifolia*	Malpighiaceae		PR	BR		
Dogwood	*Lonchocarpus guatemalensis*	Fabaceae				HR	CR
Fig	*Ficus* spp.	Moraceae					
Give and Take	*Crysophila argentea*	Palmae				HR	CR
Gumbolimbo	*Bursera simaruba*	Burseraceae	CM			HR	CR
Hog plum	*Spondias mombin*	Anacardiaceae				HR	CR
Ironwood	*Dialium guianense*	Caesalpinaceae				HR	
Locust	*Hymenaea courbaril*	Caesalpinaceae			BR	HR*	
Logwood	*Haematoxylon campechianum*	Caesalpinaceae	CM			HR	CR
Mahogany	*Swietenia macrophylla*	Meliaceae				HR	
Madre cacao	*Gliciridia sepium*	Fabaceae			BR	HR	
Mampola	*Luehea seemanii*	Tiliaceae				HR	CR
Mayflower	*Tabebuia rosea*	Bignoniaceae			BR	HR	
Negrito	*Simarouba glauca*	Simaroubaceae			BR		
Oak	*Quercus oleoides*	Fagaceae		PR			
Pimenta (palm)	*Paurotis wrightii*	Palmae		PR	BR		
Pine	*Pinus caribeae*	Pinaceae		PR			

Common name	Botanical Name	Family	Habitat Type				
			CM	PR	BR	HR	CR
Pokenoboys	*Bactris major*	Palmae				HR*	CR
Polewood	*Xylopia frutescens*	Annonaceae			BR	HR	
Prickly yellow	*Zanthoxylum kellermanii*	Rutaceae			BR	HR	CR
Provision tree	*Pachira aquatica*	Bombaceae	CM			HR*	CR
Quamwood	*Schizolobium parahybum*	Caesalpinaceae			BR	HR	CR
Ramon	*Brosimum alicastrum*	Moraceae				HR	CR
Red fowl	*Pithecellobium sp.*	Mimosaceae				HR*	CR
Red mangrove	*Rhizophora mangle*	Rhizophoraceae	CM				
Santa Maria	*Calophyllum brasiliense*	Guttiferae				HR	CR
Sea grape	*Coccoloba uvifera*	Polygonaceae	CM				
Silver thatch palm	*Thrinax radiata*	Palmae	CM		BR	HR	CR
Soap-seed tree	*Sapindus saponaria*	Sapindaceae	CM			HR	
Suppa palm	*Acrocomia mexicana*	Palmae		PR	BR		
Swamp kaway	*Pterocarpus officinalis*	Fabaceae	CM				
Trumpet	*Cecropia obtusifolia*	Moraceae			BR		
Tubroos	*Enterolobium cyclocarpum*	Mimosaceae			BR	HR	CR
White mangrove	*Laguncularia racemosa*	Combretaceae	CM				
White maya	*Miconia argentea*	Melastomaceae		PR	BR		
Wild cotton	*Cochlospermum vitifolium*	Cochlospermaceae		PR	BR		
Wild grape	*Coccoloba belizensis*	Polygonaceae				HR*	CR
Yaha	*Curatella americana*	Dillenaceae		PR	BR		
Yemeri	*Vochysia hondurensis*	Vochysiaceae			BR	HR	

COMMON FRUIT TREES FOUND in NORTHERN BELIZE

Common name	Botanical Name	Family	Habitat Type	
Cashew	*Anacardium occidentale*	Anacardiaceae	PR	
Coconut	*Cocos nucifera*	Palmae	CM PR	BR
Craboo	*Byrsonima crassifolia*	Malpighiaceae	PR	BR
Custard apple	*Annona reticulata*	Annonaceae	PR	BR
Guava	*Psidium guajava*	Myrtaceae	PR	BR
Mango	*Mangifera indica*	Anacardiaceae	PR	BR
Papaya	*Carica papaya*	Caricaceae		BR
Pear (Avocado)	*Persea americana*	Lauraceae	PR	BR
Soursop	*Annona muricata*	Annonaceae	PR	BR

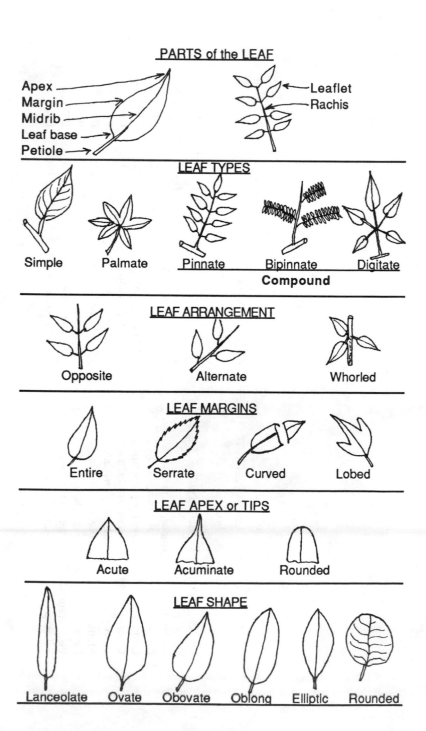

PARTS of the LEAF

Apex
Margin
Midrib
Leaf base
Petiole

Leaflet
Rachis

LEAF TYPES

Simple   Palmate   Pinnate   Bipinnate   Digitate

Compound

LEAF ARRANGEMENT

Opposite   Alternate   Whorled

LEAF MARGINS

Entire   Serrate   Curved   Lobed

LEAF APEX or TIPS

Acute   Acuminate   Rounded

LEAF SHAPE

Lanceolate   Ovate   Obovate   Oblong   Elliptic   Rounded

KEY TO COMMON HARDWOOD TREE SPECIES

LEAVES SIMPLE

1. LEAVES ALTERNATE on the stem
   2. Leaf margins Serrate (saw-toothed)
      a) leaves green on both sides; leaves 3-5" long; base of leaf unequal; leaf with one major midvein; BAY CEDAR (*Guazuma ulmifolia*)
      b) leaves brownish beneath, dark green above; with 3-5 major veins; leaves mostly 4-7 " long; trunk often buttressed......MAMPOLA (*Luehea seemanii*)

   2. Leaf margins Entire (no teeth)
      3. Leaves clustered at branch tips
         a) branches armed with sharp spines; leaves 1 1/2 - 4" long; bark grayish black............ BULLET TREE (*Bucida buceras*)
         b) trunk, stems and leaves containing a white milky latex; bark with narrow vertical cracks; often with machete scars.............. CHICLE (*Manilkara zapota*)

      3. Leaves NOT clustered at branch tips
         4. Trees containing a white milky latex
            a) branches very leafy; leaves 3-7 " long; with roundish orange fruits, 3/4" dia..... RAMON (*Brosimum alicastrum*)
            b) leaves with obvious midvein; trunks smooth..........................FIG (*Ficus* spp)
         4. Trees without a milky latex
            5. Leaves large, roundish
               a) leaves large, roundish with wavy margins; veins lateral...................... WILD GRAPE (*Coccoloba belizensis*)
               b) leaves with cordate base, thin, apex tapered......COWFOOT (*Piper auritum*)
            5. Leaves narrow, short, hairy beneath; small trunked tree............................... POLEWOOD (*Xylopia frutescens*)

Bay cedar (*Guazuma ulmifolia*) - Sterculiaceae
Bay Cedar, Bastard Cedar (Bz)- Pixoy, Xuyuy (Maya)
Caulote, Guacimo (Guat)

A common tree reaching to 60 ft (19 m). The bay cedar is commonly found in secondary growth and secondary forest areas from sea level to 3,500 ft (1100 m). The tree produces flowers and fruits twice a year. The fruits are eaten by many animals including monkeys and cattle. The gelatinous sap of the tree is said to treat elephantiasis and is used to induce sweating (sudorific). The bark may also be stripped and used for cordage.

Mampola (*Luehea seemanii*) - Tiliaceae
Mampola, Caulote (Bz)- Kazcat (Maya)- Tapasquit,
Guacimo (Guat)

Common in lowland forest and frequently with plank buttresses. Grows to over 100 ft (30 m). It produces small but very fragrant, cream-colored flowers in the early dry season.

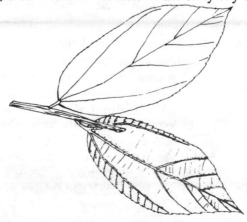

Bullet tree (*Bucida buceras*) - Combretaceae
Bullet Tree, Bully Tree (Bz)- Pucte, Pocte (Maya)-
Cacho de Toro (Guat)

Commonly found in coastal swamps or inland in wet forest areas and along rivers. The tree gets its name from its very hard and durable wood which was used for construction, railway ties, and charcoal. The bark is also used in tanning.

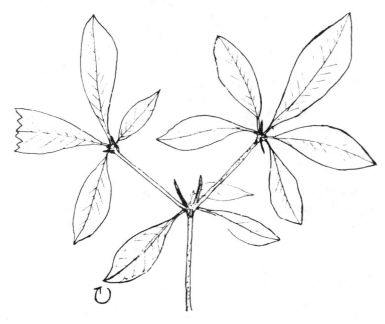

Chicle (*Manilkara zapota*) - Sapotaceae
Chicle, Sapodilla, Sapote (Bz)- Mui, Tzaput, Ya (Maya)-
Zapote, Chico-Zapote (Guat)

This tree is the source of chicle, the original form of chewing gum. The harvesting and history of chicle are mentioned elsewhere in the guidebook. Because of the chicle industry that once thrived in Belize, most adult chicle trees bear the machete scars of the "chicleros" who depended on the trees for their livelihood. The tree grows in mixed limestone forests.

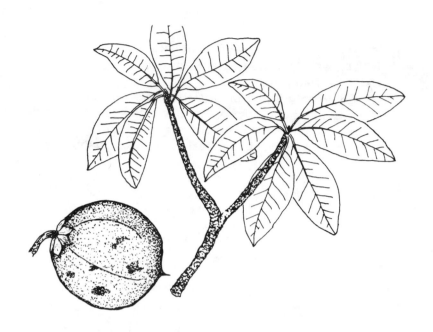

Ramon (*Brosimum alicastrum*) - Moraceae
   Ramon, Breadnut (Bz)- Ujushte, Ox (Maya)- Ramon,
Capomo (Guat)

     A medium to large-sized tree commonly with a leafy
crown. The tree is common on limestone soils. The leafy
branches of this tree are often cut and fed to horses and other
livestock. The pulp of the orange fruits is edible as are the
seeds. The ancient Mayans commonly planted this tree near
dwellings for food.

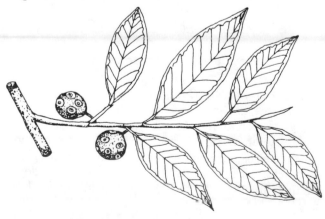

Wild grape (*Coccoloba belizensis*) - Polygonaceae
  Wild Grape (Bz)- Bul (Maya)- Uva de Monte, Uva (Guat)
    A tree commonly found in wet forest areas. The tree gets its common name from its long-strands of berries resembling small grapes which are eaten in some regions. Young trees often have very large, rounded leaves.

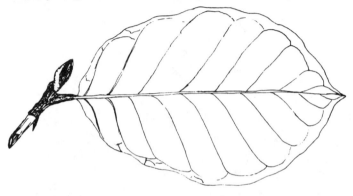

Cowfoot - (*Piper auritum*) - Piperaceae
  Cowfoot, Bullhoof (Bz)- Xaclipur, Obet, Maculan (Maya)-
  Cordoncillo, Santa Maria (Guat)
    A small tree-like shrub with stout branches. It is one of the more common shrubs found on abandoned lands throughout Central America. Crushed leaves smell of sarsaparilla and are used as a food flavoring throughout Central America.

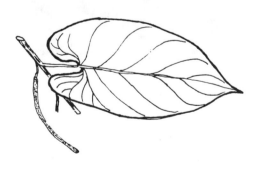

Polewood (*Xylopia frutescens*) - Annonaceae
Polewood (Bz)- Sina (Maya)- Malagueto, Palanco (Guat)
A shrub or small tree with light bark and long slender branches. The straight trunks of smaller trees are used as poles or "palancos" for pushing small boats in shallow water and also for fish spears.

LEVES SIMPLE

1. LEAVES OPPOSITE on the stem

   6. Leaves in Whorls of Three
     leaves 3-5" long; flowers yellow (April-May);
     mostly in broken ridge...............................YEMERI
                        (*Vochysia hondurensis*)
   6. Leaves Paired, not whorled

      a) Trees with white milky latex; leaves oblong-
         lanceolate, 3-7" long; fruits large, paired...........
         COJOTONE (*Stemmadenia donnell-smithii*)

      a) Trees without milky latex; leaves with many
         parallel, lateral nerves, dark green; trunk with
         a yellowish sap.......................... SANTA MARIA
                  (*Calophyllum brasiliense*)

LEAVES DIGITATE

1. Leaves with mostly **5** - leaflets
   Leaflets 4-8" long on long petioles; fruits bean-like up
   12" long; deciduous in dry season; often a large tree
                MAYFLOWER (*Tabebuia rosea*)

1. Leaves with mostly **7** or more leaflets

   2. Trunk smooth, often buttressed; leaflets broad, 5-7"
     long, pale beneath; fruit ovoid, large, up to 10" long
         PROVISION TREE (*Pachira aquatica*)

   2. Trunk often covered with short, conical spines; with
     horizontal branching; leaflets thinner than above......
         COTTON TREE (*Ceiba pentandra*)

Yemeri (*Vochysia hondurensis*) - Vochysiaceae
Yemeri, White Mahogany (Bz) Saguc (Maya)- San Juan,
Palo Bayo (Guat)

A medium-sized tree with smooth, gray bark common in the broken ridge. When the tree is in flower from May to June, the bright yellow flowers render the tree very conspicuous.

Cojotone (*Stemmadenia donnell-smithii*) - Apocynaceae
Cojotone (Bz)- Tonche' (Maya)- Cojon, Copal,
Huevos de Caballos (Guat)

Frequent in thickets and forest. The tree has large conspicuous fruits made up of two fleshy, rounded pods that resemble testicles--thus the common name. The tree also exudes a sticky, milky latex that is used in El Salvador to fasten cigarette papers and has similar properties to "gutta-percha". Gutta-percha is a rubbery substance derived from latex that is used for waterproofing or even electrical insulation.

Santa Maria (*Calophyllum brasiliense*) - Guttiferae
Santa Maria (Bz)- Bari, Ocu (Maya)- Mario, Santa Maria, Leche Amarilla (Guat)

A fairly common tree found in mixed forest ranging from Mexico to Brazil. The leaves are very attractive and in fact the latin name, Calophyllum, means beautiful leaf. The trunk exudes a yellowish latex when cut. The tree is also cut for its valuable lumber throughout Belize.

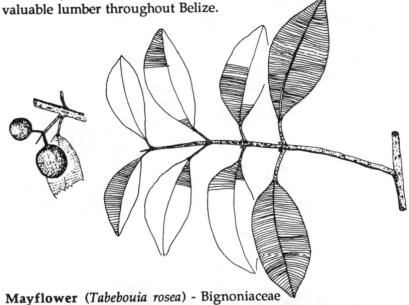

Mayflower (*Tabebouia rosea*) - Bignoniaceae
Mayflower, Roble, May Bush (Bz)- Hokab (Maya)

An often large tree with plank buttresses and bark with course vertical fissures. The tree produces large pinkish-white flowers from March to May. The tree is deciduous in the dry season. The wood was commonly used to make cattle and oxen yokes.

Provision Tree (*Pachira aquatica*) - Bombaceae
Provision Tree, Santo Domingo (Bz)- Uacoot, Cuyche (Maya)-   Zapoton, Zapote Bobo (Guat)

A tree only found in wet areas often forming dense groves. The trunk usually has many thin buttresses. The large ovoid fruits can reach over 12 in (30 cm) long and can weigh 6 lbs (2.7 kg). The seeds are roasted and eaten and the bark used to make tea.

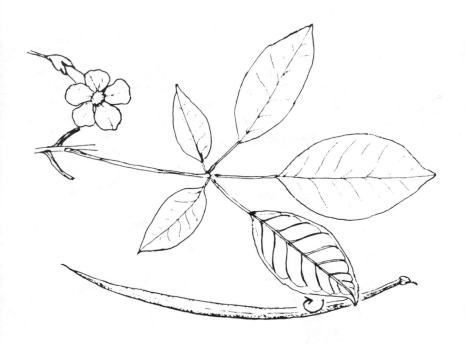

ABOVE: *Tabebuia rosea* (Mayflower) - showing flower, leaf and long slender fruits

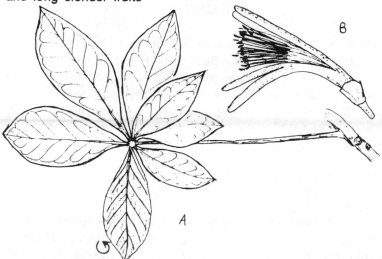

ABOVE: *Pachira aquatica* (Provision Tree) - showing A) leaf and B) large, distinctive flower

Cotton Tree (*Ceiba pentandra*) - Bombaceae

Cotton Tree, Kapok, Ceiba (Bz)- Yaxche, Mox, Inup (Maya)-
Ceiba (Guat)

A large and distinctive tree up to 200 ft (62 m) tall in some areas of the world (the species is pantropical). The columnar trunk is often buttressed and covered with short, hard, conical spines. The seeds of the fruit are embedded in a cottony material known as "kapok". The kapok was at one time used commercially for stuffing pillows, furniture, mattresses and even life preservers. The seeds also contain an oil which can be used to make soap or burned in lamps like oil.

LEAVES COMPOUND

1. LEAVES PALMATE

Leaves large, 10-13 lobed; small tree with horizontal
branches and a slender, hollow trunk............TRUMPET TREE
(*Cecropia obtusifolia*)

1. LEAVES PINNATE
2. Leaves ONCE PINNATE

3. LEAFLETS ALTERNATE
4. Trunk Armed with pyramid-like spines
with 6-8 leaflets, oblong-elliptic, 5-6" long;
leaflets shiny above................. PRICKLY YELLOW
(*Zanthoxylum kellermanii*)

4. Trunk Unarmed

5. With mostly 10-20 Leaflets
Leaflets dark green above, much paler
beneath; 2-4" long; leathery, margins
often curved..................................NEGRITO
(*Simarouba glauca*)

5. With only 5-9 Leaflets
a) tree with blood-red sap; leaflets
mostly 7-9; 4-7" long; in wet areas
SWAMP KAWAY (*Pterocarpus officinalis*)
b) leaflets mostly 5-7; leaflets 1-3" long
sap NOT red............................IRONWOOD
(*Dialium guianense*)

3. LEAFLETS OPPOSITE

6. Leaves with only TWO leaflets
a) Trunk with slender spines; leaflets small,
1-2" long; tree found mostly in wet
areas; pods slender, coiled...... RED FOWL
(*Pithecellobium* sp)

a) Trunk smootish; leaflets larger, 1.5-4"
long; legume pod 4" long, 2" wide, brown
LOCUST (*Hymenaea courabil*)

6. Leaves with MORE than TWO leaflets

7. Trunks ARMED with Spines

a) with 3 leaflets; spines large, conical and numerous; in very wet areas; flowers large, orange................COPNA
(*Erythrina fusca*)

b) usually with 6 leaflets, heart-shaped, small; spines small, pointed; smaller tree with gray bark and fluted trunk......
LOGWOOD (*Haematoxylon campechianum*)

7. Trunks UNARMED
8. BARK SMOOTH

9. Bark Reddish
bark thin and peeling; with 6-10 leaflets
....GUMBOLIMBO
(*Bursera simaruba*)

9. Bark NOT Reddish

10. Leaves with a winged rachis with 6-12 leaflets; common tree on rivers and in wet areas...... BRI-BRI
(*Inga edulis*)

10. Leaves without a winged rachis

11. With mostly 3-7 Leaflets
a) Leaflets rounded, 1-3" dia; bark thin, reddish-brown; in wet areas
....................BLACK POISON WOOD
(*Metopium brownei*)

b) Leaflets oblong with tapered tips, 3-6" long; with pinkish flowers in April and May................DOGWOOD
(*Lonchocarpus guatemalensis*)

11. With mostly more than 7 leaflets

12. With 7-13 leaflets

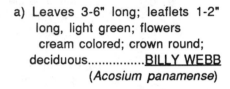

a) Leaves 3-6" long; leaflets 1-2"
   long, light green; flowers
   cream colored; crown round;
   deciduous................<u>BILLY WEBB</u>
        (*Acosium panamense*)

b) Leaves 8-12" long; leaflets
   dark green; bark with strong
   odor.................<u>CABBAGE BARK</u>
        (*Andira enermis*)

12. With 10-30 leaflets

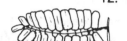

1-2" long, oblong, finely hairy;
seed pod large, 1-3 ft long.......
        <u>BUCUT</u> (*Cassia grandis*)

8. BARK ROUGH, with fissures

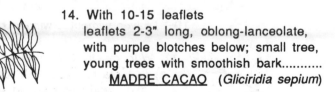

13. Leaflets asymmetrical; 6-10 leaflets per
    leave, even-pinnate, 2-5" long; bark
    dark colored.........................<u>MAHOGANY</u>
            (*Swietenia macrophylla*)
13. Leaflets symmetrically shaped

14. With 10-15 leaflets
    leaflets 2-3" long, oblong-lanceolate,
    with purple blotches below; small tree,
    young trees with smoothish bark...........
        <u>MADRE CACAO</u> (*Gliciridia sepium*)

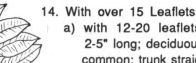

14. With over 15 Leaflets
    a) with 12-20 leaflets, broad-elliptic,
       2-5" long; deciduous in dry season;
       common; trunk straight.... <u>HOG PLUM</u>
            (*Spondias mombin*)

b) with 18-26 leaflets; leaflets smaller,more narrow than in hog plum, bark similar; bark with strong odor...... CEDAR (*Cedrela mexicana*)

2. LEAVES TWICE-PINNATE

15. Branches with hollow thorns containing stinging ants leaflets bright green; hollow thorns from whitish to black..............COCKSPUR (*Accacia* spp.)

15. Branches without hollow thorns

a) Bark smoothish; large tree; often buttressed; with ear-shaped fruits; small white flowers; deciduous in dry season.......................TUBROOS (*Enterolobium cyclocarpum*)

b) Bark somewhat rougher than above, often with a reddish tint; produces bright yellow flowers and small, flat droopy pods; leaves very large, fern-like..QUAMWOOD (*Schizolobium parahybum*)

Trumpet (*Cecropia obtusifolia*) - Moraceae
Trumpet Tree, Trumpet (Bz)- Pacl, Choop, (Maya)-
Guarumo, Yaruma (Guat)

The trumpet tree is one of the typical pioneer trees which occupies forest gaps. The tree can grow quickly--up to 20 ft (6 m) in the first year alone, and is common along roadsides. The hollow trunks house species of *Azteca* ants which help defend the plant. The "wool" material separated from the leaves and stems is said to be smoked by Mayans in Mexico. The name trumpet eludes to the belief that the hollow stems were used by the Mayans to make wind instruments.

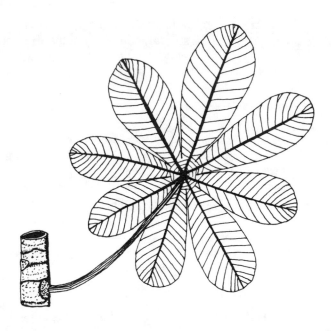

ABOVE: *Cecropia obtusifolia*, note straight and crisp leaf edges
BELOW: *Cecropia peltata*, leaf edges wavy, not as deeply lobed

Prickly Yellow (*Zanthoxylum kellermanii*) - Rutaceae
   Prickly Yellow (Bz)- Lagarto, Cedro Espino (Guat)
      The latin names comes from "xanthos" = yellow, and
"xylon" = wood, in reference to the yellow wood and roots of
trees in this genus. The large conic prickles on the tree make it
conspicuous in the forest. Crushed leaves have a lemonish odor.

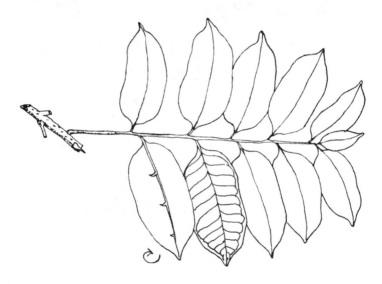

Negrito (*Simarouba glauca*) - Simaroubaceae
   Negrito (Bz)- Pasac, Aceituno (Maya)-
   Jocote de Mico (Guat)
      The leaflets of the tree are very dark green above and
very much paler beneath. The tree produces fruits in March
and April. These fruits are black and edible, tasting like
olives. The seeds contain an oil which can be used in cooking or
for making soap. The wood burns even when green.

Swamp Kaway (*Pterocapus officinalis*) - Fabaceae
   Swamp Kaway, Kaway (Bz)- Sangre, Sangre de Drago,
   Sangregado (Guat)
      The tree has smooth gray bark which when pierced
yields a blood-red sap. The sap has been used as a medicine
under the name "dragon's blood". The smooth barked tree is
common in wet swampy areas near the coast and is often has
many thin buttresses.

BELOW: *Pterocarpus officinalis* (Swamp Kaway)

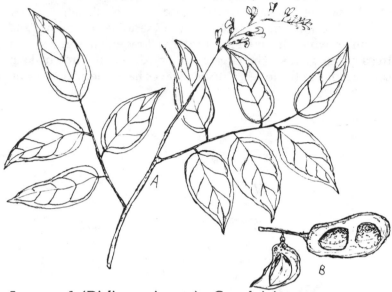

Ironwood (*Dialium guianense*) - Caesalpiniaceae
Ironwood, Wild Tamarind (Bz)- Cuatchi, Chate, Uapake
(Maya)- Paleta, Tamarindo, Palo de Lacandon (Guat)
    A common tree of the Atlantic lowlands of Central
America. The tree gets its common name for its very hard and
heavy wood. The wood may weigh up to 55 lbs per cubic foot
(0.8 kg dm^3) and does not float.

Copna (*Erythrina fusca*) - Fabaceae
Copna, Coama, Tarpon (Bz)
    The large orange flowers of this tree make it very
conspicuous when it flowers in March and April. The flowers
are relished by the baboons who seem undeterred by the many
sharp, conical spines on the trunk and branches of the tree. At
night, the three leaflets of the leaf, droop downward giving
the tree a wilted appearance.

Locust (*Hymeneae courabil*) - Caesalpiniaceae
Locust (Bz)- Pac, Pacoj (Maya)- Guapinol,
Hoja de Cuchillo (Guat)
    The latin name of the genus is named after Hymen, the
god of marriage because of the paired leaflets. The pulp

surrounding the seeds is edible and tastes faintly like banana. The trunk also exudes a pale gum known commercially as "copal" used in the manufacture of varnish or burned as incense.

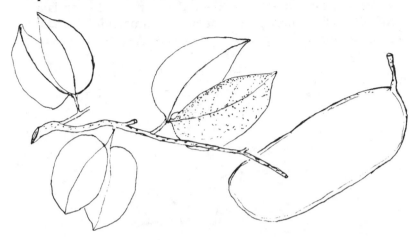

Logwood (*Haematoxylon campechianum*) - Caesalpiniaceae
Logwood (Bz)- Ek (Maya)- Tinta, Campeche,
Palo de Tinta (Guat)
A once very abundant tree in low forests and thickets. Its harvest for logwood dye represents the early history of Belize and is explained elsewhere in the guidebook.

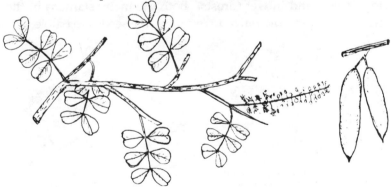

Gumbolimbo (*Bursera simaruba*) - Burseraceae
Gumbolimbo, Birch (Bz)- Chicah, Cacah (Maya)- Jiote, Ohaca, Ohic-Ohica (Guat)
The red peeling bark renders the tree obvious. It is one

of the more common trees planted as a living fence post. The wood of the tree is not durable but is often used for making match sticks. The resinous sap from the tree was burned as incense in many churches in Central America. The sap is also used as an all-purpose glue. The name "gumbolimbo" is said to be derived from the spanish "goma elemi", meaning resinous sap.

Bri-Bri (*Inga edulis*) - Mimosaceae
Bri-Bri, Guamo (Bz)-Uatop, Bitze (Maya)-Guajiniquil (Guat)
A medium-sized tree with a spreading crown common along rivers and in wet forests. Both the many stamens in the large flowers and the pulp surrounding the seeds are edible.

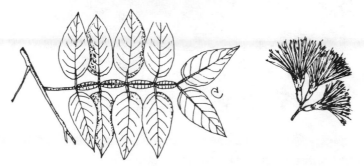

Black Poisonwood (*Metopium brownei*) - Anacardiaceae
Black Poisonwood, Honduras Walnut (Bz) Chechem (Maya)-
Palo de Rosa, Chechem Negro (Guat)

A shrub or tree with thin reddish-brown bark. Both the bark and leaves have poisonous properties similiar to poison ivy.

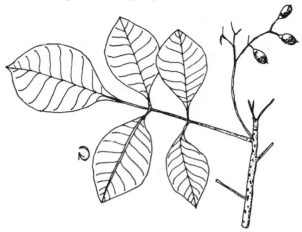

Dogwood (*Lonchocarpus guatemalensis*) - Fabaceae
Dogwood, Ridge Dogwood, Turtle-Bone (Bz)- Ixec-subin, Xuul (Maya)- Palo de Gusano (Guat)
A tree with conspicuous pinkish flowers when it flowers in the dry season. It may be that this species was used by the Mayans to make an intoxicating beverage. The bark was soaked in water and honey and then fermented to produce a drink called "Balche'". Balche may have been made from the bark of a close relative of this species.

Billy Webb (*Sweetia panamensis*) - Fabaceae
Billy Webb (Bz)- Guayacan, Quina Silvestre (Guat)
The slightly scaly bark has a bitter taste and is used to make a remedy for coughs and fever. The tree also has a very hard, durable wood that is suitable for heavy construction.

Cabbage Bark (*Andira enermis*) - Fabaceae
Cabbage Bark, Cornwood, Barley Wood, Black Blossom Berry (Bz)- Carbon, Almendro, Iximche
The name cabbage bark comes from the fact that the rough bark of adult trees resembles the rough trunk of the cabbage palm. The tree is unusual in that it only produces flowers and fruits once every two years. When in flower, the dense clusters of purple flowers are very showy. The tree has a very hard wood which is used for construction.

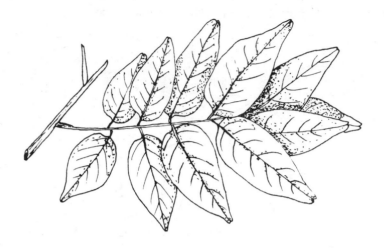

ABOVE: *Sweetia panamensis* (Billy Webb)
BELOW: *Andira enermis* (Cabbage Bark)

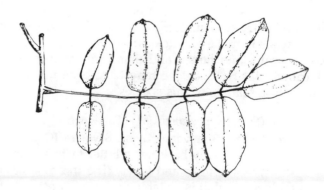

Bucut (*Cassia grandis*) - Caesalpinaceae
   Bucut, Stinking toe, Beef-Feed (Bz)- Mucut (Maya)-
   Carao (Guat)
      A common tree in Belize. When in flower in April it is
one of the most beautiful trees in Belize. The numerous pink
flowers are produced after the tree has shed its leaves. The
large pods reach 3 ft (1 m) long and are said to have purgative

properties. The pods have a strong, disagreeable odor, hence the name stinking-toe. Its wood ashes are used in making soap.

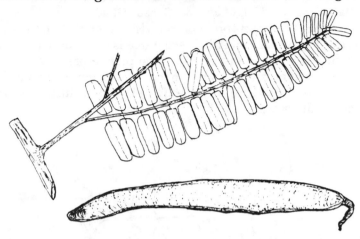

Mahogany (*Swietenia macrophylla*) - Meliaceae
Mahogany,Caoba (Bz)- Chiculte, Punab (Maya)

A once common forest tree but heavily logged. The mahogany tree has long been an integral part of Belize and its history and legacy are explained elsewhere in the guidebook.

Madre Cacao (*Gliciridia sepium*) - Fabaceae
Madre Cacao, Matasarna (Bz)- Zacyab, Cansim (Maya)-
Matasarna, Madrial, Madre de Cacao (Guat)
One of the most common and well known trees in Central America. This small to medium-sized tree is commonly planted as a living fence post and also in cacao plantations as a shade tree for the understory cacao, hence the common name. It produces an abundance of attractive pink to whitish flowers during the dry season.

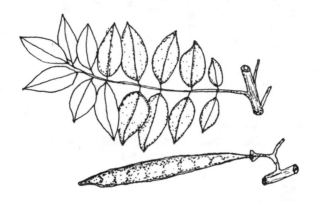

Hog Plum (*Spondias mombin*) - Anacardiaceae
Hog Plum (Bz)- Poc, Kinim, Canabal (Maya)- Jobo, Jocote
Jobo, Ciruela de Monte (Guat)
The hog plum produces plum-like yellowish fruits which are edible but not especially tasty. The wood of the tree is very soft and not at all durable. It is a common tree in the Belizean forest. Another member of the genus, *Spondias purpurea* , also occurs in Belize and is distinguished from *S. mombin* , by having much smaller leaves (see illustration).

Cedar (*Cedrela mexicana*) - Meliaceae
Cedar (Bz)- Kulche (Maya)- Cedro (Guat)
Cedar is closely related to mahogany and is also a very prized timber. The wood is scented and faintly resembles the scent of the coniferous cedar. The wood is durable, beautiful, and workable and used for furniture, boat-building and cigar boxes.

TWO SPECIES OF SPONDIAS (Hog Plum):
Above is *Spondias mombin* with its larger, fuller leaves; Below is shown *Spondias purpurea* at the same scale.

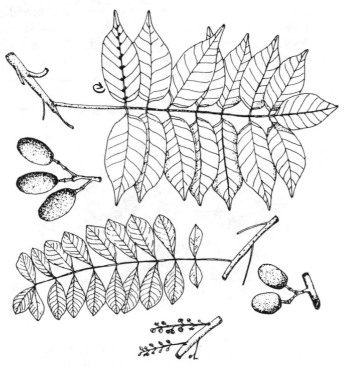

BELOW: *Cedrela mexicana* (Cedar) - it superficially resembles the hog plum but has more fissured bark and a strong odor.

Tubroos (*Enterolobium cyclocarpum*) - Mimosaceae
  Tubroos, Guanacaste, Ear-Tree (Bz)- Pich (Maya)-
  Guanacaste (widespread)

An often giant tree with a thick trunk and broad crown, it ranges from Mexico to Venezuela. The ear-shaped fruits are broad and flat and much esteemed by cattle. The tubroos is the most common tree used for making carved out canoes called "dories". When the tree reaches adequate size, it is felled and hand carved into the shape of a canoe. The wood is light yet very durable and a good dory can last as long as ten years.

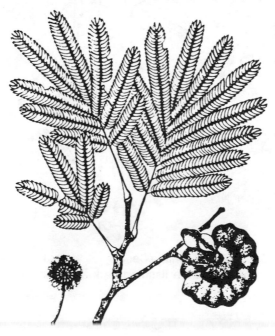

Quamwood (*Schizolobium parahybum*) - Caesalpiniaceae
  Quamwood, Quam, Zorra (Bz)- Copte (Maya)- Plumillo,
  Zorra (Guat)

Often a tall tree found in wet to dry mixed forest. The tree sheds its leaves in the dry season and produces attractive bright yellow flowers in March and April. The name "quamwood" is so given because the curassow is known to feed on the seed pods of the tree. The thin-barked tree may also have high buttresses.

BELOW: *Schizolobium parahybum* (Quamwood) - showing bipinnate leaf and seed pod

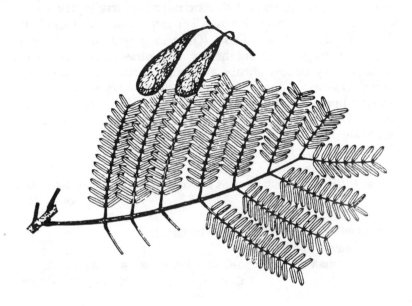

PINE RIDGE TREE KEY

The pine ridge forests of Belize are not as diverse in tree species as some other forests in Belize. The dominant trees include the Pine (*Pinus caribeae*), Oaks (*Quercus* spp.), and Pimenta (*Paurotis wrightii*). Nonetheless, the pine ridge supports a wide variety of low shrubs and herbaceous plants including many grasses, sedges, and small wildflowers which are not treated here. The following key is for 8 of the most common trees. The cultivated fruit trees are given special attention in a separate list.

1. Trees Coniferous
   a) PINE TREE with needles in bunches of 3.......*Pinus caribaea* (Caribbean Pine)

1. Trees BROADLEAVED; NOT Coniferous
   2. Leaves PALMATE
      small shrub or tree; with large yellow flowers...............
      Cochlospermum vitifolium (Wild Cotton)

   2. Leaves SIMPLE
      3. Leaves OPPOSITE
         a) Leaves large, broad, 5-veined; dark green above and whitish below...*Miconia argentea* (White Maya)

         b) Leaves clustered at end of branches; bark dark brown, rough; with yellow edible fruits; shrub to medium-sized tree...............*Byrsonima crassifolia* (Craboo)
      3. Leaves ALTERNATE
         4. Leaves rough and sandpapery, rounded; viney shrub to small tree......*Curatella americana* (Yaha)

         4. Leaves smooth

            5. Leaves in alternate fasicles; oblong-lanceolate and firm; small tree with twisting branches;with large gourd-like fruits
               ....*Cresentia cujete* (Calabash)

5. Leaves single
   a) Leaves thin, deltoid ovate and truncate at base, on thin petioles; shrub or small tree fruits turning dark red..........*Blxa orellana* (Annata)
   b) Leaves thicker, leathery; tree with rough bark....................*Quercus oleoides* (Oak)

Pine - *Pinus caribaea*   (Pinaceae)
Pine, Caribbean Pine (Bz)- Huhub (Maya), Pino, Pino Blanco (Guat)

The caribbean pine is found on sandy soils ranging from the southern Yucatan, through Belize and into Honduras and Nicaragua. The tree may reach to 100 ft (30 m) tall but is commonly shorter. It is found from sea level up to around 1,500 ft (470 m) in elevation. The caribbean pine has needles in bundles of mostly 3 and can be distinquished from the other species of pine found in the Mountain Pine Ridge of Belize (*Pinus oocarpa*) which has needles in bundles of 5.   The caribbean pine is one of the dominant trees in the pine ridge of Belize and has been an important timber tree in Belize for many years.

Pine forests or pine forest remnants make up around 20% of the forest cover in Belize. The wood of the pine is commonly used for construction and pine has been harvested extensively in Belize from the turn of the century to the present time.   The pine also contains a thick resin which has been used as a glue, water repellant, and burned as an insect repellant. The high resin content of the wood also makes the wood burnable even when fresh cut.

Wild Cotton - *Cochlospermum vitifolium* (Cochlospermaceae)
Wild Cotton (Bz)- Tsuyuy, Cho (Maya)
    The wild cotton is commonly found in highly disturbed and secondary growth areas in broken and pine ridge and other dry brushy areas. It is a small, deciduous tree reaching from 5-20 ft (1.5-6 m) tall. The very large, bright yellow flowers make the tree conspicuous in the later stages of the dry season when the tree is in bloom. The flowers are mostly 3-6 in (7-15 cm) wide, have 5 broad petals, and numerous orange stamens.

    The wood of the tree is very soft and weak and the brittle branches are easily broken. The branches also root very easily when planted in the ground. The stamens have been used as a substitute for saffron in Guatemala and the bark fiber can be used for making rope. The common name "wild cotton" is in reference to the silky fibers found in the seed pods of the tree. The whitish, silky fibers resemble the "cotton" found in Ceiba tree pods.

Wild Cotton Tree Leaf

White Maya - *Miconia argentea*   (Melastomaceae)
White Maya, Maya, White Moir (Bz)- Jolte (Maya)
A large shrub or small tree with light brown or pinkish bark which peels of in square chunks on larger trees. The white maya is found mostly in broken ridge forests but is also found in the pine ridge and sometimes in lowland forests. The tree is very common in disturbed areas and in secondary growth. The white undersurface of the leaves is most evident on windy days.

The white maya is a member of the Melastome Family. The Melastomes (Melastomaceae) are a large family in Belize containing nearly 100 species of trees, shrubs and herbs. The genus *Miconia* alone contains some 40 species.

Craboo - *Byrsonima crassifolia*   (Malpighiaceae)
Craboo, Wild Craboo (Bz)- Nance, Chi, Xacpah (Maya)
A shrub or tree reaching from 5-35 ft (1.5-10 m) tall with dark brown bark and dark green foliage. The craboo is found in pine forests to wet thickets and is also commonly planted. The fruit of the craboo is edible although somewhat tart and can be found in many markets. The rind of the fruits have been used to produce a dye used for making inks and dyeing cotton. The bark of the tree has also been commonly used for tanning.

373

BELOW: *Miconia argentea* (White Maya)

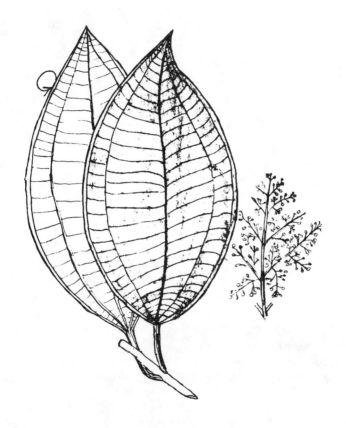

Yaha - *Curatella americana*   (Dilleniaceae)
   Yaha, Sandpaper Tree (Bz)
      The sandpaper tree gets its name from its rough leaves which contain silica and feel very rough to the touch. The leaves can be used as an inexpensive sandpaper substitute. The seeds of the tree are roasted and eaten and sometimes used to flavor chocolate. The yaha is commonly a shrub or small tree rarely reaching 15 ft (5 m) high and often has horizontally spreading branches which may resemble vines.

ABOVE: *Byrsonima crassifolia* (Wild Craboo) - showing
leaves, flower and fruit
BELOW: *Curatella americana* (Yaha) - leaves are sandpapery
to the touch; young leaves may be deeply toothed

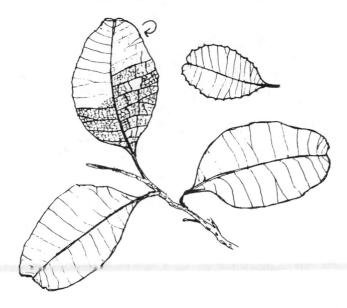

Calabash - *Cresentia cujete* (Bignoniaceae)
Calabash, Wild Calabash (Bz)- Hom, Luch, Huaz (Maya)

A small tree often with a thick, twisted trunk commonly found in wetter regions of the pine ridge. The dark green spathulate leaves are in clusters on the long twisted branches. The name "calabash" comes from the spanish word "calabazo" meaning gourd or pumpkin in reference to the often very large gourd shaped fruits of this tree. The gourds were once used for food and water storage. Cups made out of the gourds known as "jicaras" were often elaborately decorated by the Mayans. The hard wood of the tree has also been used to make ox yokes, tool handles, and stirrups.

ABOVE: *Cresentia cujete* (Calabash) - A) branch showing clumped leaves; B) calabash flower; C) view of entire tree in fruit

376

Annata - *Bixa orellana* (Bixaceae)
Annata, Annato, Ricatta (Bz)- Achiote (widespread)

This is a shrub or small tree which is commonly planted or cultivated. The tree has dark brown bark and a yellow-reddish sap. The tree is cultivated for the red-orange dye obtained from the dried seeds which is known as annata or ricatta in Belize. The dye is used in cooking to color a wide variety of foods and imparts some flavor. The plant also produces nectar on the main stems and at the base of the flower stems which is eaten by ants which, in return, provide some protection for the plant. The latin name is one of the more ironic botanical names in the neotropics. The genus *Bixa* was named in honor of the indigenous Indians of Darien in what is now Panama and the species name *orellano* is named after an associate of the conquistador Pizarro.

Oak - *Quercus oleoides* (Fagaceae)
Oak, Live Oak (Bz)

Perhaps the most common of the 8 species of oaks known to occur in Belize. The live oak is found in lowland pine forests, hillsides, and dry plains throughout Belize. This species of oak is usually a small tree with leaves mostly 2-3 in (5-7.5 cm) long and with ovoid acorns about 3/4 in (2 cm) across.

THE TREE PALMS

The Palm family (Palmae) has a wide distribution throughout much of the tropical world. In Belize, there are some 20 tree palm species and numerous other shrubby and herbaceous palms (especially species of *Geonoma* and *Chamaeodora*).

KEY TO COMMON BELIZEAN TREE PALMS

1. Palms ARMED with Spines
   2. Leaves PALMATE

      a) Palm found in Pine Ridge; only frond stems armed; 5 to 15 feet high; often clumped.....*Paurotis wrightii* (Pimenta palm)

      b) Palm found in forest; trunk armed with dense down-turned spines 3-4" long............*Chrysophila argentea* (Give and Take palm)

   2. Leaves PINNATE

      3. Trunk larger; standing erect
         4) Trunk diameter less than 5 inches; stem with black, needle-like spines; common in wet forest areas; clumped...................... *Bactris major* (Pokenoboy palm)

         4) Trunk diameter greater than 5 inches
            a) Large tree to 35 feet; densely armed with straight spines; fruits unarmed; leaves up to 12 feet long.................*Acrocomia mexicana* (Suppa palm)

            b) Smaller tree armed with compressed, black, 2-edged spines; fruits armed; leaves 3' long ....*Astrocaryum mexicanum* (Warree Cohune palm)

<u>1. Palms UNARMED</u>

2. Leaves PALMATE
   a) Leaf blade with well developed rachis, about half the length of the leaves; trunk tall, slender; in forests near sea level; fruits blackish....................................
   Sabal morrisiana (Sabal or Botan Palm)

   b) Leaf blade with very short rachis; trunk with thick pads of wool-like fibers; smaller palm than above.....
   ....*Thrinax radiata*
   (Silver Thatch Palm)

2. Leaves PINNATE

   a) Trunk ROUGH with old leaf bases still attached; Common palm; leaves large, plume-like sometimes to 30 feet long or more; nuts in large pendant panicles; nuts about 3 inches across ....
   ....*Orbigyna cohune* (Cohune Palm)

   b) Trunk SMOOTH; tall palm from 30-60 feet; top of trunk with a large green sheath; common in wetter areas, often rising above surrounding canopy
   ....*Euterpe macrospadix* (Cabbage Palm)

Pimenta Palm or **Palmetto Palm** - (*Paurotis wrightii*)

The pimenta or palmetto palm is a rather small palm reaching mostly from 10-20 ft (3-6 m) high. It is found most commonly in moist or wet regions of the pine ridge and often grows in dense clusters. In some areas there may be as many as 3,400 stems per acre. The stem of the palm can be stripped of the persisent leaf sheaths and used for making light-weight cages or lobster pots. The trunks are used for temporary fence posts.

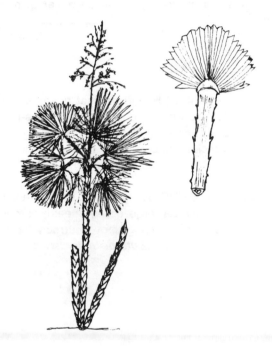

Give and Take Palm (*Chrysophila argentea*)

A slender, single-trunked palm reaching 12-20 ft (4-6 m) and densely armed with down-turned, branching spines. This palm is very striking in appearance and has from 10-15 fan-leaved fronds which are shiny green above and silvery-white beneath.

BELOW: *Chyrosophila argentea* (Give and Take Palm) - note long, barbed spines densely covering the stem

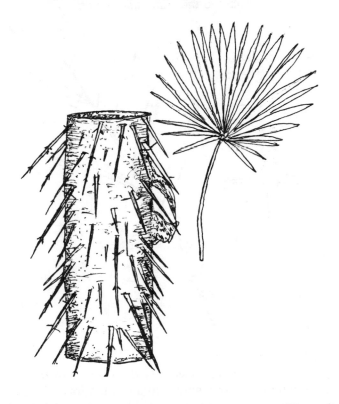

Pokenoboy Palm (*Bactris major*)

The common name, "pokenoboy" palm, is an abbreviated version of an older name for the plant "pork-and-doughboy". The palm gets this name because the hard, fire-resistant wood of the trunk is used to make a two-pronged cooking tong called a "kis-kis" in Belizean Creole. Making a kis-kis can be hazardous work, however, as the trunks, stems and leaves of the palm are densely covered with long, needle-like black spines which can inflict painful wounds. The palms often grow in dense thickets in wet areas of forests and pastures and pose a formidable barrier to travel unless one wields a machete. The pulp within the moderately hard shells of the palm is edible and when ripe tastes similar to black cherry.

BELOW: Pokenoboy Palm showing needle-like spines covering both the the trunk and fronds

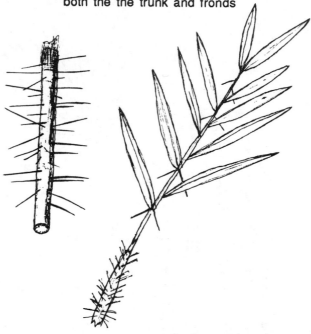

Suppa Palm (*Acrocomia mexicana*)

The suppa palm is widely distributed in the Yucatan, Belize, Guatemala, and south to El Salvador. The palm is found in open forests, and on dry hillsides and plains. The tree is also sometimes planted for ornament and for its edible fruits. The suppa palm may reach to over 30 ft (9 m) tall with its trunk and frond stems covered with long, sharp, dark-colored spines. The fronds may reach 12 ft (4 m) long and are somewhat feathery.

The fruits of the palm are in large, heavy, pendent clusters. Individual nuts are about 1.5 in (4 cm) across. The pulp inside the nut is edible and quite sweet. The coconut-like tasting kernels of the nuts are edible raw or boiled with sugar and eaten. A sap from the trunk of the tree can be drawn and fermented to make a delicious palm wine. The hard nut shells have also been used to make rosary beads, rings, and other jewelry items.

BELOW: *Acrocomia belizensis* (Suppa Palm) - frond close-up shows needle-like spines covering the frond mid-rib

Warree Cohune Palm (*Astrocaryum mexicanum*)

This is a common palm in dense, wet lowland forest and ranges along the Atlantic coast from southern Mexico through Belize to Honduras. It is a small palm reaching from 2-15 ft (0.6-5 m) high and is armed with stout, flattened, 2-edged spines. The common name "warree cohune" is in reference to the spiny covering of the fruit which resemble the stout bristles on the common peccary, known as a "warree" in Belizean Creole.

Sabal or **Botan Palm** (*Sabal morrisiana*)

This tall, unarmed and slender palm is found in forests at or near sea level. The fronds are fan shaped and reach to 6 ft (2 m) across. The leaves are a prime choice for thatching because they are very durable. Because of its value as a thatch palm, the sabal is often left standing when land is cleared.

Silver Thatch Palm (*Thrinax radiata*)

An unarmed palm reaching to 35 ft (10 m) tall with fan-shaped leaves. The fronds are about 3 ft (1 m) across, roundish and flat, divided to the center, and have leaflets tips gracefully arched downward. The whitish fruits of this palm are small, about 1/4 in (0.5 cm) across, but are grouped in large pendent clusters. The fruits are edible. The fibrous mats on the trunk have also been used to stuff pillows and mattresses.

Left: *Sabal morrisiana* (Sabal Palm)
Right: Frond close-up of *Thrinax radiata* (Silver Thatch Palm)

Cohune Palm (*Orbigyna cohune*)

The cohune palm is perhaps the most characteristic tree in the forests of Belize. The cohune is common and abundant throughout much of Belize reaching from sea level up to 1,800 ft (560 m). The cohune can grow to 50 ft (16 m) tall or more and has very large, plume-like fronds which can reach to over 30 ft (9 m) long. Because the trunk of the cohune is very hard, it is frequently left when land is cleared. This may be one reason why the cohune is so abundant in some areas. However, the cohune forest association in a naturally occuring community which is common in Belize on well-drained but moist, deep, organic soils.

The cohune palm has been used for generations by Belizeans for a wide range of purposes. The fronds of the palm can be used to make a reasonably durable thatch or even a bed-roll. The stout midribs are used for light-weight framing and the cross-entwined leaves make up the thatch or webbing. The apical meristem at the top of the trunk can be eaten also. The large and heavy pendent clusters of nuts have been used for a variety of purposes. The pulp of the fruit is edible, the nuts also yield a rich oil used for cooking, making soap, and many other uses. The extremely hard nuts have also been used to make charcoal. In fact, the British during World War I, imported tons of the nuts to make charcoal for gas masks used to protect soldiers from poison and mustard gas in the trenches of Europe. The cohune nuts are produced in large clusters of 800-1,000 nuts weighing potentially well over 100 lbs (30 kg). The stalks of these pendent nut-clusters can be dried and mashed to make a delicate but durable fly-brush.

The cohune palm also plays an important role in soil formation. When a cohune dies, it rapidly decays and leaves a cylindrical stump hole behind. These holes can reach to 3 ft (1 m) deep and play an important role in soil aeration and redistribution of surface soils. The persistent litter beneath cohunes also has been shown to contain a relatively high proportion of nitrogen and the abundant cohune litter may act as a nutrient reserve slowly releasing valuable nutrients into the soil.

BELOW: *Orbigyna cohune* (Cohune Palm)

Cabbage Palm (*Euterpe macrospadix*)
    A common palm in wet, inland areas. The cabbage palm has a large green sheath at the tip of its trunk and leafy fronds. The palm is often an emergent tree rising above wet swampy forests. Because the wood is water resistant and floats well, it has been used historically in raft making for moving non-floating logs and goods up and down Belizean rivers. It is also used for pilings on docks.

BELOW: *Euterpe macrospadix* (Cabbage Palm)

COMMON FRUIT TREES of BELIZE

Cashew (*Anacardium occidentale*)

The cashew tree is widely cultivated on well drained and sandy soils throughout Belize and throughout the new and old world tropics in general. It is a small to medium-sized tree reaching to 30 ft (9 m). The cashew is one of the best known trees in Central America owing to it its edible and tasty nuts and its juicy and edible "fruit". The large yellow to reddish "fruit" upon which the cashew nut is perched, is actually an engorged hypocarp and is not a true fruit. This hypocarp contains a bitter-sweet juice which is used to mix with rum or to make cashew wine.

The cashew nut is harvested during the mid to late dry season (March to April) when the nuts mature. Because the seeds contain oils (cardol, cardonal, and anacardic acid) which can blister human skin, the nuts are first roasted before eaten. World wide, the annual production of cashew nuts is second only to the almond in the world nut trade. The common name "cashew" is derived from the Brazillian-Portuguese word "caju" which was first noted by the french naturalist Thevet in 1558, the european "discoverer" of the cashew tree.

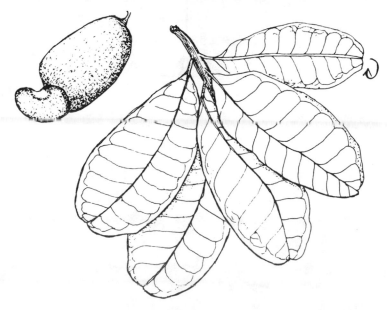

Coconut (*Cocos nucifera*)

The coconut is widely planted throughout the tropical regions of the world. In Belize, coconuts are found both in coastal regions and cultivated inland. Recently, however, a devastating leaf blight is killing many coconuts throughout Mexico and the Caribbean islands.

Custard Apple (*Annona reticulata*)

The custard apple is a small to medium-sized tree mostly 10-30 ft (3-9 m) high with chocolate colored bark. It gets the name "custard apple" in reference to its large, globose fruits. The fruits are reddish-brown to purplish and mostly from 3-6 in (7-15 cm) across. The pulp of the fruit is cream-colored,very sweet and of a consistency not unlike custard although the pulp is somewhat gritty. The pulp is embedded with many dark colored seeds. The fruits develop from March to May and are sold in markets.

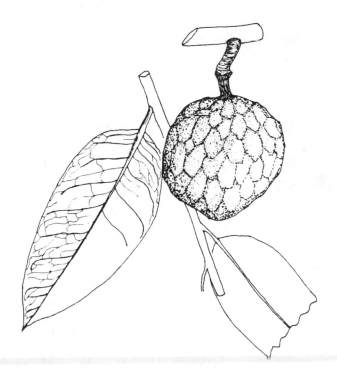

Guava (*Psidium guajava*)
     The guava is a small tree mostly 10-30 (3-9 m) high which is commonly cultivated in tropical America. The tree has smooth, red-brown mottled bark which flakes off exposing younger greenish bark beneath. The edible fruits of the guava are round or pear-shaped and moslty 3 in (7 cm) long. The fruits are greenish-yellow skinned and have a strong musky odor. The pulp of the fruit is juicy and soft and contains many small, kidney-shaped seeds. The guava fruit is high in vitamin C and pectin. The guava fruit is most often prepared into as thick jelly or "guava paste" which is cut into thin squares and is a common dessert throughout Central and South America. Many animals also eat guava fruits and frequently spread the indigestable seeds over a wide area where they often germinate and grow.

Mango (*Mangifera indica*)
     A native of tropical India, the mango is widely cultivated throughout the tropical world. The mango tree is medim-sized reaching to 50 ft (16 m) with dark green, evergreen foliage and a dense crown. The aromatic fruits of the

mango are oblong, elliptic or lopsided and are moslty 3-6 in (7-15 cm) long. The immature fruits are green and when ripe turn from a yellowish orange to dark red or deep purple depending on the variety being grown. Immature fruits contain oils which can cause severe rashes and blisters as well as swelling, itching and dermatitis. Mature fruits, however, are sweet and delicous and one of the prized fruits of the tropical world. The juicy pulp of the fruit is yellow to orange colored and often fibrous. The fruit also contains a single, large, ellipsoid seed.

Papaya (*Carica papaya*)

The papaya is a small "tree" commonly 10-15 ft (3-5 m) high with a simple trunk bearing obvious triangular leaf scars. The large palmately-lobed leaves are clustered at the top of the stem. The fruits of the papaya are highly variable in size and shape varying from roundish to pear-shaped. Commonly the fruits are from 6-12 in (15-30 cm) long although they can reach much larger sizes and weigh up to 20 lbs (9 kg). The fruits are yellow-orange at maturuity and often streaked with green. The fruits are soft skinned and have an abundant fleshy, yellow or orange pulp which is very juicy and sweet.

Partial List of Wildlife Found in the Community Baboon Sanctuary

A question mark (?) following any species means that it probably occurs in the sanctuary but has not yet been confirmed.

MAMMALS

Order: Marsupialia
Southern or White eared opossum
Didelphis marsupialis
Four eyed opossum
Philander opossum

Order: Carnivora
Coati, Quash
Nasua narica
Racoon, Coon
Procyon lotor
Kinkajou
Poto flavus
Tayra, Bush dog
Eira barbara
Skunk, Polecat
Mephitis mephitis
Otter, Waterdog
Lutra longicaudis
Gray fox
Urocyon cinereoargenteus
Jaguar, Tiger
Felis onca
Red tiger, Mountain lion, Puma
Felis concolor
Jaguarundi
Felis yagouroundi
Ocelot, Tiger cat
Felis pardalis
Margay
Felis wiedii

Order: Rodentia
Deppe's squirrel, Cohune squirrel
Sciurus deppei
Yucatan squirrel, Pine ridge squirrel
Sciurus yucatanensis
Mexican porcupine, Porcupine
Coendou mexicanus
Paca, Spotted cavy, Gibnut
Agouti paca
Agouti, Rabbit
Dasyprocta punctata

Order: Edentata
Tamandua, Antsbear
Tamandua mexicana
Silky anteater (?)
Cyclopes didactylus
9-banded armadillo, Dilly, Hamadilly
Dasypus novemcinctus

Order: Sirenia
Manatee, Sea cow
Trichechus manatus

Order: Perissodactyla
Baird's tapir, Mountain cow
Tapirus bairdii

Order: Artiodactyla
Collared peccary, Pecari
Dicotyles tajacu
Red brocket deer, Antelope
Mazama americana
White tailed deer, Deer
Odocoileus virginiana

Order: Primates
Black howler monkey, Baboon
Alouatta pigra

Birds Found Within the Sanctuary
list compiled by
Jevra Brown and *Susan O'Connell*

Key to habitats: F - forest and clearings;
R - river and river edge; P - pine ridge;
V - village; * - common in the sanctuary

Tinamous (Family: Tinamidae)
Little Tinamou
R   *Crypturellus cinnamomeus*
Thicket Tinamou, Bawley, Blue Legged
Partridge
R   *Crypturellus soui*

Cormorants (Phalacrocoracidae)
Olivaceous Cormorant, Shag
R   *Phalacrocorax olivaceus*

Anhingas (Anhingidae)
Anhinga, Snake Bird
R   *Anhinga anhinga*

Herons and Bitterns (Ardeidae)
Great Blue Heron, Full Pot, Toby Full Pot
R   *Ardea herodias*
Pinnated Bittern, Barking Gaulin
R   *Botaurus pinnatus*
Cattle Egret, Gaulin
*PV   *Bubulcus ibis*
Green-backed Heron, Poor Joe
R   *Butorides striatus*
Great Egret, Gaulin
*R   *Caserodius albus*
Little Blue Heron, Carpenter, Blue Gaulin
*R   *Egretta caerulea*
Snowy Egret, Gaulin
R   *Egretta thula*
Bare-throated Tiger Heron
R   *Tigrisoma mexicanum*

Storks (Ciconidae)
Jabiru, Turk
     Jabiru mycteria
Wood Stork, Turk
     Mycteria americana

Ibises, Spoonbills (Threskiornithidae)
Roseate Spoonbill
R   *Ajaia ajaja*
White Ibis, White Curlew, Coco
R   *Eudocimus albus*

Swans, Geese, Ducks (Anatidae)
Blue-Winged Teal, Duck
R   *Anas discours*
Black-bellied Whistling Duck,
Whistling Duck
R   *Dendrocygna autumnalis*

American Vultures (Cathartidae)
Turkey Vulture, John Crow
*FPV   *Cathartes aura*
Black Vulture, John Crow
*FPV   *Coragyps atratus*

Kites, Eagles, Hawks (Accipitridae)
Black Collared Hawk, Fishing Hawk
F   *Busarellus nigricollis*
Roadside Hawk, Chicken Hawk
*FPV   *Buteo magnirostris*
Gray Hawk
F   *Buteo nitidus*
Common Black Hawk, Water Hawk
     Buteogallus anthracinus
Hook-billed Kite
F   *Chondrohierax uncinatus*
Black Shouldered Kite
     Elanus caerulens
Plumbeous Kite
     Ictinia plumbea

Falcons, Caracaras (Falconidae)
Aplomado Falcon
P   *Falco femoralis*
Laughing Falcon, Water Hawk, Guaco
*FPV   *Herpetotheres cachinnans*
Collared Forest Falcon
F   *Micrastur semitorquatus*

Chachalacas, Guans, Curassows (Cracidae)
Plain Chachalaca, Cocrico
*F   *Ortalis verula*

Partridges, Quail (Phaisianidae)
Black-throated Bobwhite, Quail
P   *Colinus nigrogularis*
Singing Quail
     Dactylortyx thoracicus

Rails, Gallinules, Coots (Rallidae)
Gray-necked Wood Rail, Top-notch-chick
*RV   *Aramides cajanea*

Sungrebes (Helliornithidae)
Sungrebe, Diving Dapper
R   *Heliornis fulica*

Jacanas (Jacanidae)
Northern Jacana, Georgie Bull
R   *Jacana spinosa*

Plovers (Charadriidae)
Killdeer
P   *Charadrius vociferus*

Limpkins (Aramidae)
Limpkin, Clucking hen
R   *Aramus guarauna*

Sandpipers (Scolopacidae)
Spotted Sandpiper
R   *Actitis macularia*
Solitary Sandpiper
R   *Tringa solitaria*

Pigeons, Doves (Columbidae)
Blue Ground Dove
V   *Claravis pretiosa*
Pale-vented Pigeon
    Columba cayennensis
Short-billed Pigeon
* FV   *Columba nigrirostris*
Scaled Pigeon
* F   *Columba speciosa*
Plain-breasted Ground Dove
P   *Columbina minuta*
Ruddy Ground Dove, Ground Dove,
  Turtle Dove
* PV   *Columbina talpacoti*
Ruddy Quail-dove
    Geotrygon montana
Grey-fronted Dove
F   *Leptotila rufaxilla*
White-tipped Dove, Ground Pigeon
FVP   *Leptotila verreauxi*

Parrots (Psittacidae)
White-fronted Parrot, Mangrove Parrot
FPV   *Amazona albifrons*
Red-lored Parrot, Corn-eater
* F   *Amazona automnalis*
Mealy Parrot, Blue-crowned Parrot
P   *Amazona farinosa*
Yellow-crowned Parrot, Yellow-head Parrot
* PV   *Amazona ochrocephala*
Yellow-lored Parrot, Watch-out Parrot
PV   *Amazona xantholora*
Aztec Parakeet, Keeti
* FPV *Aratinga aztec*
White-Crowned parrot
* FPV *Pionus senilis*

Cuckoos (Cuculidae)
Groove-billed Ani, Tick Bird
* FPV *Crotophaga sulcirostris*
Squirrel Cuckoo, Rick Quam
* F   *Piaya cayana*
Striped Cuckoo
V   *Tapera naevia*

Goatsuckers (Caprimulgidae)
Lesser Nighthawk
FV   *Chordeiles acutipennis*
Common Nighthawk
FV   *Chordeiles minor*
Common Pauraque, Who-you
* V   *Nyctidromus albicollis*

Hummingbirds (Trochilidae)
White-bellied Emerald
F   *Amazilia candida*
Azure-crowned Hummingbird
F   *Amazilia cyanocephala*
Rufous-tailed Hummingbird
* FVP *Amazilia tzacatl*
Buff-bellied Hummingbird
P   *Amazilia yucatanensis*
Green-breasted Mango
FV   *Anthracothorax prevostii*
Little Hermit
* F   *Phaethornis longuemareus*
Long-tailed Hermit
* F   *Phaethornis superciliosus*

Trogons (Trogonidae)
Citrolline Trogon, Ramatutu
* F   *Trogon citreolus*
Violaceous Trogon, Ramatutu
F   *Trogon violaceus*

Kingfishers (Alcedinidae)
Amazon Kingfisher
    Chloroceryle amazona
Green Kingfisher
R   *Chloroceryle americana*
Belted Kingfisher
* R   *Megaceryle alcyon*
Ringed Kingfisher
* R   *Megaceryle torquata*

Motmots (Momotidae)
Blue-crowned Motmot
F   *Momotus momota*

Puffbirds (Bucconidae)
White-necked Puffbird
F   *Bucco macrorhynchos*

Toucans (Ramphastidae)
Collared Aracari, Phyllis
F   *Pteroglossus torquatus*
Keel-billed Toucan, Bill Bird
P   *Ramphastos sulfuratus*

Woodpeckers (Picidae)
Pale-billed Woodpecker
F   *Campephilus guatemalensis*
Lineated Woodpecker, Red-head Wood-
  pecker
* F   *Dryocopus lineatus*
Golden-fronted Woodpecker
* FV *Melanerpes aurifrons*
Acorn Woodpecker
P   *Melanerpes formicivorus*
Golden-olive Woodpecker
F   *Piculus rubiginosus*
Smoky-brown Woodpecker

Ovenbirds (Furnariidae)
Buff-throated Foliage-gleaner
F   *Automolus ochrolaemus*
Rufous-breasted Spinetail
F   *Synallaxis erythrothorax*
Plain Xenops
F   *Xenops minutus*

Woodcreepers (Dendrocolaptidae)
Tawney-winged Woodcreeper
*F   *Dendrocincla anabatina*
Barred Woodcreeper
F   *Dendrocolaptes certhia*
Ruddy Woodcreeper
*F   *Dendrocincla homochroa*
Wedge-billed Woodcreeper
F   *Glyphorynchus spirurus*
Streak-headed Woodcreeper
F   *Lepidocolaptes souleyetii*
Olivaceus Woodcreeper
F   *Vittasomus griseicapillus*
Ivory-billed Woodcreeper
*F   *Xiphorhynchus flavigaster*

Antbirds (Formicariidae)
Dusky Antbird
F   *Cercomacra tyrannia*
Black-faced Antthrush
F   *Formicarius analis*
Dot-winged Antwren
F   *Microrhopias quixensis*
Great Antshrike
F   *Taraba major*
Barred Antshrike
*F   *Thamnophilus doliatus*

Tyrant Flycatchers (Tyrannidae)
Tropical Pewee
V   *Contopus cinereus*
Yellow-bellied Elaenia
FVP   *Elaenia flavogaster*
Boat-billed Flycatcher
F   *Megarynchus pitangua*
Ochra-bellied Flycatcher
F   *Mionectes oleagineus*
Dusky-capped Flycatcher
        Myiarchus tuberculifer
Brown Crested Flycatcher
        Myiarchus tyannulus
Sulphur-bellied Flycatcher
F   *Myiodynastes luteiventris*
Greenish Elaenia
F   *Myiopagis viridicata*
Social Flycatcher
*FVP   *Myiozetetes similis*
Northern Bentbill
F   *Oncostoma cinereigulare*
Royal Flycatcher
F   *Onychorhynchus coronatus*

Great Kiskadee, Kiskadee
*FVP   *Pitangus sulphuratus*
White-throated Spadebill
F   *Platyrinchus mystaceus*
Vermillion Flycatcher, Robin Red-breast
*VP   *Pyrocephalus rubinus*
Rufous Mourner
F   *Rhytipterna holerythra*
Common Tody Flycatcher
        Todirostrum cinereum
Slate-headed Tody-flycatcher
F   *Todirostrum sylvia*
Yellow-olive Flycathcer
F   *Tolmomyias sulphurescens*
Scissor-tailed Flycatcher
P   *Tyrannus forficatus*
Tropical Kingbird
*FVP   *Tyrannus melancholicus*

Manakins (Pipridae)
White-collared Manakin
*F   *Manacus candei*
Red-capped Manakin
F   *Pipra mentalis*
Thrushlike Manakin
        Schiffornis turdinus

Cotingas (Cotingidae)
Rose-throated Becard
F   *Platypsaris aglaiae*
Masked Tityra
F   *Tityra semifasciata*

Swallows (Hirundinidae)
Grey-breasted Martin
V   *Progene chalybea*
    Northern Rough-winged Swallow
RV   *Stelgidopteryx serripennis*
Mangrove Swallow
*R   *Tachycineta albilinea*
Tree Swallow, Christmas Red
VP   *Tachycineta bicolor*

Jays (Corvidae)
Brown Jay, Piam Piam
*FVP   *Cyanocorax morio*

Wrens (Troglodytidae)
Spot-breasted Wren
F   *Thryothorus maculipectus*
House Wren
V   *Troglodytes aedon*

Gnatcatchers (Sylviidae)
Blue-gray Gnatwren
P   *Polioptila caerulea*
Long-billed Gnatwren
        Ramphocaenus melanurus

Thrushes (Turdidae)
Veery
F   *Catharos fuscescens*
Wood Thrush
F   *Hylocichla mustelina*
Clay-colored Robin, Cusco
*V   *Turdus grayi*

Mockingbirds (Mimidae)
Gray Catbird
FVP   *Dumetella carolinensis*
Tropical Mockingbird, Nightengale
*VP   *Mimus gilvus*

Vireos (Vireonidae)
Rufous-browed Peppershrike
VP   *Cyclarhis gujanensis*
Lesser Greenlet
F   *Hylophilus decurtatus*
Tawny-crowned Greenlet
F   *Hylophilus ochraceiceps*
White-eyed Vireo
F   *Vireo griseus*
Red-eyed Vireo
F   *Vireo olivaceus*
Mangrove Vireo
FP   *Vireo pallens*

Wood Warblers (Parulidae)
Yellow-throated Warbler
FVP   *Dendroica dominica*
Grace's Warbler
VP   *Dendroica graciae*
Magnolia Warbler
FV   *Dendroica magnolia*
Yellow Warbler
FV   *Dendroica petechia*
Gray-crowned Yellowthroat
F   *Geothlypis poliocephala*
Common Yellowthroat
RVP   *Geothlypis trichas*
Worm-eating Warbler
F   *Helmitheros vermivorus*
Yellow-breasted Chat
F   *Icteria virens*
Black-and-white Warbler
FV   *Mniotilta varia*
Kentucky Warbler
F   *Oporornis formusus*
Ovenbird
F   *Seiurus aurocapillus*
Northern Waterthrush
R   *Seiurus noveboracensis*
American Redstart
FV   *Setophaga ruticilla*
Golden-winged Warbler
F   *Vermivora chrysoptera*
Blue-winged Warbler
R   *Vermivora pinus*

Hooded Warbler
     Wilsonia citrina

Honey Creepers (Coerebidae)
Bananaquit
F   *Coereba flaveola*

Tanagers (Thraupidae)
Red-legged Honeycreeper
F   *Cyanerpes cyaneus*
Gray-headed Tanager
F   *Eucometis penicillata*
Yellow-throated Euphonia
F   *Euphonia hirundinacea*
Red-throated Ant-tanager
F   *Habia fuscicauda*
Red-crowned Ant-tanager
F   *Habia rubica*
Summer Tanager
FV   *Piranga rubra*
Scarlet-rumped Tanager
F   *Ramphocelus passerinii*
Crimson-collared Tanager
F   *Ramphocelus sanguinolentus*
Yellow-winged Tanager
V   *Thraupis abbas*
Blue-gray Tanager, Bluebird
*VP   *Thraupis episcopus*

Finches, Sparrows (Fringillidae)
Green-backed Sparrow
F   *Arremonops chloronotus*
Olive Sparrow
F   *Arremonops rufivirgatus*
Blue-black Grosbeak
F   *Cyanocompsa cyanoides*
Blue Bunting
F   *Cyanocompsa parellina*
Thick-billed Seed-finch
F   *Oryzoborus funereus*
Indigo Bunting
     Passerina cyanea
Black-headed Saltator
*FV   *Saltator atriceps*
Grayish Saltator
F   *Saltator coerulescens*
Buff-throated Saltator
F   *Saltator maximus*
Variable Seedeater, Che-che
FVP   *Sporophila aurita*
White-collared Seedeater, Che-che, Ricey
*FVP   *Sporophila torqueola*
Blue-black Grassquit, Chi-che
F   *Volatinia jacarina*

Blackbirds (Icteridae)
Red-winged Blackbird
P   *Agelaius phoeniceus*
Yellow-billed Cacique, Bamboo Cracker
* F   *Amblycercus holosericeus*
Melodius Blackbird, Blackbird
*FVP   *Dives dives*
Northern Oriole
FV   *Icterus galbula*
Yellow-tailed Oriole
*FV   *Icterus mesomelas*
Black-cowled Oriole
    Icterus prosthemelas
Orchard Oriole
FV   *Icterus spurius*
Montezuma Oropendola, Yellow Tail
FVP   *Psarocolius montezum*
Great-tailed Grackle
    Quiscalus mexicanus
Eastern Meadowlark
    Sturnella magna

REPTILES
partial list by *Jevra Brown*

Squamata (Lizards)
Iguanidae
Anole
    Anolis spp.
Striped basilisk, Cock malakka, Jesus
Christ lizard
    Basiliscus vittatus
Scaley-tailed iguana, Wish-willy
    Ctenosaura similis
Iguana, Bamboo chicken
    Iguana iguana

    Sceloporus variabilis (?)
    Sceloporus spp.

Scincidae (Skinks)
    Ameira undulata `(?)
Snake-waiting-boy
    Mayuba brachypoda

SNAKES

Colubridae
Black tailed indigo, Blacktail
    Drymarchon corais
Shovel toothed snake, Double snake,
Half and half snake
    Scaphiodontophis annulatus
Speckled racer, Green snake, Guinea hen
snake
    Drymobius margaritiferus

Black striped snake
    Coniophanes imperialis (?)
Green vine snake, Green tommygoff
    Leptophis ahaetulla
Green-headed tree snake, Green head
    Leptophis mexicanus
Monkey snake, Bocatura clapansaya
    Spilotes pullatus

    Leptodeira annulata (?)

Micruridae - Coral snakes
Coral snake, Bead and coral
    Micurus diastoma (?)

Crotalidae - Pit vipers
Fer-de-lance, Yellow-jawed tommygoff
    Bothrops asper
Rattlesnake
    Crotalus durissus

Boidae - Boas
Boa, Wowla
    Boa constrictor

Crocdylidae-crocodyles
Morelet's crocodile, Alligator
    Crocodylus moreleti

Cheldridae - Turtles
Central American river turtle, Hickatee
    Dermatemys mawii
Mud turtles
    Kinosternum spp.
Black belly turtle
    Kinesternum spp.
Ornate terrapin, Bokatura
    Trachymys scripta
Loggerhead
    Stauriotypus triporcatus

AMPHIBIANS
partial list by *Jevra Brown*

Frogs and Toads

Hylidae - Tree Frogs)
Red-eyed tree frog
    Agalychnis callidryas

    Hyla microcephala
    Hyla staufferi
    Hyla spp.
    Smilisca baudinii
Bufonidae (True Toads)
    Bufo valliceps
Marine toad, Spring chicken
    Bufo marinus

Acknowledgments

We wish to thank all the people from the Community Baboon Sanctuary area for their past and future help. We especially want to thank Clifton Young and Fallet Young who have been an immense help in the initial formation of the sanctuary. Additional thanks go to the chairmen and village council members of all participating communities. The support of the Belize Audubon Society has been instrumental in maintaining the Sanctuary. We especially thank Jim and Lydia Waight, Mick Craig, Victor Gonzalez, Dora Weyer and Dolores Godfrey. Thanks also to the Belize Ministries of Natural Resources, Agriculture, Forestry and Fisheries for their help. Special thanks go to Mr. Oscar Rosado for his gracious cooperation and guidance. Thanks for financial support to World Wildlife Fund - U.S., Zoological Society of Milwaukee County and Lincoln Park Zoological Society. Their staffs, especially Dennis Glick, Steve Cornelius, Nancy Hammond, Dr. Gil Boese, and Dr. Dennis Merrit, have shown faith in good times and bad. Thanks also to Peace Corps Volunteers Bill Lindsley and Al Aquilar for help in mapping, to Leo Bradley for historical information, to Fallet Young and Vallen Pope and many other persons for guiding us in the forest, to Dail Murray for help publicizing the project. Special thanks to Susan O'Connell whose baseline information on howlers will guide the management and to Jevra Brown for her valuable work on many aspects of the sanctuary. Thanks also to Jack and Patty Pfitsch and the Wauzeka Public Schools for help with printing the guidebook. A final thanks to Dave Hackett for help in indexing this book.

CREDITS

The following figures in order of appearance have been redrawn from the following drawings or photographs:

hanging howler (1); roaring howler (2) 9:1134; howler throat structures (3) 2:206; barbeque (39) p.10; false eggs and sticky hairs on passionflowers (4) Fogden,P. 1987 Jan.-Feb.:16; fig wasp cycle (5) 138-9; parasol ant queen (6) p.46 and (7) p.76.; minima ants (6) p.163; bullhorn acacia (6) p.53; sloth (4) 1986,Jan.-Feb. :back cover; edentate vertebrae (8) p.130; armadillo skull (8) p.134; tamadua skull (9); edentate pelvic girdle (8) p.131 ; tamandua (2)1:65; jaguar (4) 1987Mar.-Apr.: cover; ocelot (13) p.170; puma and puma kitten (11) p. & 13; horse, peccary and deer skulls (8) p.229, 235, & 242 ; tapir feeding (10) p.539; digestive tracts (9) p.47; ungulate feet (9); tapir ranges (2) 17:2365; peccary range, marking behaviors (14) p. 5, 120, 129, & 130; manatee skull (8) p.218; manatee kiss, courtship & copulation (15); hummingbird map (16); hummingbird wing (5); humingbird flight (5) p.89; hummingbird tongue (5) p.89; hermit breeding lek, feeding graph, aggressive graph, aggressive behavior, male on perch (20); black & white warbler range map (21); black bird range map, gaping, oropendula nests (22); range of guan, chachalacha & currasow (23); turkey range (24)p.15; currasow trachea (2); turkey courtship (25)p.19; toucan feeding (5)p.84; aracari bill fencing (19)p.273; hickatee shell (27); hickatee range (18) ; hickatee range in Belize (26); crocodile and alligator heads (28); crocodile ranges (2); Morelet's crocodile range in Belize (29); crocodile head profiles (30); crocodile nests; young crocodile in egg (7) p.143; female carries young (7) p.143; snake Jacobsen's organ (32) p.96; boa (32) p.64; rattlesnake glands (33) p.59; pit organs (34) p.97; boa legs (33) p.29; iguana aggressive display (31) p.259; tadpoles (36) p35; frog calling (35) p.72; hylid seasonal graph (36); red eyed tree frog; frog resting (37) p.199; 3 hylid species (36); bat eating frog (38) p.78-9; sharks(40)p.78.

Reference Nos. (1) Hladik,C.M. 1972. Les Hurleurs de Barro Colorado. *Science et Nature*, 110:31 (2) Burton, M. & R. 1969. *Intl.Wildlife Encycl.* Marshall Cavendish Corp, NY. (3) Schultz, A.H. 1969. *The Life of Primates*, 2:206, Universe Books, NY (4) *Int.Wildlife* (5) Ayensu, E.S. 1980. *Jungles*, Smithsonian Inst. Press, Washington, D.C. (6) Wilson, E.O. 1971. *The Insect Societies*,Harvard Univ. Press, Cambridge, MA; (7) Whitfield, P. 1979. *The Animal Family*, W.W. Norton & Co.Inc., NY (8) Vaughan, T.A. 1972. *Mammalogy.* W.B.Saunders Co, Phila. (9) MacDonald D. 1984. *The Encyclopedia of Mammals.* Facts on File Publications, NY. (10) *National Geographic Book of Mammals* (2 vols). 1981. National Geographic Society, Washington, D.C. (11) Turbak,G. 1988. *America's Great Cats.* p. & 13, Northland Press, Flagstaff, Ariz. (12) Wexo, J.B. 1981. *ZooBooks. The*

Big Cats (13) Graves, E. 1976. *The Cats*, Time Life Films, NY. (14) Sowles,L.K. 1984. *The Peccaries*, UnivAriz Press,Tucson AR (15) Hartman, D.S. 1979. *Ecology and Behavior of the Manatee* (Trichechus manatus) *in Florida*. Special Publication No. 5 The American Society of Mammalogists. (16) Grant, K.A. and V. Grant. 1968. *Hummingbirds and their flowers*. Columbia University Press, NY. (17) (18) Alvarez del Toro, M. Mittermeier, R.A., and Iverson, J.B. 1979. River turtle in danger. *Oryx* 15:170-173. (19) Skutch, A.F. 1983. *Birds of Tropical America*. Univ.of Texas Press, Austin. (20) Stiles, F.G. & L.L. Wolf. 1979. Ecology and evolution of lek mating behavior in the long-tailed hermit hummingbird. *Ornitholopgical Monographs* No. 27. A.O.U., Wash, D.C.(21) Lincoln, F.C. and S.R. Stevenson. 1979. *Migration of Birds*. Circular 16. U.S. Fish and Wildlife Service, U.S. Dept. Interior (22) Orians, G.1985. *Blackbirds of the Americas*. Univ. of Washington Press, Seattle. (23) Delacour, J. & D. Amadon. 1973. Curassows and related birds. *Amer. Mus. Nat. Hist.* (24) Lint, K.C. 1977-8. Ocellated turkeys. *J. World Pheasant Assoc.* p. 14-21. (25) Steadman, D.W., J. Stull, and S.W. Eaton. 1978-9. Natural history of the ocellated turkey .*J. World Pheasant Assoc.* p.15-37. (26) Moll, D. 1986. The distribution, status, and level of exploitation of the freshwater turtle *Dermatemys mawei* in Belize, Central America. *Biol. Conserv.* 35:87-96. (27) Pritchard, P.C.H. 1979. Taxonomy, evolution, and zoogeography. PP1-42. In: Harless, M. and Morelock, H. eds. *Turtles : Perspectives and Research*. John Wiley and Sons, NY. (28) Wexo, J.B. 1986. *Alligators and crocodiles*. Zoobooks Wildlife Education Ltd , San Diego. (29) Abercrombie, C.L. et al. 1980. Status of morelet's Crocodile *Crocodylus moreleti* in Belize. *Biol.Conserv.* 17:103-113. (30) Alverez del Toro,M. 1982. *Los Reptiles de Chiapas*. Inst.Hist.Nat. Tuxtla Gutierrez, Mexico. (31) Burghardt, G.M. & A.S.Rand. 1982. *Iguanas of the World*, Noyes Publ., Park Ridge, NJ. (32) Echternacht, A.C. 1977. *How Reptiles and Amphibians Live*. Gallery Press, NY. (33) Carr,A. 1963. *The Reptiles* , Time Inc. NY. (34) Gamow,R.I. and J.F. Harris. 1978. The infrared receptors of snakes. *Sci.Amer*, 228:94 100. (35) Mattioon, C. 1987. *Frogs and Toads of the World*. Facts on File Publ., NY. (36) Duellman, W.E. 1970. The Hylid frogs of middle America. *Monogr. Mus.Nat. Hist.*, Univ. Kansas vol 1&2. pp. 1-753. (37) Duellman, W.E and L.Trueb. 1985. *Biology of Amphibians*. McGraw-Hill, NY. (38) Tuttle, M.D. The amazing frog-eating bat. *Natl.Geog.* 161:78-89, (39) Dobson, N. 1973. *A History of Belize*. Longman Caribbean, Jamaica. (40) Ommanney, F.D. 1964. *The Fishes*.Time, Inc., NY.

The following artwork and photographs are gratefully acknowledged: cover poster by Caroline Beckett, photo of R.Horwich by Bengt Arne Runnerstrom, hickatee drawing by A. Neil and manakin drawings by Bernard Lohr.

COMMUNITY BABOON SANCTUARY EDUCATIONAL
NATURE TRAIL

A trail system is being maintained for use by tourists to see wildlife. Since the sanctuary lands are privately owned and because there are some forest dangers, we ask all tourists to contact the Sanctuary Manager before going into the forest. Initially all tourists should have guides for orientation and protection. The trails are marked with numbered signs. The numbers correspond to the following educational signs.

1.   Amate - The Great Fig Tree
The fruits of this large riparian fig (*Ficus glabrata*) are relished by the monkeys, birds, and other animals. The fig is capable of setting fruit 3 to 4 times per year. While the tree is in fruit, the monkeys may stay on this same tree for days or weeks at a time, feeding on the fruits and young leaves. This giant fig also has the distinction of having been the focus of the film, *"Amate"*, filmed by Richard Foster. Fig trees and specific species of wasps have co-evolved one of the most unique pollination systems in the plant world.

Fig   flowers are born on the inside wall of a rounded enclosure called a synconia. This structure eventually becomes the ripe fruit, if pollinated. Each enclosure produces 3 types of flowers: male, female, and gall flowers. The gall flowers are not true flowers but act as an incubator for the wasp larvae. Here's how   the pollination/incubation system works.
- a) The male wasp hatches first from the gall flowers and while still inside the developing fig, inseminates the still unhatched female.
- b) The male flies out a special opening in the fruit and soon dies.
- c) The impregnated female emerges from the gall flower and inadvertently collects pollen on its back from the male flowers within the fruit.
- d) The female leaves through the opening in the fig and flies to another ripening fig of the same species.
- e) The female enters the new fig and while searching for an appropriate gall flower in which to lay her eggs, she inadvertently pollinates the female flower with the pollen on her back.
- f) The eggs incubate in the climate controlled interior and eventually hatch and continue the cycle.

2.   Born to Dye - Logwood (*Haematoxylon campechianum*)
The early history of Belize is largely concerned with the

harvesting of this tree for the dark blue dye (haematoxylin) contained in its wood. British settlement of Belize in the mid-17th century by small bands of buccaneers was for logwood logging operations. The small, twisted logs were often bundled together on cabbage palm rafts and floated to Belize City. From there they were shipped to England to be pulped to remove the dye. Logwood was the major export timber of the British colony until the mid 18th century when mahogany exports exceeded logwood. The dye has since been replaced by synthetic dyes but in recent years there has been some increased interest in natural dyes.

Logwood is found in wet, low forests and thickets. The tree does not attain great heights but may reach large diameters. It often forms dense thickets and is also a prized choice for fence posts and building posts because the dye protects the wood from decay.

3. Communists ? - Some Are More Equal Than Others

A closely knit flock of black birds may be seen flitting through nearby pastures or secondary growth areas. Sometimes called tickbirds or witch birds, anis are often seen following cattle or horses, snatching insects which are flushed up. Anis are members of the cuckoo family which exhibit unique breeding systems such as brood parasitism (when one species lays its eggs to be reared by another species). Anis also exhibit an interesting system of communal nesting whereby the group lays eggs in a single nest and all care for them together.

Anis live and breed in stable groups of 2-8 adults which defend group territories. The groups are composed of equal numbers of males and females which pair off during the breeding season. One nest is constructed by the group with all females laying eggs into a communal cutch. All group members contribute to incubation and rearing of the young. However, as in many social systems, not all members benefit. The female who benefits most is the oldest, dominant female who lays her eggs last, and may roll other eggs out of the nest, similar to other brood parasite cuckoos. She also incubates and feeds the nestlings less than do the other females. The dominant female also picks a dominant male as her mate who compensates for her laziness by contributing the greatest amount of work, incubating the eggs most of the time.

4. The Cohune Palm - 1001 Uses

The hardy cohune palm (*Orbigyna cohune*) is one of the most abundant and conspcicuous trees in Belize. The cohune is often spared when clearing for plantations or pasture because the tree has many uses. The abundant nuts may be eaten or processed into palm oil for cooking. The nuts have also been used to make charcoal. During World War I, the British actually harvested tons of cohune nuts in order to make charcoal for gas masks. The fronds have long been used for roof thatching on houses and are still used for kitchen and shed roofs. The apical meristem or "heart" of the palm is sometimes harvested and eaten when a tree is cut. They are said to have the taste of cabbage.

Besides being very versatile, the cohune is also exceptionally hardy. Its wood is very hard to cut, it survives burnings, and it can be completely stripped of its leaves and still survive. Unlike many trees which drop their leaves in the dry season, the cohune is green the year round, providing shade for both cattle and crops.

5. "Watcho" - Plant Defenses
Vulnerable and tasty plants must somehow protect their leaves, stems, and flowers from plant-eating animals. Plants have countered the attacks of animals through the evolution of spines, thorns, tough leaves, and chemical defenses. Several examples of protective spines, thorns, and prickles can be found in the sanctuary.

Defensive structures range from long needle-like spines found on the pokenoboy palm, to recurved spines found on basket tie -tie, to large conical projections found on the cotton tree, to tiny prickles. Spines may arise from modified branches or even leaves. Spines may be found on small herbs, bamboo, vines, or trees. Some spines release irritating compounds when touched to further irritate and warn away the unwary traveller. Some thorns even act as hosts for biting ant species as in the *Acacia*'s.

6. Mutualism
The cockspur or bull horn acacia and a species of ant of the genus *Pseudomyrmes* have formed an obligatory symbiotic relationship where both depend on each other for survival. The leguminous tree provides a home for the ants who hollow out the thorns. If you look carefully, you will see the round entrances below the thorn tip. When the plant is disturbed, the ants will attack and bite the intruder, either you or some other potential enemy of the plant. They also protect the acacia from other viney plants which could choke out sunlight from the intolerant tree and damage or even kill it. You will notice that the acacia is not covered by vines while the other species nearby probably are. The plant in turn provides the ants with high protein food sources known as Beltian Bodies at the tip

of the leaflets and some sugar producing nectaries on the upper leaf surfaces which it specifically produced for the ants to eat. The tropics are full of these special and often agriculturally important plant-animal partnerships.

7. "Sensible" Weeds - *Mimosa pigra*

This common pasture legume gets its name because its leaves fold up during hot, dry weather and at night to help conserve water, a most sensible thing to do. Sensible weed, along with numerous other leguminous plants (including many types of "sensitive plants") are the first colonizers in cleared pasture areas and are part of the first phase of succession. The nitrogen fixing legumes provide the soil with a natural fertilizer, replenishing the depleted pasture soils. The sensible weed is also protected by defensive thorns. These thorns protect the plant from browsing cattle and account for the abundance of the plant in pastures.

8. Plants Without Shame - Strangler Figs

There are three different species of strangler fig represented at this location. Strangler figs are the menacing killers of the plant world, slowly and methodically strangling their hosts and establishing themselves. Strangler figs start from seeds deposited by birds, monkeys or bats in another tree's canopy. In Belize, stranglers commonly start off in the canopy of cohune palms. The roots of the developing strangler grow downward, either through the air or down and around the host tree's trunk. Over a number of years the fig roots which branch and encircle the host tree, eventually fuse, engulfing the entire trunk of the host tree. The enormous pressure exerted by the strangler roots eventually girdles or strangles the host tree trunk, killing the host tree. Eventually the dead host rots, thus leaving the center of the strangler trunk hollow.

9. Impenetrable Tangle

Bamboo, a member of the grass family, is well adapted for the riverbank where you now see it growing. This water loving plant can survive the annual floods which accompany every wet season. Without the bamboo, this riverbank would soon wash away. Like any grass, it grows from the base up. This means it will quickly resprout if the tip is eaten or broken off. The new sprouts are sometimes eaten by cattle. As the plant ages, it becomes silicated, hardens, and grows spines. Once these defenses are developed, the bamboo often forms an armored thicket, forbidding to any potential consumer or traveller.

The bamboo thicket you are about to walk through shelters a variety of animals. The giant blue morphos butterfly and the industrious wee-wee ant are both permanent residents. Game animals such as the peccary, gibnut, and armadillo find cover in this dense thicket from local hunters. Baboons which inhabit the canopy above, are often found along the trail and fence line. A wide variety of birds are also found along the bamboo trail. The yellow-billed cacique, a shy black bird with a pale yellow bill and eye, is called the "bamboo cracker" because of the sound it makes, like cracking bamboo.

10. Pasture Regeneration

Pastures, like other cleared areas, can regenerate back to forest if the soils have not been completely destroyed. The process of vegetational changes and regeneration over time are termed succession. Succession is a complex process that is not completely understood or predictable. However, certain patterns are obvious and are briefly summarized.

1) In the first years after a pasture is abandoned, the area is overrun by a wide variety of light loving shrubs, herbs, and vines. Many of these plants have spines or thorns which keep large plant-eating animals away. These early colonizers grow rapidly and set seed quickly.

2) Into the third and fourth year after abandonment, the area is overrun by many fast growing smaller trees which begin to dominate the growth, and shade out the early colonizers. Many of the young trees arise from resprouting stumps, now free from grazing pressure. They are often from seeds of the trees left standing in the pasture.

3) After 7-10 years of regeneration, a secondary growth area arises with the trees 20-30 ft (6-10 m) high and a less dense understory. Many of the earliest colonizers are no longer present, being shaded out by the developing canopy. At this stage, many secondary forest trees form a conspicuous element of the plant growth. After 15-20 years, the early stages of a secondry forest growth become established with a more or less closed canopy and a less dense understory. The understory now contains many shade tolerant tree seedlings which will become members of the mature forest.

4) If left undisturbed for 50 years or more, a well developed secondary forest will become established with a well developed canopy and with sparse understory growth.

11. Lifeline to Civilization

The Delize River has always played a prominent role in village life. Prior to 1958, when the first access road was built into the area, the river was the primary means of transportation and communication. The river Cayo Boats transported passengers, supplies, and mail from Belize City to all the villages up to San Ignacio. Today the river is still used for fishing and short distance transportation by dory. The Belize River is not always a kind provider. During the wet season (July through November) the river floods as high as this sign. The high waters may carry away large trees and erode away unprotected banks.

12. Adventitious Roots and Epiphytes

Tropical plant roots are diverse in their structures, functions, and their origins. The classic root burrows into the soil beneath the plant, seeking nutrients and water, while anchoring the plant. However, many tropical plants are epiphytes (air plants) or start off as epiphytes, and their roots face an entirely different set of circumstances. Plant epiphytes have adapted to their aerial situation through the evolution of aerial roots and by developing roots which form from branches, stems or even leaves. The latter innovative solutions are called adventitious roots.

Plants living their entire life above ground (true epiphytes) never have roots which reach the forest floor. Epiphytes obtain needed water and minerals from the often humid air and sometimes by penetrating roots into their hosts. Different species of epiphytes can often be found in distinct parts of the tree canopy. Some species are only found at specific heights above ground, in a certain degree of shading, at a particular distance from the center of the tree or on a specific plant part (trunk, branch, leaf, etc.).

Plants starting their life up in a tree may send down aerial roots to obtain needed water and minerals. Adventitious roots may also arise from parts of leaves and stems near the ground. Adventitious roots are also common on vine species which require a secure anchorage. Roots may arise from different parts of the main vine stem securing the vine to nearby plants or soil.

13. Forest Architects

Termites, the master builders of the insect world, build custom nests as varied in design and material as human homes. Termite nests may be above or below ground, in trees, carved from wood or fashioned from wood, soil, saliva, and excrement into solid adobe-like nests or light paper carton nests. The large dark nest above you serves to protect the termite colony from light while allowing for ventilation to keep the nest cool. To avoid any exposure to light, they also build covered passageways or galleries between the nest and food sources.

14. Tree Stabilizers

Most of the nutrients in the rain forest are contained in the living plants and subsequently the topsoil is very shallow and nutrient deficient. Trees, thus, send most of their roots out near the surface to capture the available nutrients. This shallow rooting system makes the tree unstable, a problem further compounded by frequent tropical rains and winds. Trees have adapted to these notable conditions by developing buttresses whose main function is to help anchor and stabilize the tree. Buttresses may take several forms, including large vertical plank buttresses, prop roots, and flying buttresses.

15. Cotton Tree (*Ceiba pentandra*) family - Bombaceae

One of the half dozen largest trees of Central America, it is locally called the cotton tree because its seeds are imbedded in a soft cottony material also known as "kapok". Kapok is traditionally used to stuff pillows and mattresses and at one time was widely exported. The cotton tree is pantropical meaning it is found in the American, African, and Asiatic tropics. The large tree has distinct horizontal branching and the trunk is often covered with large conical spines.

16. Plantation - Slash-and-Burn Agriculture

You are standing in a traditional slash-and-burn agricultural plot, locally called plantations or milpas. The plots, usually about one acre, are cleared by hand (with only machetes and axes) during the dry season (from February to May). The felled trees are left to dry out for a month or more before burning. The burning is done in accordance with each particular farmer's planting program. Many farmers burn in late May in anticipation of the first rains of the rainy season. Planting is done immediately after the burn. The major crops planted are rice, beans, and corn. Other crops planted include peppers, cocoa, yams, potatoes, plantains, bananas, and cassava. It requires a great deal of manual labor to help control the weeds. Slash-and-burn agriculture is an extremely labor intense practice if is is to be done successfully.

17. Succession - The Early Years

Succession is the process whereby a disturbed area regenerates back into a mature plant community. In this disturbed area, a slash-and-burn agricultural plot, you can see the first phase of succession represented by a dense and varied growth of herb, vine, and shrub species. The forest surrounding the clearing is about 35 years old with many of the larger trees considerably older than 35 years. The first clearing was done in early 1985 followed by a second clearing to the west in 1986. The clearings allowed direct sunlight to reach the ground and this stimulated a variety of light loving plants to germinate and grow from seeds already in the soil or transported from nearby clearings by birds, insects, or the wind. These early colonizers of the clearing grow quickly and if unchecked by the farmer, they will overrun the plantation and choke out the crops. The more common and conspicuous species found are *Heliconia, Canna, Ceropia, Piper,* bamboo and several resprouting cut tree trunks. This luxuriant growth is beneficial in that it stabilizes the soil and starts the process of soil nutrient regeneration via decaying leaves and plants.

18. Conservation In Action

The owners of this plantation are active and exemplary members of the sanctuary. They are practicing conservation and helping maintain a balance between their own needs and the needs of the monkeys and other wildlife in the region. This owners conservation effort can be summarized into 3 main courses of action.

1. He left a strip of forest along riverbanks to limit erosion and preserve the habitat.
2. He left a strip of trees across the large clearing so the monkeys can move across the clearing
3. He left known food trees for the monkeys during land clearing

These relatively simple actions, if practiced on a large scale, can go a long way in protecting fragile environments and can be beneficial for both people and wildlife.

19. Hermits, Hummers, and Heliconia

The banana-like *Heliconia* species are common plants of early tropical succession. Their flowers are almost exclusively pollinated by hummingbirds. Characteristics of *Heliconia* flowers and their hummingbird visitors show they are co-evolved species. Hummingbirds can be split into two groups to show this: hermits and non-hermits.

In general, non-hermits have short straight beaks and are territorial, defending an area of flowering plants for their own use. *Heliconia* species pollinated by non-hermits have clumped distributions, short straight flowers, and produce copious, concentrated nectar. This creates a situation energetically beneficial for the hummingbird who, in turn, may protect the *Heliconia* from "nectar-robbers" who often destroy these flowers.

Hermits have long, curved beaks, visit scattered flowers along regular foraging routes, and are dependent upon *Heliconia* nectar. Hermit pollinated *Heliconia* have scattered distributions and long, curved flowers shaped specifically for the hermit pollinator species. These *Heliconia* species also have different pollen deposition sites and different flowering seasons to avoid cross pollination.

20. Tubroos, Guanacaste, Elephant Ear
(*Enterolobium cyclocarpum*) Family-Leguminosae

This large forest tree ranges from Mexico to Venezuela. The tree has a broad spreading crown and may reach 6-9 ft (2-3 m) in diameter. The tubroos has large ear shaped fruits easily detected when in fruit. The "ears" are relished by cattle and that is one reason why the trees are left in pastures. A second reason is that tubroos wood is very water resistant and easy to work and hence it is the first choice wood for making dugout canoes, locally called dorys. A large tubroos can produce 2 or 3 doriess.

This particular tubroos is a common resting spot for a local troop of baboons. Several species of epiphytes are also found on this mammoth tubroos.

21. "Wee-Wee's" - Leafcutter ants
The industrious leaf cutter ant known as the "wee wee" ant in creole, is responsible for the small road crossing this path. These roads are maintained between favored food trees and their large subterranean nest mounds. Leaf cutters are the only vegetarian ants in the world. They do not actually eat leaves but use the leaves to grow a fungus, on which they do feed. Because of a preference for the tender young leaves of fruit trees, they can cause great damage to crops. Endless columns of these ants can be seen ascending a tree trunk, cutting pieces of leaf, then carrying the leaf fragment back to their nest. There the leaf matter is chewed up, mixed with saliva, and fertilized with feces. Special fungus is planted on this medium, then tended by the ant farmers. Without the ants to care for it, the fungus cannot survive and it is only found in leafcutter ant nests.

22. The trumpet tree - (*Cecropia obtusifolia*)
The local name of this tree aludes to traditions where the stems of *Cecropia* were used for making ceremonial trumpets by indigenous Mayans. The trumpet tree is common and conspicuous in clearings and forest edges. It grows very rapidly and its leaves are eaten by monkeys and other herbivores. The tree has combatted

herbivorous attacks through a unique co-evolution with ants of the genus *Azteca*. The *Cecropia* trunk has large hollow chambers which provide shelter for the ants. It further accomodates the ants by producing both a nutrient rich solution from special structures inside the trunk and a high energy carbohydrate food source from structures on the outside of the trunk. The ants in return patrol their home and protect the tree from herbivorous insects and small animals. When disturbed, the ants scramble and attack the intruder. Although the ants do not sting, they have strong jaws and secrete caustic chemicals that they rub into their bites.

23. Bananas and Wee-Wee's

Bananas, and the closely related plantain, are commonly planted in small groves like this one. There are numerous different varieties of banana and plantain, all belonging to the genus *Musa*. Bananas and plantains are often planted on leaf cutter ant nests (locally called wee-wee nests) because the nests provide good aeration and drainage during the rainy season. The banana plant's "trunk" does not contain any woody material but is made up of tightly wrapped leaf sheaths. The banana flower starts off from the base of the plant and grows up through the leaf sheath through the top of the plant and then arcs downward. After fruiting once, the plant dies. The ovaries of the common banana develop into fruits without fertilization. The aborted ovules are present in the mature fruit, only as small brown spots. All reproduction is entirely vegetative, bananas cannot be grown from seed.

24. Pokenoboys (*Bactris major*)

This small but well defended palm is abundant in wet and swampy forests. It is one of the worst pests in the lowlands of Central America often forming dense thickets. The long slender spines are numerous and can inflect painful wounds. The palm is not without its local uses, however. The trunk of the tree is very fire and heat resistent. Its wood is used to make the "kis-kis", a pair of tongs used to remove food and biscuits from hot fires. The mature fruits are also edible tasting similar to black cherries.

25. Basket Tie-Tie (*Desmoncus schippii*)

This very wicked looking plant is unusual for a number of reasons. Although it is a palm, it takes the form of a vine, climbing upwards over other forest trees and is known as a rattan palm. The entire vine is covered with small but needle sharp spines. The leaf tips are also modified into a series of reverse-hooked spines which may catch your hair if you're not careful. By catching an animal's hair, the vine is passively moved across forest pathways. Its name comes from the fact that this spine covered vine is used to make traditional baskets. After removing the outer spiny covering, the vine is then split into strips for weaving into baskets.

Common Birds of the Sanctuary

a) **Cattle Egret** (*Bubulcus ibis*) - "gaulin" in creole
A small white egret with yellow feet. It often follows cattle feeding on the insects they stir up. Originally from Africa, it is now very common in Central America and is spreading north through North America.

b) **Gray necked wood rail** (*Aramides cajanea*) - "top notch chick" in creole
Gray neck and head, cinnamon brown sides, black belly and tail. Look for this chicken-sized bird on riverbanks making a loud cackling chicken-like sound.

c) **Amazon parrots** (*Amazona* spp.)
Several species are found in the sanctuary including the yellow headed (*A. ochraocephala*), white fronted (*A. albifrons*) or "mangrove" in creole. All are stocky with short squarish tails. Noisy and gaudily colored in greens, reds, yellows, and white they are conspicuous when flying overhead.

d) **Olive throated or Aztec parakeet** (*Aratinga astec*) - "keeti" in creole
Smaller than a parrot, the tail and wings are pointed. This all green parakeet is the only variety found in the sanctuary. Parakeets and parrots are responsible for considerable damage to fruit trees and corn crops.

e) **Kiskadee** (*Pitangus sulphuratus*) - "kiskadee" in creole
A large flycatcher with bright yellow breast, white throat, black and white striped head. A loud conspicuous bird often found perching within the village and in pastures. It has several   calls one of which sounds like its name.

f) **Brown jay** (*Psilorhinus morio*) - "piam-piam" in creole
A large, sooty-brown jay with dark head, cream breast, brown back and tail, with white markings on the tail tip. Its creole name comes from the sound it makes.

g) **Tropical mockingbird** (*Mimus gilvus*) - "nightingale" in creole
A gray pastoral bird with white belly and white markings on its dark tail. It is similar to the common U.S. mockingbird but without the white wing patches. Their songs mimic medleys of other bird songs.

h) **Yellow billed cacique** (*Amblycercus holosericeus*) - "bamboo cracker" in creole

A shy blackbird with a pale yellow bill and eyes. Commonly found in bushy thickets and bamboo, it eats insects found in dead bamboo stalks. Its creole name comes from the cracking call noise it makes.

i) **Melodius blackbird** (*Dives dives*) - "blackbird" in creole
A large entirely black bird often found in pastures and around the village. Its calls are many and varied, mostly loud, clear, and liquid but sometimes shrill. It is one of several birds called "blackbird" in creole. Others include the ani, cacique and grackle.

j) **White collared seedeater** (*Sporophila torqueola*) - "chechi" in creole
A small finch often found fluttering amongst tall grass or rice. The male is black, brown, and white with a collar. The female is buff brown with white wing marks. In large numbers, these birds can cause considerable damage to a rice crop.

INDEX

Boldface print refers to illustrations. All tree and shrub species are indexed under, trees and shrubs. Major tree species information occurs on pages 49-58 and 338-391. Definitions of some technical terms are found in the Glossary, pp. 322-325.

413

predation of, 36; resting, 36; roaring, 28-30; scent marking, 30-31, 32; sex, 32-33; social behavior, 26-27; tail, prehensile, 36; territory, 26-30, 36
howler, black and gold, 24; geographic range, 41
howler, brown, 24; geographic range, 41; extinction, threat of, 41
howler, mantled 24, 25, 37; geographic range, 25-26, 41; extinction, threat of, 41
howler, red, 24; geographic range, 40
howler, red-handed, 24; geographic range, 41; extinction, threat of, 41; weight, 25
hummingbirds, 214-221; adaptations, 214, 217; flight, 215; geographic distribution, 214, **214**; hibernation, 216; pollination, 216-217, of orchids, 129, of passionflowers, 132; hermits, 216, 408-409; hermit, activity rhythms, 218-219; hermit, breeding territories (leks), 217-221; hermit, feeding, 219; hermit, little 216; hermit, long-tailed, 216-217, 217-221
hunting, 15, 38, 40, 42, 62, 153-154, 156, 198; camps, 90; hickatee, 263-265; limpkin, 247; manatee, 206; pet trade, 153; turkey, 243
hylids (see tree frogs)
hyoid, 28-29, 173
Icteridae (see blackbirds)
iguanas, 291-300; green iguana 291, 292-293, 294, 295-300; feeding, 291-293; reproduction, 295-300; spiny- tailed iguana, 291, 293, 294, 298, 299, 300; territory and aggression, 293-295
insects (see also ants, bees, butterflies, wasps), 118, 124, 163; defense against, 119, 120-121
jabiru, 155, 156, **156**
jaguar, 154, 156, 161, 172, **172**, 173, 179, 243; geographic range **180**
jaguarundi, 174, 177-178
jay, brown, 411
keys; hardwood trees, 343, 349, 354-357; palms, 378-379; pine forest trees, 370-371
kiskadee, 411
land use (see agriculture)
limpkin, 247-248; calls, 247; evolutionary relationships, 247; extinction, threat of, 247; feeding, 247-248; reproduction, 248
liverworts, 105
leaf cutter ants (see ants)
leaf fall, 71, 74
lianas (see vines)
lichens, 104-105, 116
living fence posts, 15, 42
logging, 38, 44-46, 49-55, 59, 62, 67, 70, 72, 99, 112, 153, 401-402
manakins, 255-258; mating system (lek), 255-258, **258**
manatee, 203-213; adaptive characteristics, 204, 208; conservation, 205-207; evolutionary relationships, 203-204, 204-205; feeding, 209-210; geographic range, 204-205, **205**, 207; habitat, 207-208; hunting, 206; locomotion, 210; reproduction and sexual behavior, 211-213, **212**; resting, 210, 211; social behavior, 210-211
mangrove forest (see forest types)
Mayans, 41, 44, 55, 87, 121, 206, 409
Maya Mountains, 60

migration, 224-228; functions of, 224; navigation, 226-228;
    stimulation of, 225
migratory birds, 155, 156, 222-231; ducks, 222, 228; doves, 227;
    falcons 227-228; flycatchers, 227; rain forests, dependence on,
    228-229; seasonal cycle, 223- 224; songbirds, 228; warblers 222-
    224, **224**, 228, 230-31; winter residents and transients, 222-223
milpa (see agriculture)
mimicry; Batesian, 135; Mullerian, 135; passionflowers,133-134, **134**
mockingbird, 411
monkey (see howler, spider monkey), 124, 125, 183
Morelet's crocodile, 266; distinguishing from American crocodile, **270**;
    geographic range, 269-269, **268**, **269**
mosses, 104, 116
moths, 76
mountain cow (see tapir)
museum, 17-18
Mussell Creek, 7, 70, 207, 260
nightingale (see mockingbird)
ocellated turkey, 16, 154, 156, 243-246; characteristics of, 244;
    feeding, 244; geographic range, **244**; reproduction 245-246; social
    behavior, 245
ocelots and margay (small spotted cats), 154, 156, 174-177; character-
    istics of, 175-176, **176**; feeding, 176-177; geographic range, **175**;
    reproduction, 177
orchids, 104, 126-129; epiphytic (list of species) 107-108, 128;
    flowers and reproduction, 126-129; parts of 126, **126**; seeds, 122,
    129; species diversity, 126; vanilla, 129, **129**
paca, 183
parrots, 153, 156, 411
passionflowers, 130-135; flower, 130-131; fruits, 131-132; plant
    animal interactions, 132, with butterflies, 132-135; species
    diversity, 131-132
peccary (see also ungulates), 183, 187, **187**, 197-202; characteristics
    of, 197-200, **200**; extinction, threat of, 198; geographic range,
    197-198, **198**; related species, 197; reproduction, 200; social
    behavior and scent marking, 201-202, **201**
phenology, 73-77; flowers, 74-76; fruit, 76-77; leaves, 74
piam-piam (see jay, brown)
pine-oak forest (see forest types)
pine ridge (see forest types)
pioneer species, 78-79, 111
Pipridae (see manakins)
pitpans, 47-48
pit vipers, 284-290; Central American rattlesnake, 289-290; charac-
    teristics of, 284; fer de lance, 154, 288; hunting with heat
    receptors, 287-288; poison and poison injection, 284-286, 288,
    289-290; rattles, 288-289, **289**; rattlesnakes, 288-290;
    reproduction, 289
plant-animal interactions; ants, 141-145, 148-151, 403-404, 409-
    410, 410; bats, 124; orchids and insects, 127-128; passionflowers
    and butterflies, 132-135
plantation (see agriculture)
pollination, 75, 76, 104